Praise for *Henry*

"Amy Mackin has written a magnificent book, eloquently and compassionately detailing the riveting account of her son's struggles inside (and outside of) the school system, along with her unceasing efforts to help him on his educational journey. It's a love story, a story about raising children with disabilities, and a beautifully written story about a mother's quest to ensure that her son receives the education he deserves. She weaves facts and figures throughout her narrative, while leaving the reader on the edge of her seat, mesmerized by this incredible story, rooting for both mother and son. I highly recommend."

— Linda Murphy Marshall, author of *Ivy Lodge: A Memoir of Translation and Discovery*

"In prose as precise as her insights, Mackin chronicles the challenges—and rewards—of raising a neurodivergent child. In addition to her first-hand experiences, the book contains plenty of research, which is woven seamlessly into the narrative and never becomes pedantic. Henry's Classroom is both moving and enlightening. Spoiler alert: The giant Elmo scene is itself worth the price of admission."

— Sue William Silverman, author of *Acetylene Torch Songs: Writing True Stories to Ignite the Soul*

"A rallying cry and a balm—I'll be giving this book to all my parenting friends, especially those with kids on the autism spectrum. From IEP meetings to birthday parties to homeschooling, Mackin effortlessly weaves relatable personal stories of raising a child on the spectrum that had me laughing out loud one minute and grabbing for tissues the next. As a mother of my own neurodivergent child, I felt so seen by the sacrifices and immense time commitment required of Mackin to meet the relentless task of strong-arming an inflexible, outdated American education system into providing proper support so that her child can thrive. This book gave me hope and should be required reading for all educators and education administrators."

—Minna Dubin, author of *Mom Rage: The Everyday Crisis of Modern Motherhood*

"A compelling fusion of gut-wrenching personal story with the policies, procedures, and legislation that contributed to the heartache. From the very first page, you will root for Henry and his mom to succeed, despite the educational and medical system stacked against them."

— Karen DeBonis, author of *Growth: A Mother, Her Son, and the Brain Tumor They Survived*

Henry's Classroom

A Special Education in American Motherhood

Henry's Classroom

A Special Education in
American Motherhood

a memoir

Amy Mackin

Apprentice
House Press
Loyola University Maryland

First Edition

Library of Congress Control Number: 2025932586

Casebound ISBN: 978-1-62720-572-6
Paperback ISBN: 978-1-62720-573-3
Ebook ISBN: 978-1-62720-574-0

Cover and Internal Design by Niki Ignacio
Promotional Development by Kate Tourison
Editorial Development by Claire Marino

Author Photo by Sarah Montani Photography

Published by Apprentice House Press

Apprentice
House Press
Loyola University Maryland

Loyola University Maryland
4501 N. Charles Street, Baltimore, MD 21210
410.617.5265
www.ApprenticeHouse.com
info@ApprenticeHouse.com

For my grandmothers, Hazel and Mary.
Their resilience and quiet rebellions flow through my veins,
and I am forever grateful.

And for my mother,
who held on to herself through marriage and motherhood.
I didn't understand how difficult that must have been
until she was already gone.

"Education is not preparation for life;
Education is life itself."

~John Dewey

Contents

PART III: TEARS AND T-SHIRTS

AUTHOR'S NOTE

I relied on personal notes, medical and school records, researched facts, academic studies, and my own memory to write this book. With the exception of my spouse, I changed the names of all individuals who appear in the narrative to protect their privacy. I also changed some minor identifying details about people and places to further maintain this privacy. No events were altered that had an impact on the accuracy of the story.

Henry was encouraged to contribute to this book, and I offered him the opportunity to suggest edits to the final manuscript. Though he supported my desire to write the memoir, he chose to step aside from any involvement in the creative process.

PROLOGUE

On a clear October morning in 2002, we sit waiting to be called in for Henry's fifteen-month checkup. I'm not at all anxious. The days of monitoring breast milk going in and poop coming out have long passed; he has sustained and survived his first cold and fever and bump on the head. He's eating solid foods, sleeping nine hours a night when he feels well, and taking reliable naps.

The only stressful part of this visit is the pediatrician's office itself. It's a madhouse, as usual. Toddlers stack large cardboard blocks on the beige industrial carpet, then squeal with excitement as they knock them over and watch them fall. Toys chime and buzz from all sides. A cartoon blares on the television mounted above us. But Henry isn't interested in playing like the other children. He's nestled in my lap, quietly leafing through one of those fabric baby books that have googly eyes to shake and laces to twist and braid. Every few minutes he tugs on my jacket, pulling it towards him as if to shield himself from the surrounding bedlam. *I'm with you, kid,* I think. I can't wait to get out of here either.

"Oh, you're a little mama's boy, aren't you, sweetheart?" a waiting grandmother comments. The young child who calls her "nana" is playing with a busy-box a few feet from where we sit. I tense up but smile at the woman. I'm sure she doesn't mean to offend me, but a relative called Henry a "mama's boy" earlier that month in a tone that suggested I was creating a spoiled monster, and I've been on the defensive ever since. A few days prior, I shot a malevolent stare at a man in the supermarket checkout line when he spoke to Henry during a meltdown—Henry's meltdown, not mine, though it might have been hard to tell at that moment. "What's all this carrying on about? I bet you can be a big boy and help your mama," the guy said, as Henry screamed and pulled on my shirt from the cart he was buckled into. I must have looked out of my mind, like a maniacal witch about to put a curse on him, because when the guy caught my glance he stepped back and muttered, "Uh, sorry."

What no one understands, what I want to holler at everyone who makes these snap judgments, is that Henry only fusses and clings to me when other people are around. He dislikes crowds and chaotic environments. At home, Henry is not needy at all. He'll sit in the living room and play by himself all afternoon with hardly a sound, until he gets hungry or is ready for his nap. "Mama's boy" is not an accurate description.

When we are called into the examination room, the pediatrician listens to Henry's heart and lungs, checks his ears and throat, and pokes around his belly. She declares him healthy, as I expected. Then she asks me a lot of questions about his behavior.

"What words does he say?" she begins.

"Mama and Dada," I reply. But as soon as I say it, it occurs to me that I can't remember the last time I heard Henry refer to me or John with words. "And he makes quite a few sounds," I add hastily. *Doesn't he?*

"How does he tell you when he wants something, like a drink or a snack or a toy?" she asks.

"I just have to figure it out," I say.

"Does he point to the cabinet the snacks are in? Does he point to the refrigerator when he's thirsty?"

"No," I answer. "Should he be?"

The pediatrician says that Henry ought to make more than sounds at this point, produce at least another consistent word or two. He should attempt to communicate with us using either spoken or nonverbal cues. She explains that he might need a little help jump-starting those skills, but a delay is not unusual for a child who has an attentive older sibling.

"Danielle may be anticipating what Henry wants before he even has to ask," she says, "so he doesn't need to work too hard to communicate. And given the family history of speech problems, he may already be predisposed to a delay. Research tells us that children with family members who have experienced speech problems have a far greater chance of developing similar issues."

She hands me a phone number for our local Early Intervention program.

I don't hesitate to call. I'm familiar with the services they provide. Henry's three-and-a-half-year-old sister Danielle also had a slight speech delay. Just after she turned eighteen months, an Early Intervention speech therapist started coming to our home twice a week. Now, you couldn't stop her from talking if you wanted to. My husband John also required speech therapy as a kid.

And then there's my brother.

"Kirk didn't speak until he was five!" my mother says on a phone call two days later, when I tell her about the referral. "The doctor said he'd talk when he was good and ready, and he did. In full sentences!"

I've heard this story many times before. She's telling

it again now to make me feel better, but it has the opposite effect. Though no one in my family has ever admitted it, ever even touched upon the subject, it's clear to me that my older brother struggled with a learning disability or developmental disorder when he was young that had gone undiagnosed and consequently untreated. There's no doubt in my mind that this lack of recognition and intervention impacted his long-term outcome, as it did for many others of our generation who never got the help they needed.

She finishes telling this familiar tale of my brother's delayed, then miraculous, acquisition of speech. "I know, Mom. I'm sure it's nothing to worry about," I say.

* * *

Occasionally, my mother and I talk about my or my brother's experiences within the public education system. She acknowledges that Kirk wouldn't have made it through high school without the work-study program—a now long-abandoned initiative that allowed students to leave class by noon so they could pull full shifts at the local grocery store or gas station. But she blames his lack of motivation and disinterest in formal schooling on lousy teachers who were unable or unwilling to engage a bored kid. She never associates the speech delay he experienced as a young child with these later problems he had as a teen. Still, her reasoning is not entirely invalid. Though I had a few wonderful teachers growing up, the public high school that both Kirk and I attended offered a mediocre education at best.

It took me decades to recognize that I was steered toward typing and shorthand classes in high school because I had trouble learning in the traditional public education format. If work-study was the way to get underperforming boys through to graduation, then secretarial courses were the default for girls who didn't show enough promise to be enrolled in the college-prep curriculum. I'd also been labeled a "weird kid" in middle school, thanks to my visible discomfort in noisy, chaotic spaces and my general clumsiness in gym class. This designation followed me into high school.

I didn't have speech problems in my early years that I know of, but I've always been slow to process other people's communication, both verbal and nonverbal. I also have trouble identifying sarcasm; I was often confused by the wisecracks my classmates made in school. A group of popular girls decided my social issues and lack of physical dexterity were reasons enough to target me with relentless verbal bullying, along with a few physical attacks. There were no support services available for these challenges, so I saw no point in complaining to anyone. If kids like me needed help adapting, they were on their own.

Although interest in the field of school counseling took hold in the progressive years of the 1960s and 70s, there was still much debate around what role these professionals should have in public education systems. National standards were not adopted until 1997. Many schools had no counselors during this time period. My high school did have a counselor on staff in the 1980s, but that person's primary responsibility was guiding working-class students toward appropriate post-graduation vocations, and helping those work-study kids like my brother find a compatible job so they could manage to get their diplomas. Providing social-emotional support and conflict mediation wasn't in the job description.

Now, forty years later and after a global pandemic that

forced school closures and resulted in a widening of education achievement gaps across the country, only twenty-three states require a counselor in elementary schools, and just thirty require a counselor in high school. My home state of Massachusetts is not one of those. Despite no mandate, our schools currently have a student-to-counselor ratio of 364 to 1, which is slightly better than the national average, though a 2020 study found that many Massachusetts high schools average 450 or more students to one counselor. Meanwhile, the American School Counselor Association has been recommending a ratio of 250 to 1 since 1965.

There was no early childhood educational assistance or screening back when Kirk and I were growing up either. Preschool was not an American norm then, but my mother worked outside the home and therefore needed some sort of daycare. My brother was one of the 10 percent of American kids enrolled in "nursery school" in the mid 1960s. Unlike the other 90 percent of young children, Kirk frequently interacted with adults beyond his own family, but those adults were not trained to detect developmental delays. Even if they had been, no services existed to help kids with less visible learning challenges—some of which are now included under the neurodivergent umbrella, such as ADHD and dyslexia.

In the 1960s and 70s, the dominant thinking in American culture was that kids with marked intellectual or developmental disabilities could not be helped in a traditional school setting. Parents were given a choice between keeping their children at home with no services or institutionalizing them where, they were told, educational and therapeutic services would be offered. Children who experienced disabilities that we refer to today as "invisible" or "hidden" languished between this binary.

We now know that the outcomes of children with developmental delays, from mild to severe, can significantly improve with appropriate therapies at home and in community settings. But the Early Intervention services Henry had just been referred to were established only in 1986, just fifteen years before his birth and well past both my brother's and my childhood years. Public responsibility for education of people with developmental and/or learning disabilities is still a relatively new concept in the American consciousness.

The social culture of semi-rural New England also didn't work in my brother's favor, or mine. We were born into an extended working-class environment where hourly wage jobs or military service after high school were the norm. Our parents and community neither prepared us for nor expected us to attend college. In that light, my brother's and later my own inability to thrive within the subpar education system our town offered didn't raise any red flags. Though I know that my parents and others like them had the same hopes for their children that most all parents do—namely, to be more successful than they had been—there was little discussion about kids meeting their full potential. The goal was to make a living, secure stable employment.

This history formed the context within which I began my own parenting journey.

But that autumn of Henry's fifteen-month checkup, I tell myself that John and I are not our parents. Our small corner of New England and the larger world around us have changed since we were kids. We have more resources now, better awareness. And I take no comfort in my mother's well-intentioned comparisons.

In the twenty years since that doctor's visit, I've acquired an unexpected but extensive knowledge of the American public education system, the medical establishment, and the cultural patterns that influence so much of our social lives in this country. I've also gained a deeper understanding of my own behavior and the experiences that have influenced my worldview. It wasn't always flattering. But to be an effective advocate for Henry, I had to confront my own biases and reckon with personal histories that I'd have preferred to ignore. The pages that follow chronicle what I learned—about my child, myself, and the larger societies we all live within.

PART I
A VACANT VILLAGE

LESSON 1

Good Help is Hard to Find

In late November of 2002, six weeks after our pediatrician made the Early Intervention referral, a group of clinicians visit our home with toys for Henry and paperwork for me. They ask Henry to perform various tasks: Can you stack these blocks, Henry? Can you sort these shapes by color? Henry sits in his booster seat at our kitchen table and complies; he's been doing these tasks on his own for months.

The following week, I meet with one of the service coordinators, who tells me that the team has determined that Henry has a developmental delay and that he qualifies for home-based, therapeutic services. We discuss logistical details including therapist assignments and weekly appointment times. I sign medical release forms and provide a credit card number—the state now requires that families make a financial contribution. Until recently, Massachusetts had provided these services for free; I didn't pay anything for Danielle's Early Intervention speech therapy. "Budget cuts," the coordinator explains.

A few days later, our assigned therapist shows up. She's a sturdy, no-nonsense middle-aged woman with short wavy hair colored a coppery red and the rugged skin of a sun worshipper.

"I'm Pat," she says, with a raspy voice that hints at a pack-a-day habit. She strides past me to Henry. He's sitting on the floor arranging plastic Fisher Price "Little People" in a toy bus. Henry's body language changes as she approaches. I know that she's encroaching, moving too quickly. He looks at me, wide-eyed and nervous, a cornered animal searching for an escape.

Pat speaks before I can intervene. "Mom's going to sit over there while we play," she says, as she points to the couch. She must sense that I'm about to leap to my son's aid. I sit as directed. She picks up one of the plastic people Henry is playing with, and he starts to cry. She touches his arm, and he begins to wail. It takes all the restraint I have to remain seated. For all I know she's conducting this therapy by the book, but I become angrier with each passing minute. Henry cries on and off throughout the session. He and I both are in a constant state of discomfort and distrust.

After about forty minutes, Pat announces, "That's enough for today. I'll see you again next week." As she gathers her things, I sweep Henry up into my arms. I catch her smile, a smirk really, that is both authoritarian and patronizing. I manage a polite goodbye, but by the time she walks out our door to her car, I'm crying right along with Henry.

The following weekend at a gathering with John's family, I describe the session to anyone who'll listen. "Oh, don't be silly," my sister-in-law says. "Henry's fine."

I should know better. John's siblings and parents engage in the same generationally acceptable denial my own do, albeit in a more sophisticated way. My parents-in-law lean toward formality in both dress and décor, despite being retired. They entertain other couples their own age and wash away any worries during happy hour. Anything uncomfortable is swept beneath the rug, like the dust and dirt the outside world brings in. My mother-in-law and her youngest daughter exude complete confidence in their respective viewpoints and are resistant to any critical examination or compromise, regardless of topic. These gatherings bring lots of small talk, but meaningful conversation is almost impossible—neither John's mother nor his youngest sister acknowledge the limitations of their own life experience.

Later, when navigating the frustrating system of special needs education, I'll occasionally find myself envious of their blissful complacency.

"His father needed speech therapy, too, you know," my mother-in-law says that day, in a tone that implies that Henry's home-based, multifaceted therapy is unnecessary. "The school offered it to him, but I told them that I could pay for my own child's speech services, and I took him to a private practice in Kingstown."

My husband had a stutter in elementary school. Like my own mother's anecdote, my mother-in-law's story does double-duty: She uses it to convince herself that she's done right by her son as well as to persuade me, the mother of her only grandchildren, that she is an experienced expert whom I should listen to. And like my mother, she appears to believe that her past experience can accurately predict my future. I wonder if, decades from now, I'll have a similar narrative that I recite to my own adult children.

"I'm sure it'll clear up," my father-in-law says, patting my shoulder gently. Though he never openly defends my husband or me in these moments, my father-in-law often tends to the wounds post-mortem with words of encouragement, a soft squeeze of the hand, a phone call or email the next day. He plays a role in John's family that's similar to my mother's in mine—a passive, patient, keeper of the peace. It's not enough for me; I'm angry. I want them, *all* of them, to fight for me and my family, to stand with us through the ordeal to come.

I don't understand that this is the best they could do; that maybe they were scared, too. In a 2017 article on self-deception, social psychologist Mark Alicke asserted, "people engage in willful ignorance because it is useful." I've come to recognize the stories that my extended family and I tell ourselves help us cope when we aren't ready to face certain realities or to reckon with our past mistakes and deficiencies.

In journalist Jessica Grose's *Screaming on the Inside*, she notes that the women she interviewed for her chapter on "Identity" universally shared one overwhelming emotion: guilt. If the women worked outside of the home prior to having children, they experienced guilt whether they went back to work or stopped working after childbirth. "They felt guilty for continuing to work and leaving their children in the care of others, and they felt guilty about leaving work and feeling lost, or never having a job they felt was a career in the first place." If they suffered from postpartum depression, they felt guilty about their inability to be happily consumed by early motherhood. If they could not live up to the "perfectly heteronormative, naturalistic, and pristine ideals of their communities" in any way, they felt guilty. "Even when they were deeply aware of the flaws in society's ideals, those ideals got in their heads," writes Grose.

I detect no hints of mom guilt from my mother, or John's, throughout my own early years of parenting. If they understand or even acknowledge those "flaws in society's ideals," I never know. In true pull-yourself-up-by-your-bootstraps New England wisdom, they show complete confidence in their parenting. My mother's apparent certitude won't waver until the last day of her life. She'll lie dying from cancer, having experienced precious little of her retirement before her devastating diagnosis, and say to me in a strained voice, "You are a better mother than I ever was." The knowledge that she carried this belief for so long, silently, still devastates me.

* * *

Henry grunts. He's been sitting in a corner of my in-laws' living room, fitting three-dimensional shapes into a plastic ball. Soon he holds the ball up, his long thin arms stretched toward me—my cue to empty it so he can start again.

LESSON 2

American Ideals Are Out of Reach

"You want the good news or the bad news first?" John asks after arriving home on a chilly December evening a few weeks later. He's giddy. In another time, I might make an educated guess as to the good news, throw my arms around him, and share in his enthusiasm. But I look up from the spaghetti I'm boiling on the stove and stare at him. Neither genuine nor feigned exuberance is possible for me by seven o'clock these days.

Catching the hint, John makes the decision himself. He goes with the good news. "I got put on General Motors."

"Oh, that's great, honey." I meant it, sort of.

In the world of digital marketing agencies, John's job security depends on which client he's assigned to. A small client whose work might dry up after one or two projects? We can expect uncertainty about whether he'll have a position there the following fiscal year. A huge client that has multiple brands on various platforms? We'll be good for years to come. The projects at GM will be more interesting, and John's job won't be in jeopardy any time soon. It may even mean an opportunity to move up, get a promotion. With me only doing the occasional freelance proofreading job, we're living on a shoestring budget, paycheck-to-paycheck and often in the red, so this is news worth celebrating. Yet, I'm not overjoyed. More than a tinge of jealousy seeps in and dampens the encouragement I should offer him. I love my kids and want to be available to them while they're small. But I'm starting to wonder if this stay-at-home mom situation is becoming unintentionally permanent. We haven't discussed it, but it seems to me that John's career growth directly correlates to a diminishing of my personal goals for the future. The higher he climbs up the corporate ladder, the more the domestic responsibilities of our life fall to me.

A shriek from the living room halts the conversation. I hold my breath. Two seconds of silence follow, then full-out crying. I run in. Henry is slumped next to the coffee table with a pink bump on his forehead. It's swelling.

"He fell," Danielle says. She'd let out the initial scream, and I assume those moments of quiet were the lapse between Henry's collision with the coffee table and him realizing that his head hurt.

"I can see that."

Sizzling and splattering sounds come from the kitchen—another pot boiling over. Since Henry has become mobile, it's a rare occasion when I can pay attention to the preparation of a meal in its entirety.

"John! Take the pot off the stove!"

I carry screaming Henry into the kitchen. John's mopping up the overflow from the pot with a kitchen towel. "Sorry. Work was messaging me," he says.

"Work is *always* messaging you," I mutter under my breath. His company issued him a Blackberry device for the sole reason, it appears to me, to further intrude on his non-working hours and our family time.

"He okay?" John asks.

"I think so."

I sit in a kitchen chair holding an ice-filled towel to Henry's head. "So, what's the bad news?" I ask, now thoroughly irritated.

I resent these work conversations that John starts up when he arrives home, not only because I'm envious of his separate existence and identity outside of being a spouse and parent, but also because I'm completely worn out by the end of the day. I want him to swoop in like a shining knight with flowers and wine, whip up dinner like a four-star chef, and then occupy the kids with a lively game of hide and seek. I want him to tell me how sexy I look in the sweatpants I've been wearing for three straight days, how radiant my makeup-free face and unwashed hair are.

The more time I spend in the house with only kids for company, the more these fantasies run rampant. Sometimes I believe one or another fairy-tale scenario is actually possible, which makes the inevitable reality even more disappointing. The truth is that this day is like most other recent days, and John is the only one who has anything new to talk about. I've become boring, if not to him, then certainly to myself. He'd first been attracted to me back in our 20s because I was so independent—living alone in my own apartment and commuting into the city every day. I appeared put-together and professional and was just as happy to attend a theatre production or a museum exhibition alone on a Saturday as I was to be out on a date with a romantic prospect. I'd seen the popular bands perform, read the latest books, and was knowledgeable about current events. But any semblance of that woman is gone now. I'm not quite sure how much of her was real to begin with.

I'd spent so much of my younger days contorting myself into what I thought people—family, friends, classmates, coworkers, supervisors—expected me to be. My existence became more about pleasing others than pleasing myself. It was a survival mechanism, to avoid the brutal bullying I dealt with as a kid. Being an outsider, a child on the fringes, was a serious liability in the town where I grew up and in the schools I attended. I learned to mimic the behavior of others to better blend in.

"I'll have to travel a lot more," John says, looking at his phone rather than at me.

I sigh. "What's 'a *lot* more'?"

"After the holidays, I'll have to spend at least two days a week in Detroit getting up to speed. Depending on the project I'm assigned to, it could increase. Some projects can be managed from here, but GM likes someone onsite as deadlines approach."

"Okay, well, we'll deal with it," I say. *More like I'll deal with it* is what I'm thinking. I remove the cold towel and lightly kiss the bump on Henry's head. Little help with the kids during the week is about to turn into zero help.

* * *

Years later I'll realize my experience is not unique. The high cost of childcare coupled with a persistent gender pay gap meant that I would stay home during daytime hours once my husband and I started a family, even without additional complications. But having a kid who needs services like group-based Early Intervention, speech pathology, or occupational and physical therapy sealed the deal. Those services are provided during weekday business hours, and transportation to them is solely the parents' responsibility. If a child qualifies for a state-funded special-needs preschool, bus access is only provided to families who fit low-income guidelines and can prove an inability to secure transportation to and from the school. When children with disabilities transition to public elementary school, they walk or take the bus within the same guidelines as those without a disability unless their Individual Education Program (IEP) specifically allows for alternative transportation. There is no assistance for kids like Henry to get to and from supplemental private therapy. Without a friend or family member who's willing to help manage these logistics, working a traditional nine-to-five job is impossible. A 2012 report from the Russell Sage Foundation notes that a third of children with disabilities live in single-parent households, and approximately 30 percent of families raising a child with a disability live in poverty. I was fortunate to have a partner with a full-time job and healthcare benefits when Henry was young, but I often questioned how single parents were expected to handle that level of care and still put food on the table.

I continued to be a stay-at-home parent by day and a part-time employee by night and weekend for most of my child-rearing years. When John stopped traveling so much, I also took evening college classes as time and finances allowed, eventually earning a bachelor's degree. Later, I'd apply for loans and complete two master's degrees as a non-traditional student. I took the lead on school projects, provided teaching assistance to professors, submitted essays for publication, and worked in part-time administrative jobs on the weekends for a large healthcare organization. But resuming a full-time career after stay-at-home motherhood proved difficult. I sent out over a hundred targeted cover letters and resumes with no response.

In early 2018, I finally got an interview for a communications job at a healthcare provider. It paid $40,000 a year. (The 2024 MIT Living Wage Calculation for Massachusetts states that a single adult with no dependents needs to make at least $58,000 a year to afford the basics of food, shelter, and transportation. With three kids to support? Over $178,000 per year.) After attending a second round of interviews and submitting a public relations plan that I'd prepared for the organization on my own time, I was offered the job. I tried to negotiate the salary, but the HR representative said there was no room for that. So I asked if there might be some schedule flexibility instead. What did they think about my working from home a day or two per week to offset commuting costs? The next day the HR coordinator called me back. "I'm sorry, but we are rescinding your offer of employment," she said. "Leadership feels that your request for remote work is an indication that you are not fully dedicated to this role."

A few months after that, a full-time position opened up at the organization where I'd been working part time. I applied and got the job. The salary was significantly higher than that earlier offer but still not what I'd hoped for, especially considering that the daily commute to Boston would cost me over $500 a month in commuter rail and subway fees. Even by 2024, after working full time for more than five years and part time for twenty years before that, my salary is half of what my husband earns. His work is not any more "skilled" than mine. He holds no college degrees, and his professional experience is far less diverse and wide-ranging. Yet, he's been consistently valued as a competent contributor over the last two decades. Until very recently, I've been viewed as a "mom" with a job on the side, even after our kids had all reached adulthood.

Researchers are investigating the root causes of this disparity. Earlier scholarship focused on gender inequities in accessing higher education, but that has equalized—women now outnumber men in finishing college. Still, the pay gap remains. A 2018 study argues that the gender pay gap is a penalty for childbearing. Additional studies have confirmed this thinking. The concept has come to be known as the "childcare penalty," a disadvantage resulting from a complex intersection of cultural and social norms, gender bias, salary inequities, lack of affordable and reliable childcare, inadequate social services, and outdated workplace cultures that value quantity of hours and physical presence over quality of work.

COVID-19 brought this issue to the forefront. More than 2 million women left the labor force in 2020, resulting in the lowest workforce participation level of women since 1988. Some of those women were forced out of female-dominated industries, like hospitality and childcare. Others quit their jobs due to the difficulty of balancing childcare and homeschooling with paid work, once daycare centers and schools closed down. Black and Latina women were especially hard-hit. The gender pay gap ensured that in the majority of heterosexual, two-parent households, it was women, rather than men, who left their paid work to focus on their children's needs.

The possible long-term economic consequences of this mass exodus received a great deal of media coverage. For a brief moment it seemed as though there was serious motivation to fix the gender pay gap along with other workplace inequities and inflexible policies that prevent women, as well as people with disabilities, from working to their full potential. But as America emerged from the pandemic, that discussion fizzled out. Some employers retained remote work, but many did not and demanded that their employees return to long commutes and traditional work hours, even when many of those jobs don't require someone onsite five days a week.

The pandemic illuminated critical deficits in America's social safety nets and healthcare infrastructure. It also revealed the value of women's work to our national economy, particularly in the field of education. A February 2024 *Wall Street Journal* report analyzed the most recent data from the American Community Survey and found that 96.7 percent of kindergarten and preschool teachers are women, and their median take-home pay is approximately $35,000 per year—less than half of the median salary for Americans who hold a four-year college degree. In an article for *Forbes*, gender bias expert Kim Elsesser argues that this statistic is likely due to economics. Despite the prevailing belief that women are more nurturing than men and therefore perform better in these roles, there is no proof to support that. Data suggests that the abysmal salaries are the reason why more men don't pursue these jobs. Gender stereotypes create a vicious cycle of inequity. Elsesser writes, "Work predominantly performed by women is often undervalued, and in fields predominantly occupied by women, there is a tendency to under-recognize their expertise and educational background." The few men who do teach preschool and kindergarten make almost 7 percent more than their women counterparts.

School and daycare closures were devastating for parents who rely on them to perform their own jobs, leading to calls for permanent subsidies that make childcare more affordable while providing early childhood educators a decent wage. Unfortunately, those appeals largely disappeared from the post-pandemic discourse. I'd hoped that my daughter's generation would find better opportunities to balance family responsibilities, health concerns, and fulfilling work. But my hopes faded along with the dying conversation.

LESSON 3

Your Medical Mileage May Vary

Winter overtakes southern New England and blankets our house in snow. Henry and I both come down with nasty colds early in the New Year. Danielle catches something two weeks later, just as Henry and I start to feel better, and Henry picks up that bug, too. Danielle has almost mastered potty training, but she begins having accidents in the night again. If I'm not up at 2 a.m. clearing stuffy noses or administering Children's Tylenol, I'm changing soaked sheets.

John is traveling to Detroit every week now, flying out of Boston on Monday afternoons and not returning until late Thursday evening, after the kids and I are already in bed. On Friday mornings he gets up early and goes back into the Boston office. By the time Saturday rolls around, I look and feel like I haven't slept in days. John spends the weekends playing with the kids. I take the opportunity to clean and shop for the week, child-free, and turn in long before John is ready for bed. We're more like roommates than lovers, sharing a space and chores but maintaining emotionally separate lives.

Eventually I get into such a routine that I almost dread John's return on Friday nights. He spends the weeks working in another city, going out for dinner and drinks with his coworkers on the company's dime, and staying in a nice company-paid hotel—a convenience that allows him to sleep until 8 a.m. every morning. I haven't had a vacation, *we* haven't had a vacation together, since our low-budget honeymoon in Florida five years ago. He's living like a person with money, though we don't have much. Even more aggravating to me, he's living like a person who has the luxury of free time—reading, watching movies in bed, ordering room service when he doesn't go out. I hate him for it. He gets the best of the kids on the weekends. I get the illnesses, toilet training, tantrums, and Henry's agonizing therapy sessions during the week.

I also get to see Henry's first gestures, watch my kids drag blankets across the house to build their first "fort" together, and attend Danielle's first school play. But I can't recognize this; exhaustion and loneliness obscure the joys.

One Monday evening—after a too-busy weekend during which few chores got done thanks to three preceding days of sick, cranky kids—I find no clean clothes in Danielle's closet. She has nothing to wear to school in the morning. Danielle refuses to re-wear something pulled from the dirty laundry hamper, but when I head toward the basement with the intention of doing a load of laundry, the stairway seems more like a trek down Kilimanjaro than a trip to the washing machine. My fatigue is so complete, so all-encompassing, that I don't trust my legs not to buckle underneath me and send me tumbling onto the concrete landing below. I call John's cell phone, crying.

"What?" he hollers into the phone. "Dani's clothes aren't washed? I can't hear you. I'm at a jazz club with some of the Tech Team. I'll call you later from the hotel."

"Fuck you," I say and slam the phone down.

* * *

At the end of January, Henry starts yet another round of antibiotics for one of the many ear infections that routinely follow any cold or sniffle. Soon after, he begins to vomit. I think he's reacting to the medicine, which often makes his stomach upset. He cries most of the night and into the next day, and within minutes loses whatever fluids or food he ingests. I call the pediatrician, who tells me to stop that antibiotic and try a new one she prescribes. But by the time John gets home from work that Friday, Henry's crying hasn't let up. I call the doctor again on Saturday morning, and she advises me to take him to the local emergency room.

John stays home with Danielle while I wait in the ER with Henry. A nurse calls his name and a doctor briefly checks him; then the nurse administers IV fluids. Henry quiets down and falls asleep on the exam table. I sit next to him, wanting to nap myself but too nervous to close my eyes.

"He was just dehydrated," the nurse says. "He'll be fine now."

We're released a couple of hours later. I carry sleeping Henry to our new minivan. The van is only new to us; we bought it used from a local dealer. It's a Chevy Lumina APV, a model that was discontinued several years before. It has a smooth white body with gray trim, massive dark windows that extend around most of its frame, and a pointed front-end, all of which make it resemble a rocket. The first time I saw John and the kids drive away in it, I conjured an image of a family who'd been dropped into a remote galaxy and who were then headed out to explore the terrain. It's a strange looking vehicle, for sure, but I love the thing. It has an incredible amount of interior space for all the kids' gear, and I can spot it in any parking lot, no matter how vast. I began affectionately referring to it as "the spaceship" after we purchased it.

I'm not even out of the hospital parking lot when Henry wakes up and starts screaming and vomiting again. I take him home hoping he'll improve. He doesn't. By dinner time, he has a fever. I give him a dose of Children's Tylenol and we settle into the rocking chair in his bedroom, where I wake early Sunday morning with him squirming in my arms. His pajamas are damp. I stroke his forehead; his skin is hot and clammy. In the soft glow of his nightlight, I look around for the thermometer, but I don't see it. Gently, I lay Henry down in his crib, then creep into my bedroom, where John is sleeping. I shuffle around as my eyes adjust to the harsh light from the hallway fixture.

John stirs, "What's going on?"

"Henry's fever is worse. I want to check it, but I don't know where I left the thermometer."

"Okay, okay, hang on." He stumbles out of bed and I go back to Henry.

"I found it," John says as he enters the room. He holds Henry and I take the temperature; it's 103. I give him more Tylenol, but he gets increasingly fussy and uncomfortable as the morning wears on. I call the doctor's office and an answering service operator promises to page our pediatrician. Meanwhile, Henry evolves from fussy to ferocious. He's inconsolable. Holding him, or just touching him, seems to make it worse.

"Something's very wrong. He's burning up. And he's curling himself in a ball, screaming like he's in pain," I tell the doctor when she returns the page.

"I can hear him," she says. "I want you to give him another dose of Tylenol to bring the fever down and take him straight to the ER in Boston. I'll call and let them know you're coming."

The traffic into Boston isn't too bad. Henry cries intermittently most of the way, but the car's movement seems to calm him some. I find a spot on the roof of the patient parking garage, which would count as a small miracle on a weekday. That's where my good fortune ends.

We check in with the front desk. And then we wait. And wait. And wait. This inner-city hospital sees the worst of emergencies—gunshot wounds, catastrophic accidents, domestic abuse, and drug overdoses. As much as I think Henry's mysterious pain is an emergency, he doesn't qualify for the top of the triage list here.

Six hours pass before Henry is evaluated. He cries almost the entirety of that time, interrupted only by a few spells when he falls into sleep out of complete physical exhaustion and then abruptly wakes up crying again five or ten minutes later. In those brief lulls, I flip through a magazine, hoping Henry might stay asleep long enough for me to become distracted by an article on some celebrity's new waterfront home or a politician's latest scandal. That doesn't happen, so I spend most of the time beating a path around eight rows of vinyl covered chairs that all face a large television mounted to an interior wall. I walk back and forth, bouncing and rocking Henry in my arms and trying to soothe him. I can't leave the waiting area and risk missing them call Henry's name. Hospitals, and all medical facilities for that matter, should hand out pagers like the hosts at chain restaurants do, so you can roam until the thing vibrates in your pocket and the little red lights flash.

When a receptionist finally calls our last name, we're directed into a room where we wait some more. An ER physician enters about fifteen minutes later and does a brief exam.

He decides to admit Henry for further observation. An orderly leads us to a semi-private room on an upper floor. Henry is given a mobile metal crib for the trip. It resembles a cage for an animal in a nineteenth-century traveling circus more than a comfortable place for a baby to rest, but I'm grateful. Once this contraption is parked and locked in place, I sit on the edge of a pale-green reclining chair beside it. My arms and legs ache. A nurse strides in, pulls the privacy curtain, and hooks Henry up to an IV that will pump fluids and pain medication into him. He still cries.

It feels like hours before a doctor enters the room and introduces himself as the attending physician for our HMO insurance plan. I have no idea why our health plan has its own physician at the hospital, but I'm too tired to question it. With scrutinizing eyes, a trim white beard, and weathered skin punctuated by a prominent nose, the doctor reminds me of a photo I saw in an essay about Ernest Hemingway in his later years. He looks wise and knowledgeable. He feels around Henry's belly and states in a solemn, grandfatherly tone, "We need to get an ultrasound of his abdomen as soon as possible. Someone will be up to transport him shortly."

I follow the rolling crib/cage to radiology and try to comfort Henry as the technician pokes and prods him in an attempt to get the necessary pictures. Henry is not a cooperative patient. His body thrashes back and forth while he releases ear-piercing screams. I've never heard such sounds from him before. A nurse pulls the rails back up around him and his cries become even more disturbing. This isn't a form of communication; it's instinct. He bangs against the metal bars like a trapped, injured primate whose very survival is at stake, his expression pained and terrified.

Another orderly wheels Henry back to our hospital room; I walk alongside him. I ask the floor nurse if I can hold my son, try to calm him down. She shows me how to steer clear of the IV, then she picks Henry up and places him on my lap. He curls into me and I envelop his fledgling body, covering his dangling feet with my winter jacket. I want to protect him, protect us, from all this chaos, to fix whatever ails him by sheer motherly will.

A while later, a young doctor enters our room and introduces himself as a pediatric surgeon. His golden complexion and sun-streaked blond hair make me wonder if he recently relocated here from some warmer locale. Boston is cold and gray at this time of year; the days are short and sunshine scarce.

"I was asked to consult with you and your doctor about our next steps," he says. *Next steps?*

The HMO physician arrives seconds later and jumps into the conversation. "We think it may be an intestinal obstruction, but we were unable to get a definitive ultrasound. An obstruction can be life-threatening. It requires surgery immediately," he says.

"I'm not comfortable going forward unless I have visible evidence of an obstruction," the younger surgeon interjects.

So someone orders another round of x-rays and ultrasounds, and again I help still Henry while the radiologist tries to get a clear picture.

"I won't do it," the younger doctor says less than an hour later, as the two physicians pick up the conversation in Henry's hospital room. The second ultrasound is also inconclusive. All they know is that Henry has enlarged lymph nodes in his abdomen.

"It could be just an inflammation," the surgeon says.

"He's been vomiting for at least forty-eight hours. Running a high fever. And he's far too irritable for simple inflammation," the older physician argues.

Irritable. That's the word he uses. It stands out to me because it seems like such an odd choice, such a mild term for the extreme anguish Henry is exhibiting, the profound pain he seems to be in.

"I am not going to open that child up and expose him to all the risks that entails without definitive proof of an obstruction," the young surgeon fires back.

It's like a scene from the set of *General Hospital*. I might find it comical in a campy way—this Ernest Hemingway doppelganger and young Dr. Physical Perfection engaging in dramatic heated dialogue—if the argument didn't determine the fate of my eighteen-month-old son.

I look down at Henry. I stroke his too-warm head and weave my fingers through his soft dark curls, now matted with sweat and tears. The two doctors continue to bicker. I silently question how much of this disagreement is about Henry and how much of it is about ego, a battle for status. I don't trust either one of them at this point. The light goes on behind the curtain that separates us from the older boy who now occupies the bed on the other side of the room. *Poor kid,* I think. *He's not going to get any rest tonight.*

The young surgeon and the older physician eventually reach a compromise, deciding that we'll watch and wait for the moment, see how Henry does over the next twelve hours.

Henry sleeps fitfully that night, with the aid of pain relievers and IV hydration, but he takes a turn for the better the next morning. He seems in less pain, less "irritable" by the time breakfast is delivered, and his fever drops a bit. He continues to improve throughout the day and into the next one. I remain by his side while John takes care of things at home. One of the moms from Danielle's preschool agrees to watch her that Tuesday afternoon so John can visit us at the hospital and bring me and Henry a change of clothes. The head nurse says Henry will likely be discharged the following morning. "Severe gastroenteritis" is the final diagnosis, probably brought on by an unspecified virus exposure, the doctor notes.

Knowing what I do now, I'd say the "irritable behavior" Henry exhibited was caused by a combination of his discomfort from the illness and the monumental sensory overload he must have been experiencing from a week of ER waiting rooms, diagnostic tests, sleep disruption, and hospital tumult. Parents experience great difficulty in getting appropriate care for their neurodivergent children within the medical system. So do neurodivergent adults. Research shows that autistic people specifically have a higher rate of premature death than the general population, and studies suggest that the numerous barriers preventing autistic people from effectively engaging with the healthcare system contribute to this mortality rate. These obstacles occur at the patient level (atypical communication, slower information processing speed, sensory sensitivities), the provider level (lack of flexibility, low knowledge about autism and related disorders, incorrect assumptions), and the systemic level (societal stigma, complexity of accessing the system, lack of supports and accommodations).

Those doctors didn't understand Henry's overwhelm, as they argued in front of us. Neither did I. But with every little setback and indignity, I was discovering who my son was, and who I would need to become as his parent.

"Mommy!"

Danielle flings her arms around my knees as I walk through our kitchen door on Wednesday afternoon, a sleepy Henry slung over my shoulder.

"Is Henry better now?" Her pleading eyes are full of genuine wonder and worry.

"Yes, baby. He's all better now." I hope I'm not lying to her.

LESSON 4

Nerves Will Fray

Winter wears on, and Henry grows more sure-footed in his mobility. But he becomes less tolerant of changes in his daily routines. Morning wake-up, mealtimes, naptime, playtime, and bedtime all have their own rituals. Henry will direct fierce protests toward anyone disrupting them. He will then attempt to right whichever routine has been wronged by repeating the process all over from the beginning. His need for structure is abnormally acute, but it makes sense to me that a kid who struggles to express himself will try to maintain extra control over his environment. Less change means less need to communicate. And I thrive on the structure as much as he does; it gives me a sense of command over my day. When I figure out his preferred routines and stay faithful to them, Henry is content and predictable.

Danielle is the exception to all of Henry's rules, the only exception, in that he seems willing and able to adjust to her extroverted nature and her desire for constant social interaction. She can do no wrong by him. He listens attentively as she reads to him, and he plays with magnetic letters, dolls, and art supplies as she instructs, even if it's not in the order he usually prefers. Many afternoons I find the two of them dancing on the brick hearth of our small dining room—Danielle in nothing but a tutu and a tiara, Henry wearing only his diaper and an abundance of Mardi Gras beads Danielle has draped around his neck. "La, la, la," Henry will "sing" along to a collection of kids' songs John has burned onto a CD. Other than a concern that we are nurturing a new family business—The Mackin Family Burlesque Show—I have no worries. Unlike my own experience growing up with my brother (who at six years old did not appreciate the arrival of a new baby sister to mix things up), no rivalry exists between these two siblings, however different they may be.

While walking and even dancing have now become part of Henry's repertoire, thanks in part to Danielle's prodding, speech has not. The few words Henry began uttering months ago, including *mama* and *dada*, have all but disappeared, and he's returned to making simple mimicking sounds and babbling. He has started pointing a bit though, and I wonder if building this skill is putting any language progress on hold, as if his brain can leap only one communication hurdle at a time.

And there are all those ear infections. By the time of Henry's eighteen-month checkup in late January, a week before he would contract that nasty stomach bug that landed him in the hospital, he'd already suffered through two more infections and a month-long series of antibiotics to treat them. Our pediatrician suspects the speech delay is associated with the constant fluid in Henry's ears. It's likely affecting his hearing and therefore his expressive communication, she explains. But she wants a full evaluation by a developmental specialist to rule out anything more serious. Two hospitals in our area have developmental medicine centers—one is a hospital dedicated to children; the other is a general research hospital. The pediatrician gives me the phone numbers for both. She also provides me with a list of local Ear, Nose, and Throat doctors (ENTs) so we can get a better handle on Henry's constant infections.

I'm able to get an appointment with an ENT within a few weeks, but there's a long wait for an evaluation at the developmental center of the children's hospital, and the general hospital isn't accepting any new patients at all in theirs. A full developmental assessment is a three- or four-hour endeavor, so they only schedule two per day. John and I have to complete pages upon pages of detailed intake forms before Henry can be put on the months-long waiting list. Once the developmental medicine center reviews this information, we'll be assigned an appointment. While we're waiting for that, Henry goes through the testing process with the ENT.

"Henry's hearing test came back functionally normal," the doctor tells me at Henry's follow-up appointment. She explains that his inner ear is vibrating appropriately and there are no apparent physical abnormalities or damage. "However, the constant infections are a problem, and the almost nonstop cycles of antibiotics need to be stopped. It's time to put ventilation tubes in and try to get this guy feeling better," she says, giving the mass of silky curls atop his head a little tousle. A few years later, a light touch to his hair will make Henry cringe and back away, but at this moment he doesn't react at all.

The procedure is called a myringotomy, in which tympanostomy tubes ("t-tubes" for short) are inserted to improve drainage of fluid from the ear. It has to be done under general anesthesia in a hospital operating room. Surgery is scheduled for March. It can't come soon enough. Within two weeks of that follow-up visit, Henry develops another ear infection, his worst yet. His fever spikes to 105. I administer perfectly timed alternating doses of acetaminophen and ibuprofen to keep it from going any higher, while continuously offering him electrolyte fluids to stave off the dehydration he experiences whenever he's feeling too ill to eat or drink.

I had recurrent, painful ear infections as a kid, too. But this procedure, the myringotomy, didn't become a common therapy until the 1980s—a decade after I needed it. My ear drum ruptured at least once that I recall and probably more times that I don't. I have some permanent hearing loss and frequent ringing in my ears that this childhood ailment may have contributed to, so I'm grateful for this relatively new surgical intervention that might help my own children avoid these consequences.

Meanwhile, Danielle is getting little attention and acting out because of it. Some days I feel like a robotic zombie, a shell of a human being. I go about what has to be done—bathing and feeding two kids, changing diapers, doing laundry, driving Danielle to preschool and dance class, and attending birthday parties or play groups when Henry is well enough—but all of it with zero enthusiasm. I have no energy to play with Danielle, bake a tray of cookies, or even watch a movie with her. And she resents it. She talks back, refuses to go to bed, and intentionally leaves messes in defiance of our end-of-day cleanup rule.

I put the kids to bed one Monday night and turn the TV on for company as I clear the dinner dishes from the table. I can barely stand up I'm so exhausted, but John's traveling and there's no fairy godmother who's going to load the dishwasher, hand-wash the pots, and wipe away the stray macaroni and squashed peas that somehow landed everywhere but back on the kids' plates. When I'm done, I walk into the living room where I plan to collapse on the couch in front of whatever sitcom or sci-fi drama is on next. I don't even have the energy at that moment to drag myself up the stairs and get ready for bed. But as I turn the corner toward the couch, I see a pile of what appears to be laundry at the bottom of the stairway. I switch on the overhead light. It's kids' clothing. I look up to see Danielle encouraging Henry to throw a pair of pants over the closed safety gate at the top of the stairs. She's giggling.

"What are you doing?" I yell.

I march up the stairs, open the gate, and spot another mountain of children's clothes in the hallway. All the clean, coordinated outfits that I washed and matched up the previous day in an effort to save myself the task of figuring out what the kids will wear this week are now tossed on the floor in a heap. Danielle pulled them off their hangers and dumped them there. She's playing a game to see how far she can throw each piece of clothing and is counting how many times she clears all twelve steps to reach the landing below. Henry must have heard the commotion and climbed out of his toddler bed to join her. The outfits from the lower bar in his closet, the ones within his short reach, are at the top of the mound.

"Why would you do this?" I holler at Danielle. "You don't think I have enough to do? Are you trying to make me angry?" She probably *is* trying to make me angry at some level, but she cannot have predicted the magnitude of the tirade her little transgression will cause.

"And egging on your brother? Teaching him to misbehave? What is wrong with you?"

I scoop Henry up and order Danielle, "Get down there and pick up all those clothes. Now!"

"No!" she screams back at me.

"Get down those stairs, Danielle. Right now!" I seethe.

"No!"

Henry starts crying. I put him back in his toddler bed. "Don't ever do something like this again, Henry, no matter what your sister tells you!" He surely has no idea what he's done wrong, just thinks he was playing with his big sister, but I'm too enraged to be rational.

Danielle is still standing in the hallway next to the pile of clothes that have yet to be thrown. "You don't want to pick up your mess? Fine, go to bed, and you can clean it up tomorrow. I don't care if you have to miss school to do it." I grab her by the arm, hard, and pull her into her bedroom. She looks up at me, the defiant pout on her face melting into something closer to fear. I've never put my hands on her like this before, never been so consumed with anger and frustration.

"I better not see you or even hear you until morning!" I leave her standing there in the middle of her bedroom and slam the door shut.

I go back downstairs, stepping over the mound of clothes that litter the last few steps. I pick up the phone and dial John's cell, but it goes straight to voice mail. "I can't do this anymore," I say after the beep. Then I hang up and cry. I slide down the wall I've been leaning against, too tired to hold myself upright any longer. I land in a crumpled heap on the floor, just like the pile of discarded clothing in front of me.

I wake up in the very early hours of the next morning, find two empty laundry baskets, then pick up all the tossed clothing and fold it, item by item. By the time the kids begin to stir, the mess is gone. I feed them breakfast, take Danielle to preschool, and go about our day as if nothing had happened.

* * *

As of this writing, there is no clinical definition of "mom rage." Writer and artist Minna Dubin popularized the term when she referred to it in a 2019 essay published in the *New York Times*. That piece was republished in the spring of 2020 when parents everywhere were trying to figure out how to care for and homeschool their children while also continuing to make a living in the midst of a global pandemic that closed schools and daycare centers. When the data on that endeavor was gathered, the results were jarring—more than half of American women who left the workforce during the pandemic did not do so because their own place of employment closed but because their children's daycare and/or school did. The enduring gender pay gap was a contributing factor. So was a set of cultural expectations that result in mothers bearing the brunt of childcare and domestic responsibilities in heterosexual partnerships, even when both partners work full-time jobs outside the home.

Lena Suarez-Angelino, a licensed clinical social worker, describes "mom rage" as a "mother's experience of overwhelming fits of anger that may arise in an instant and interrupt normal daily life" and that "may be exacerbated by both external circumstances and by a mom's internal state." These episodes are inextricably entangled with feelings of parental guilt and shame. Guilt is associated with how we behave—the actions we do or do not take—and is caused by the "external circumstances" Suarez-Angelino refers to. For example, studies show that mothers experience more parenting guilt than fathers, because American social behavior associated with being a good mother is at odds with cultural norms associated with professional success—mothers should be self-sacrificing and nurturing; professionals should be self-serving and ambitious.

We feel guilt when we don't behave in accordance with these standards.

Shame, on the other hand, is associated with how we feel about ourselves, or our "internal state." It's the difference between recognizing that you did something bad or made a mistake and thinking that you're a fundamentally bad person who is incapable of doing anything right. Suarez-Angelino explains, "Mom rage packs a double punch in that mothers experience both."

There's an ongoing debate on how much of mom rage should be attributed to a mental health issue versus a societal problem. Women are pushing back against the idea that they need to "fix" this for themselves through counseling and other means. Libby Ward, a self-identified maternal wellness advocate who posts on social media under the title "Diary of an Honest Mom" argued this point in a TikTok video that went viral in 2022. Ward asserts that women and mothers experience valid anger about things that are "unequal and unfair" and that society gaslights this anger. One of the cultural phenomena that contributes to this has been discussed on social media and dubbed "Default Parent Syndrome." The term describes a gender bias among two-parent heterosexual households that manifests in an assumption by both a woman's inner circle and the larger society around her that if a child needs something, it is she, the mom, who will drop everything to tend to that need. Being the "Default Parent" is associated with feelings of burnout and chronic fatigue, resentment toward one's children and/or partner, and a general decline in a woman's mental health.

Emerging evidence supports these anecdotal experiences that are shared on social media. In a spring 2023 report, the Pew Research Center found that, among dual-income heterosexual partnerships, "even when earnings are similar, husbands spend more time on paid work and leisure, while wives devote more time to caregiving and housework." Another recent research study showed that, for two-parent heterosexual households, when school principals were sent a message and asked to phone a parent back, they called mothers more. Interestingly, a significant number of mothers were called first even when fathers were listed as having more availability and flexibility to discuss their child with the school. The researchers conclude, "our findings underscore a process through which agents outside the household contribute to within-household gender inequalities." It's a damaging cycle of systemic bias informing and perpetuating endemic inequality.

In 2023, three communication researchers at Ohio University published the results from their study exploring the maternal anger experiences of sixty-five mothers in the U.S. They explain that gendered ideas of socially acceptable emotional experiences are learned very early on, well before school-age, and women are continually socialized to understand their anger expressions as inappropriate throughout their lives, despite experiencing anger just as intensely as men. The researchers note that within this social environment, women who discuss "mom rage" are vulnerable to potential stigma, no matter how normal and valid their anger may be. Presented with a lose-lose choice between societal judgment and frustrated isolation, it's no wonder more women don't seek help when they need it.

Cultural and societal expectations play a significant part in the overworking of mothers and the resulting exhaustion and anger. Given these intersecting considerations, it can be difficult for a woman to know if she's dealing with a personal mental health issue or the consequences of American society's impossible demands on mothers generally. Studies show that anger can also be a symptom of or coexist with postpartum depression, though these connections are still not well understood. The communications researchers note in their paper that, "Despite the complexities surrounding anger experiences and expressions, and the potential implications for mothers' wellbeing, little empirical research has explored what characterizes mothers' experiences of 'mom rage' or the factors that contribute to it."

I was not prepared for these feelings as a new mother. And no one told me how to deal with them when they happen, much less how to differentiate clinical depression from exhausted disillusionment. Either way, whatever the root causes, I believe there's something wrong with me in these moments. Motherhood is promoted as a joyful, even spiritual, state in American culture, and I feel deep shame whenever frustration and anger dominate my experience.

LESSON 5

Expect an Emotional Rollercoaster

Henry's ear operation takes place on an unusually mild, late-winter day. It starts off smoothly enough. We make the half hour drive to the community hospital and check him in. He's brought into pre-op, where his train-themed fleece pajamas are swapped out for a tiny hospital gown. The anesthesiologist puts him under as I hold him in my lap and John reads him a few lines of a favorite story. Within the hour, a nurse fetches us from the waiting room. Soon after, Henry is back in my arms shaking off the artificial sleep.

As we await discharge orders, Henry becomes fussy. We get him dressed in the soft pajamas he arrived in. I sit in yet another standard-issue vinyl hospital chair and cuddle his body against mine, gently rubbing his back. A few minutes later, he starts to thrash and then vomits—blood. He heaves again, his entire body moving with the force of it. Large clots of blood land on him, on me, and on the floor. He's now screaming, and I don't know if it's from pain or just the shock of his body's expulsion. There's blood dripping from his mouth and down his neck. A scene from some Anne Rice novel flashes across my mind.

John opens the door of our recovery room and calls to a nurse at the far end of the hallway for help. She says someone will be right in. The surgeon enters shortly thereafter and tells us that he made the decision to remove Henry's adenoids, which were very enlarged, while Henry was under anesthesia. "It's not unusual for a child to vomit up some of the tissue that's made its way down into the stomach," he explains. The surgeon assures us that it's nothing to worry about. "It looks much worse than it is," he says. I glance down at my son who is blotted in red from neck to feet. The nurse tells us we can head home whenever we feel ready. She leaves our discharge orders on the side table. Henry calms down, but no one comes in to help us clean him up, so John holds him while I make my way to the desk where we initially checked in. "Can I help you?" the woman behind the 'Registration' sign asks.

"My son's been discharged," I say, "but he vomited all over himself. Can I have a clean blanket or gown to wrap him in for the ride home please?"

The woman looks me up and down suspiciously. I'm wearing a light gray knit top that's now stained with fresh blood splotches. *Does she think I'm lying?* She gets up and opens the door of a supply closet behind her. She removes one clean blanket from a shelf and hands it to me. It's one of those multiuse thin cotton covers with a blue and red stripe across the hem— the kind that all hospitals stock, identical to the blankets my newborn babies were both swaddled in after their births.

"You'll have to return that when you're through with it," she says, as she turns back to her work.

Are you kidding me? But she clearly isn't. I think, *Yeah, okay lady, I'll be sure to wash this when I get home, pack it up, and drive the half hour back here to return this measly piece of fabric to you.* I take the blanket and decide right then that we'll be changing doctors to someone who is affiliated with a different facility. I am never stepping foot inside this hospital again.

I walk back to the recovery room, where John and I remove Henry's blood-soaked pajama top and bottoms and wrap him up in the blanket. We carry him out to the car, strap him into his child seat, and drape his winter coat over his torso to keep him warm. His feet are covered in blood-spattered Thomas the Tank Engine socks. At home, a little ibuprofen seems to curb any residual discomfort. Once he's settled into his own bed he sleeps the remainder of the day away.

As we wait for the physical improvement his surgery promises and the answers the upcoming developmental evaluation might provide, Henry grows increasingly frustrated. He seems to understand the world more and more, recognizes what he wants and when he wants it, but he can't communicate those desires. At home, I often figure it out through the process of elimination. "Do you want a drink, Henry?" I ask, as I hold out a cup. "Are you hungry?" I say, as I pull out a box of crackers. But if we are at someone else's house where it isn't so easy to make these connections? Forget it. He'll have an uncontrollable meltdown.

The therapist from Early Intervention continues working with Henry, but the sessions aren't getting any better. Both Henry and I are anxious wrecks by the time she leaves each week, and his communication is not improving. After three months, I decide to ask for a new clinician. I'm not sure why it takes me this long. I guess I want to believe this pairing will eventually be successful, or maybe I just don't want to create any more confrontation in my life—there's always the chance that the next person could be an even worse fit.

"Well, sometimes pushing a child out of his comfort zone allows him to progress," the Early Intervention administrator says when I call the office. My voice shakes as I explain the situation and ask to try someone new. It feels impolite, what I'm saying, and I don't want to offend the therapist or the program in general. Maybe my mother-in-law is right—Pat knows what she's doing and I should let the woman do her job. The pushback from the administrator confirms my vacillation and I feel defeated, ignorant. Am I the one doing something wrong? Of course I want Henry to progress, but speech therapy for Danielle was never like this. She loved her therapist and couldn't wait for her to come over each week. Henry is a different kid; isn't it possible that he might need a different kind of help? But what do I know? Still, with John's encouragement (*we're paying for it, so we should have someone both you and Henry like*, he says), I hold my ground. I want to try someone else.

A week later the new therapist arrives. She introduces herself to me and then asks if she can meet Henry. I show her to the living room where Henry is seated on the floor playing with his Matchbox cars. She watches him for a few minutes.

"Does he always play like this with his cars?" she asks.

"What do you mean?" I reply.

"Does he always assemble them in a line like that?"

"Yes. He always makes a long line. Sometimes he sorts them within the line by size, color, or style. He can sit for hours doing that."

She nods. I think it's amazing that a twenty-month-old can arrange such a large grouping so meticulously and amuse himself with it for so long. I wonder if she thinks so, too.

The therapist then approaches Henry slowly. She lowers herself to the floor and sits cross-legged about a foot and a half away from him.

"Hi, Henry. My name is Rose. Can I play with you?"

Henry ignores her.

"Can I have one of your cars?"

Henry doesn't respond.

She reaches out to touch a miniature Ford Mustang, and Henry's body begins to shake. He makes a primitive sound, the beginnings of a cry.

Rose pulls her hand back. "Okay, Henry. That's alright," she says. "I brought some of my own toys."

She riffles through her large canvas bag and pulls out a wooden puzzle. Rose removes the geometric-shaped pieces and arranges them around the rectangular base. Each piece has a small white peg in the middle to hold it by. She talks as she works, "There's the red triangle. Oh, look; here's the green square."

Henry glances over at the toy. He sits atop folded little legs that are barely able to carry his own weight. His big blue eyes are squinted and skeptical. He wrinkles his button nose, causing lines to form across a complexion so fair that his skin almost glows against the wild mop of dark curls surrounding it. *My beautiful boy*, I think, *is already jaded*. His demeanor is so cynical of the adults who are tasked with helping him, like they belong to a species altogether different from his own.

"Would you like to play with my puzzle?" Rose asks him.

Henry cautiously assesses the situation and then moves a few inches closer to her.

"This is how you do it." She demonstrates how to pick up a large wooden piece by its attached peg and then fit it into its appropriate place on the board. Rose hands Henry a piece—a yellow circle. He can't pinch his fingers around the peg, so he takes the puzzle piece from her with his whole hand and tries to manipulate it into one of the openings.

"Oops. Doesn't fit there," Rose confirms.

Henry keeps trying. He finally maneuvers the piece into the correct spot and Rose exclaims, "You got it! It fits!"

Henry smiles. So do I.

* * *

After Rose works with Henry for several weeks, she suggests we enroll him in a weekly group session at the Early Intervention center that she works out of—a spot has just opened up. In this setting, Henry will be encouraged to communicate with group facilitators and other children using recognizable sounds or sign language. Not only will it be good for Henry's communication skills, Rose says, but it might also offer me some helpful tools to manage the social interactions and unexpected routine changes that are so difficult for him.

We arrive at our first session the following Thursday and wait in the reception area until the group facilitator is ready for us. The center is housed in a 1980s-era single-level office building. The expansive interior is split down the middle, with an open play and therapy area on one side and administrative offices and conference rooms on the other. The long, narrow reception area straddles the two halves at the front, forming a T-shape. The play area has distinct sections—a reading nook with low bookshelves and beanbags to sit on, a flat rubber surface for ride-on toys, a corner with puzzles and building blocks, and an area with crescent-shaped tables for arts and crafts or snack time.

When the group officially starts, Henry and the rest of the kids are guided into the play area, and I'm directed into one of the adjacent conference rooms. One very long table spans most of the room, and multiple whiteboards line an interior wall. Two large windows on the west side look out over the weed-infested parking lot of a crumbling brick factory building that looms beyond. Glass inserts on the east side of the room overlook the other half of the center where the children play.

Parents enter the conference room and begin chatting, but I'm more interested in the activity happening on the other side of the space. I stand by the glass inserts and watch. Most of the children appear to have a combination of physical and developmental challenges resulting from disorders like Down syndrome or cerebral palsy. They all seem genuinely excited to be there—pleased to see the other kids and eager to engage with the adult staff. Henry, on the other hand, identifies the darkest, quietest corner of the room within the first thirty seconds, grabs a board book on the way, and toddles himself into seclusion. He seems to want no part of the interactions taking place around him.

It happens to be this month's "parent-to-parent" day, so once the kids are settled, the adults all sit down at the conference room table. The program coordinator introduces me as a new member and explains that this meeting is conducted every third Thursday of the month to give parents and caregivers an opportunity to ask questions and discuss challenges related to our "special needs children." The terminology takes me aback. It sounds so permanent. I don't think about Henry as a child with special needs; he's just a bit behind by current metrics. Danielle's speech delay required intervention too, but she caught up with her peers within a year or so and has gone on to be a typically developing preschooler. And like our pediatrician noted seven months earlier, with speech impediments running on both sides of the family, it isn't surprising that John's and my kids have these issues.

A social worker writes out talking points on a whiteboard while the other parents and caregivers in the room commiserate about the lack of accessible playgrounds in our area. They share tips on where to find babysitters who know how to adjust hearing aids, put on leg braces, or manage sleep apnea. I smile and nod and try to empathize, but Henry has no physical disability that requires specialized equipment, and he sleeps ten hours straight now. He only wakes in the middle of the night if he's ill. He's exhausted by the end of a normal day and a breeze to care for in the evenings; he just wants to be left alone in his room after dinner. John and I haven't gone out together in over two years, but I blame that on a lack of discretionary funds to both pay a babysitter *and* afford a nice dinner and/or tickets to a show.

I know that if I attempted to put Henry in daycare and go back to work during the day at this point, problems would surely arise. You'd have to possess some psychic ability to understand why Henry fell apart when he did if you aren't familiar with his daily routines. Even if you are familiar, any number of things in a foreign environment might set him off—things that he hadn't been exposed to before and to which his reactions were impossible to predict. At home, there are far fewer variables. Still, he sometimes develops a new compulsion or order of things that eludes me for a time. When I finally figure out what's frustrating him or what he needs, it feels like a miraculous triumph—a success emerging from hours of careful deduction, trial and error. But I'm confident that, as his communication skills improve, these compulsions and their associated meltdowns will become less frequent and eventually disappear altogether.

The coordinator starts the formal parent discussion. I keep quiet, content just to listen. But when the conversation turns toward specific therapies and opinions on the best practitioners in the area, the social worker turns to me and invites my input. I don't know what to say. Henry isn't communicating; I don't know why. He has no diagnosis and, up until recently, I didn't realize he was all that far behind. I can't remember exactly how much Danielle was talking when she was Henry's age, but lots of people tell me that boys develop on a different timetable than girls. My mother, who's worked as a home-health nurse for forty years, is convinced that Henry's just a late bloomer, and my in-laws dismiss any concerns as foolish.

"It's some kind of speech and motor skills delay," I tell the group. "That's really all we know at this point. We don't use any special therapies or practitioners, other than his regular pediatrician and these Early Intervention services. He does see an ENT for recurrent ear infections, but he had ear tubes put in, and now that's mostly cleared up." Some of the other parents nod in acknowledgment, but the social worker offers an uneasy half-smile that makes me wonder if she knows something that I don't.

It's time for the kids to have a snack. Through the glass I can see a young woman arranging portable plastic dividers to wall-off the play area. The kids are split into groups of six and directed to sit at one of the three large crescent-shaped tables. A facilitator sits in the middle of each table, flanked by a semicircle of children who are facing her. Our parent discussion hour is up, and I'm grateful. It was not helpful for me, and depressing. I heard lots of complaints about standards of care, insurance coverage limits, and lack of resources, but very few solutions.

The coordinator tells us that we can spend the remainder of the session waiting in the reception area or we can sit in the now vacant part of the divided play area and peek over the barricades to watch as the kids perform tasks around eating and drinking. We aren't allowed to speak to our children or in any way try to gain their attention. "The kids need to do this on their own," the social worker says.

I choose to watch, and I quickly conclude that Henry has the most deficient communication skills of the group. The other kids seem to know the words required for this activity but are working on better articulation, or they're mastering sign language instead. I'm not sure that Henry even has the words in his head.

According to Early Intervention's recent evaluation, both Henry's receptive and expressive language skills are approximately one year behind—no better than that of an eight-month-old. A gap of an entire year is a lot for a child who isn't even two yet. To add to the frustration, his motor skills are also several months behind, making the physical act of communicating with gestures much more challenging. Still, he moves around fine at home and plays with little difficulty. He's never around children his own age; his social experiences are mostly defined by Danielle and her friends. This group session is the first true comparison to his peers that I've seen, though every child in this room has some sort of disability or developmental delay that muddies my assessment.

A staff member pulls jugs of apple juice and water from a nearby storage cabinet and places them on the tables. Child after child says "drink" or signs it, and their respective facilitator responds by pouring a few tablespoons of juice or water into small plastic cups and handing them out. Henry grabs the whole bottle of juice and pulls it toward him.

"No, no," the facilitator says firmly as she takes the bottle back. "Tell me what you want, Henry."

He reaches for one of the plastic cups that has already been filled, but the facilitator pulls it away. Henry bangs his hands on the table in frustration.

"Tell me," the woman repeats.

Henry glares at her. I imagine him thinking, *Listen, you dimwitted shrew, what do I have to do to make you understand that I want a drink? Is reaching for the bottle not obvious enough? Grabbing the cup isn't clear?* The apple juice turns into Jack Daniels in my mind, and Henry morphs into a talking baby making inappropriate adult-like comments within a ridiculous family sitcom—a talking baby who no one but other inappropriately adult-like talking babies can understand. Like Stewie from *Family Guy*, but without the destructive bent.

The scene becomes so unbearable to witness that even these dreamed-up scripts fail to distract me from the reality of the situation. I stand and silently plead with Henry, hoping a kind of parent-child telepathy exists between us that will allow him to hear me. *You have to conform, Henry. You have to behave like everybody else, so people don't have to work so hard.* It's a lesson I learned after years of being dismissed or demeaned when I attempted to advocate for my own needs or revealed personal preferences that others viewed as unusual or inconvenient. My adult life has been a constellation of assimilations— some concentrated, some scattered, depending on the specific circumstances—connected by blissful pockets of solitude. I don't imagine this will ever change.

My attempt at clairvoyant communication fails. Henry

doesn't say or sign a word. While the facilitator puts away the juice and crackers and the other children pick up toys to a prerecorded cleanup song, Henry remains at the table, banging his fists on it with such anger that I think his knuckles might bleed. Clearly, he is not going to recover from this injustice soon enough to participate in cleanup or whatever other end-of-session rituals are scheduled.

"Can I get him? Please, can I get him now?" I yell across the room. I'm about to leap over the barricade like a mommy ninja when the facilitator nods to another employee who then pulls one of the modular dividers back. I descend upon the table, pick Henry up in one swift swoop, and hold him tightly against me. "I'm sorry," I say, as I hurry out of the building with my inconsolable toddler. I don't know if I'm apologizing to the staff or to Henry.

Despite this less than stellar beginning, Rose insists the group is good for Henry and cautions that if we relinquish our spot we'll be hard-pressed to get it back, so I agree to give it more time.

For several weeks, the one-sided dialogue between the facilitator and Henry continually repeats itself until Henry begins to cry or scream, sometimes collapsing in a frustrated heap, with seemingly no understanding of why this woman won't give him a drink or a cracker or a toy that he wants to play with. That's my cue. Once he starts full-on crying and disrupting the entire group, I'm summoned. I hold him close, willing some of the tension to leave his body and sink into my own, but I feel otherwise helpless to improve the situation. And guilty. I, his mother, am taking him to a place where he's made to sit and watch food and toys being shared with every other kid but him. A place where he is pushed to create communication that he finds excruciatingly difficult, but that seems relatively effortless and instinctual for his peers. A place where his mind is being manipulated to work in a way that it obviously isn't designed to. These exchanges that continue week after week make me profoundly uncomfortable. I feel like I'm living a scene out of *The Miracle Worker*. But surely we've advanced beyond the nineteenth-century methods that Annie Sullivan employed to teach Helen Keller. If this were happening anywhere other than in a therapeutic context, I would deem it cruel. Still, the cruelty that awaits Henry if he doesn't learn how to communicate his needs in socially appropriate ways will be worse. The world will not bend for him.

After enduring what seems like an eternity of this agony but is closer to a couple of months, Henry sits in a chair at the snack table when the facilitator once again says, "Tell me what you want." Henry lifts his left arm in front of him, makes a fist with his right hand, then bangs that fist forcefully against his left elbow—the sign for "cracker." She gives him a handful of Pepperidge Farm Goldfish and then looks over at me as I sit in my designated corner, to make sure I saw it.

Henry scoops the treats into his mouth with no fanfare, never looking at me, never offering a hint as to whether he understands the significance of this achievement or not. But a surge of emotion rises through my body with such uncontrollable force that I have to leave the room. Tears blur my vision as I scramble toward the lobby. The velocity and intensity of feeling is so unexpected and so impossible to hide that I feel like an irrational absurdity of a mother. I struggle to find a tissue in my voluminous diaper bag under the watchful eyes of a confused and concerned receptionist.

"Are you okay?" she asks.

"I'll be fine, thanks," I reply, avoiding her gaze. "I'm just going to step outside for a moment. I need a little air."

I lean against the glass of the front entrance, grateful for the spring breeze that still holds a slight chill of winter in its gentle current. The muscles of my body are loose, shaky, and I slide down to a crouch, surrendering, my head in my hands. Before this moment I could never have imagined the unadulterated, insuppressible relief a few little goldfish-shaped crackers would bring me. This emotional eruption is unlike anything I experienced during Danielle's toddlerhood. I'm in unchartered motherhood territory, and I don't know how to navigate this space. I assumed that once Henry acquired essential communication skills, we'd be nearing the end of our journey through therapeutic intervention and life would go back to "normal." Now I wonder if we've only just begun.

After pulling myself together, I go back inside and watch Henry help clean up; he gathers puzzles and blocks and drops them into appropriate storage boxes. I leave that day with a content child rather than a sobbing one for the first time since we started the group, and I praise him all the way home. But beneath this joy lurks a terrifying thought. Will every accomplishment, every uttered word or gesture, every milestone no matter how small, prove equally elusive?

* * *

Psychologist Kalman Heller writes of complex conditions, such as autism, Tourette syndrome, and bipolar disorder: "Each of these disorders has books, websites, and national organizations devoted to them. Parents often know more about the specific disorder than any individual professional involved in treating the child because they devote hours to researching out all available information."

It's true. Complex conditions manifest in a variety of ways in individuals, and parents understand the unique challenges of their young children better than any medical expert who spends an hour with them once or twice a year. Dr. Heller adds, "Yet, as I recently listened to a group of such parents share their pain and frustration, I could hear some common issues being expressed repeatedly: the need for parental support systems, the reality that in many situations nothing really works to resolve the challenges their children present, the lack of social opportunities for their children, the impact on marriage, the impact on siblings, and fears about the future."

Amen to that. The cumulative effects of this nonexistent support nearly broke me, and my marriage. I needed to know that I wasn't alone, but that reassurance rarely came. I struggled to care for myself and my family during the early years of Henry's life. My desire to provide him with the best possible environment in which to thrive, while also ensuring that his siblings felt equally loved and supported, gutted me. I couldn't meet the emotional, physical, and financial demands of keeping my family healthy, happy, and moving forward. I felt demoralized, hollow.

Dr. Heller describes his feelings of powerlessness as he recognizes the isolation many parents feel while acknowledging how difficult it is for a medical provider who has never been in these parents' shoes to provide adequate, meaningful support. The emotions a parent goes through as they watch their child struggle or be "othered" in a specific environment can be overwhelming, but many lack the time or energy to go searching for a support group of parents with similar challenges. And back in the early 2000s, these groups were rare, especially for those who lived outside of major metro areas. Although I did meet a few parents in a psychologist's office whose children struggled with similar issues to Henry's, I never found a consistent group with whom I could share information or frustration. Fortunately, more of these groups exist now than when Henry was small, thanks to increased acknowledgement of neurodiversity as well as new tools and virtual spaces that the digital revolution has made possible. These communities can be invaluable for a parent navigating special-needs education and medical systems.

Researchers have begun looking at the effects of raising neurodivergent children on parents and caregivers, with a focus on autism. Their work so far confirms the importance of group support. A 2007 needs assessment of mothers found that "the most stressful factor that parents with autistic children have experienced is limited acceptance of autistic behavior by society members and failure to receive social support." A 2021 study of families raising autistic children suggests that there hasn't been much improvement in the fifteen years since. The latter study identifies continuing challenges that fall into two categories: (1) family related issues; and (2) education and treatment problems. The family issues include three categories of consistent problems: financial, psychological, and family relationships. Education and treatment challenges involve three other categories: schooling, transportation, and quality in facilities. These were my family's primary challenges at the turn of the millennium, and they continue to plague families today.

Research is scant when it comes to how neurotypical children are affected by having siblings with neurological and developmental disorders. In a 2003 study from the United

Kingdom, neurotypical siblings of children with autism reported feeling neglected by family members as well as experiencing financial repercussions due to family resources being diverted toward therapy for the child diagnosed with autism. In another study, neurotypical siblings reported feelings of embarrassment and shame that negatively affected their friendships and their parental and sibling relationships. A South African study found that some neurotypical siblings felt the need to ease their parents' stress. However, in that same study, siblings reported developing positive character traits as a result of having an autistic sibling, including patience, tolerance, and acceptance of difference. A significant percentage of adolescents surveyed were inspired to pursue professional careers focused on helping others as a result of having a sibling with a disability.

For me, this limited research confirms what I've observed from my own children's relationships with one another and with my husband and me—support should come in the form of a holistic approach that considers the effects on and experiences of the entire family.

LESSON 6

Let Yourself be Ridiculous Sometimes

"You sure this is a good idea?" John asks. I'm studying online listings for costumed character appearances. We've planned a small backyard get-together in July to celebrate Henry's second birthday, just family and a few friends, but I want to make it memorable. Henry loves Elmo and is mesmerized every time the furry red Muppet appears on the TV. So I've decided to join the ranks of parents who hire performers to show up at their kids' parties dressed as popular television or film characters. It seems harmless enough, but John has reason to be concerned.

A month earlier, we'd taken a family road trip to Pennsylvania. Our first stop was Sesame Place in Philadelphia. We had a pleasant visit to a theater there where we watched actors recreate an episode of *Elmo's World* live, but Henry was otherwise agitated by the amusement park. When I tried to coax him into a kiddie pool or onto the carousel, he latched his little body onto my leg so tightly that I thought he might cut off my circulation. Danielle ran ahead to explore the next attraction while Henry fussed and whined and attempted to climb back into the double stroller that I'd loaded down with a mountain of snacks, drinks, sunscreen, and diapers. I eventually gave up on forcing Henry to engage, rearranged our belongings, and let him get into the backseat of the stroller. He pulled the sun hood forward as far as it would go.

In a Sesame souvenir shop I bought a small board book and an oversized Elmo towel to drape over the entire buggy. Shielded from the sun's bright rays, and with the shrieks and giggles of surrounding children muffled by the heavy fabric, Henry withdrew into his mobile cocoon with the new book. He stayed there until we left the park at the end of the day. Similar scenarios unfolded on visits to the Philadelphia Zoo, the Franklin Institute, and Adventure Aquarium during our holiday. Because of those experiences, John thinks I'm throwing away money by arranging this birthday visit, and risking the enjoyment of everyone else. If Henry becomes overwhelmed, he argues, the day could turn into a disaster.

"We'll have them cut it short if it doesn't go well," I say. "I'll tell the guy to leave if Henry's rattled."

"But why do we need to do this?" John pushes back.

I can't answer. Maybe it's the rookie-parent foolishness I've suffered with ever since Danielle was born—an impulse that prompts otherwise reasonable adults to do things like spend two full days creating an exact architectural replica of Sesame Street out of chocolate cake, as if a toddler won't completely ignore that effort and dive face-first into frosting at the earliest possible opportunity. Or maybe it's just another example of my continued effort to fit in, to keep up with the maternal Joneses all around me, to normalize our family.

I yearn to be like the moms and dads at Danielle's preschool who share videos of their small children relishing in elaborate celebrations. Their kids ooh and ahh over candlelit cakes and gifts wrapped in brightly colored paper. They gleefully sing along with a favorite television character or Disney princess who's made a surprise visit to their soiree. Aunts and uncles and grandparents clap along, delighting in the little one's joy. *This is what good parents do*, I think. *This is how to make birthdays special.* I'd done it for Danielle. She was all about art projects that year, so we spent her last birthday at a local craft store, where she and her preschool friends built, painted, and adorned their own wooden jewelry boxes. While the boxes dried, the kids feasted on a cake I decorated to look like a giant bejeweled butterfly.

John's hesitancy is a reminder that Henry isn't like other toddlers and the things that amuse most young kids won't necessarily excite him. He still isn't interested in playing or interacting with children his own age. His nonverbal communication has improved a little with Rose's help and the torturous repetition of his weekly Early Intervention group, but discerning his wants and needs is still a frustrating process of elimination that few friends or family can endure. While other two-year-olds we know are exploring and experimenting, Henry rarely strays from a structured schedule and often becomes upset when circumstances force a change in his routine. None of this dissuades me though, and I book Elmo's appearance.

The day of the party arrives. Henry plays with a shape sorter at my feet and the adults sit around in lawn chairs socializing. The rest of the kids enjoy the yard. It's a spectacular summer afternoon and we're all happy to be outside after a harsh winter that produced snow well into April. John mowed the lawn the day before, and I mulched around the shrubs, pulled weeds, and planted flowers. My yard will never look pristine, but I did what I could with fifty bucks at Home Depot's garden center and a few hours of my own labor.

We've prepared several activities for the kids. John and I

picked up a few ride-on toys at local yard sales and cleaned them up to look like new. We positioned them at a starting line for the kids to drive down "Sesame Street." It's just a linear stretch of our yard covered in some old roofing shingles with a line of yellow duct tape down the middle, but it's effective. John has manufactured a version of cornhole using a massive sheet of thick cardboard that he cut out and painted to look like Elmo. The kids will try to throw small red bean bags into Elmo's smiling mouth.

On the TV show, Elmo has a pet goldfish named Dorothy, so I counted out hundreds of goldfish crackers and filled a large plastic fishbowl with them—whoever guesses closest to the right amount will win a prize. I wanted to award a real goldfish, but John reminded me that not everyone would appreciate that, so I went with a stuffed Elmo instead. (I never actually present it, though; before I identify the winner, a concerned parent informs me that if I give a toy to one child, I should give one to all, so there will be no hurt feelings.)

Finally, I bought plastic daisy yard decorations at the Dollar Store, drew faces on them to resemble the talking flowers on *Sesame Street*, and then stuck them in the ground among the live ones I'd planted. If I'd been more forward-thinking, I would've taken photos of it all before the guests arrived and later pitched our display to one of the popular parenting magazines—"Best Themed Birthday Parties on a Budget!" I'm proud of our creativity.

About an hour into the festivities, Danielle runs toward us. "Henry! Look! There's someone here to see you!" A seven-foot Elmo emerges through the trees at the back of our yard carrying a bouquet of multicolored balloons. I hold my breath.

Henry gazes at the oversized red figure but doesn't move,

as if temporarily stunned. A few seconds later he scrambles to his feet and begins running—straight for Elmo. I follow, with camera-ready John directly behind me. Henry reaches Elmo and leaps into his arms as the absurdly tall monster bends down to greet him. I take the balloon bouquet from a large fuzzy paw, and Henry throws his arms around Elmo's neck, burying his face in the matted fur of the costume.

"Well hello, new friend," the man says in his best imitation of Elmo's high-pitched, guileless tone. I turn toward the lawn chairs to see most everyone with their hands over their mouths in disbelief. None of us has seen anything like this from Henry; it's the most enthusiastically he's ever greeted anyone.

Elmo walks around with Henry in his arms for the remainder of the hour we've paid for, and then some. "I've got to go now," Elmo finally says. "But I'll see you soon on *Sesame Street*." Henry reluctantly lets his feet touch the ground as Elmo lowers him onto the lawn.

"Bye bye, everyone," Elmo singsongs, and we all wave as he turns to exit back through the trees, beyond which his car is parked and where he can discreetly climb out of his costume. John distracts Henry, and I catch up to Elmo to give him a few extra dollars for his trouble. "Sorry about that," I whisper, apologizing for the fact that he had to carry a two-year-old child around for over an hour on an eighty-degree afternoon while encased in what must have been a sweltering polyester monster suit. "But you made his day."

"Are you kidding?" he replies in a grown man's rasp. "He made mine. Kids who respond like that are why I do this job."

As Elmo disappears into the grove between our back-yard and the abutting side street, I turn to see John stepping through our patio door carrying the edible block of *Sesame*

Street that I toiled over for the previous forty-eight hours. It has a plastic Elmo toy positioned in the center like a monument. "Time for cake!" I cheer.

The cake sits on a thick piece of foil-covered cardboard, and John holds it just far enough away so that Henry can blow out his two candles without touching any of it. But as soon as John sets the cake down on the patio table, Henry demolishes a miniature street corner with one quick swipe, like Godzilla stepping on Manhattan. As Henry shoves a fistful of frosting into his mouth, I slide the cake out of his reach and start slicing up the undamaged portion for our guests.

Birthday presents are opened; games are played; and squealing kids are treated to wagon rides around the yard as fast as John can pull them. Henry mostly observes the action from a quiet corner, happy to let his gregarious older sister take the lead and absorb the spotlight.

* * *

I'm not aware of any research studies exploring the role of fictional characters in the lives of children with disabilities. But the connection Henry formed with Elmo (and later with other characters) was far more intense than the attachments I'd observed by other children, including Henry's siblings. Danielle liked Dora the Explorer and later Kim Possible, but Henry seemed to be attempting a sort of understanding with Elmo that came to fruition when the character showed up in the flesh, or rather in the fur, in our own backyard.

In *Life, Animated*, Ron Suskind writes about his son Owen's connection with and use of Disney characters to communicate and access emotions that his autism spectrum disorder otherwise impedes. Henry was in his mid-teens when I first came across the book, and I found that the Suskinds' experience and my family's journey were similar in some ways but very different in others. Still, when I read about Owen's attachment to these characters, I was reminded of Henry's early fondness for Elmo. I didn't understand it at the time, but after several years of watching Henry struggle to navigate social norms and societal structures that his peers adapted to with relative ease, I came to recognize how comforting that muppet's fictional neighborhood must have appeared to Henry. A recurring character on *Sesame Street* who was a perpetual three and a half years old, Elmo always found himself surrounded by kind and wise adults of both the human and furry sort. He often asked them to explain words and ideas—he was too young to grasp the nuances of relationships or to recognize that a word or phrase could take on new meaning depending upon the context. Henry, too, struggled to understand his environment back then. He just didn't yet have the voice or vocabulary to ask the questions.

Today I like to think that Elmo gave Henry something no one else could at that time—the knowledge that he wasn't alone. Maybe Henry wasn't holding onto Elmo solely for his own comfort at that party. Maybe he was also consoling, as if to say: "I get it, buddy; I know what you're going through. I don't understand much about this world, either."

On that second birthday I believe my son exhibited an emotion that would often prove difficult for him to express in the years that followed, and sometimes still does—empathy. A sensitive child who experienced a full range of human emotions, Henry didn't quite know what to do with all those feelings. Long spells of silence eventually erupted into screams and sobs, followed by more days or weeks of self-inflicted solitude.

The adults who tried to help him probably appeared demanding and intimidating much of the time. But Elmo wasn't. He was a kindred spirit also trying to make sense of a confusing and unpredictable place, and his neighbors on *Sesame Street* were patient and approachable.

Rookie-parent decision or not, the money I paid for Elmo to visit us that day was worth it. Henry may have no memory of that warm and cloudless afternoon, but I carry it with me as a reminder of my son's capacity for love and compassion. It rarely manifested itself in the way it did for other children who hugged, applauded, and openly encouraged or engaged their classmates or caregivers, but it was there nonetheless. These emotions existed in and maybe even fueled Henry's obsessions with a seldom-remembered U.S. president and a struggling Star Wars Jedi. They dwelled in his reverence for a particular classical composer who violated accepted musical norms, and for a certain Red Sox outfielder who had a bad game on the most important of days. My heart sang as I watched a friendship blossom between Henry and a foster child who was new to our town—two kids marginalized but united. And my heart broke as I watched him deeply grieve the loss of our sweet goofy cat who never left Henry's side from the very first day we brought him home from the animal shelter.

Assisting and advocating for a child who develops and behaves outside the "normal" parameters is an education in itself, and I've learned as much about my own strengths and limitations as those of Henry's. I look harder now for a human connection that may at first seem nonexistent. I try to give others the benefit of the doubt when it feels like they're failing us and to pay closer attention to the inherent struggles that we all face, no matter where we come from or how different our personal goals and motivations may be. As Henry carves out his own life as a young adult and I navigate middle age, we both continue to learn resilience in a complicated and often disconcerting world. And when those paths seem fraught with challenges, it's helpful to remember the ever-present possibilities for joy and wonder—like the arrival of an unexpected, understanding friend on a warm and welcome sunny day.

LESSON 7

The Best Laid Plans Will Go Awry

It's mid-August and Danielle is getting ready to start her second year of preschool. I've scheduled daily therapy sessions for Henry around her drop-off and pick-up times. At our last visit to the pediatrician, when I explained that Henry seems to have lost the few words he'd gained in the months prior, the doctor was concerned. "All the studies show the more therapy at his young age, the better," she said. "While the brain is still developing, it can forge new pathways, find a new route to the same skill if the original one was broken."

Broken? "What do you think is wrong?" I asked. I'm still of the mind that much of Henry's symptoms are lingering effects from the constant fluid that's been in his ears. The audiologist at the ENT's office explained that it's as if he was hearing underwater all those months before the t-tubes procedure. And since babies mimic what they hear, both his receptive and expressive language would have been affected. More than one doctor we've come in contact with suggests the same thing; so has Rose and others from Early Intervention.

The pediatrician said it's far too early for any diagnosis one way or another and that we shouldn't get bogged down with labels, but rather focus on getting Henry as much help as possible to meet his milestones. So that's what I'm doing. Rose comes to the house twice a week. I bring Henry to the Early Intervention center for the group session every Thursday, and the other two days I take him to a private speech therapist. I'm happy to have found one who takes our health insurance, but the $40-per-appointment copay cuts into what little disposable income is left after the bills are paid each month, so I pick up some freelance proofreading work that I can do in the evenings once the kids are in bed.

Henry's frequent ear infections have ended thanks to his t-tubes, and we're all getting a decent night's sleep now. John has been put on a new project that's managed out of the Boston office, so his business trips are fewer and farther apart. With him home more of the time, I decide to sign up for a continuing education class that meets one night a week at a local art school. It doesn't offer college credit, but it's inexpensive and interesting. Increased rest and a break from the monotony of motherhood improves my mood and John's and my relationship.

* * *

"What's that, Mommy?" Danielle asks. I'm scrutinizing pregnancy tests in the health and beauty aisle. I want the one that offers the fastest results, but I must choose quickly. Now three months into her senior preschooler status, Danielle declares that she is far too big to sit in a shopping cart, even those ones shaped like trucks and busses that have big front seats, so the grocery store is a challenge. Fortunately, Henry is still small enough and happily restrained.

"Nothing, sweetie. Just grown-up stuff."

I didn't go back on birth control after I stopped nursing Henry. Frankly, my marriage hadn't required it. At this time last year, I thought John and I might be headed for divorce. But we got through that rough patch and even started discussing the possibility of a third child, despite having sold most of our baby gear in a neighborhood yard sale a few months earlier. We aren't actively trying to get pregnant but taking a "let's see what happens" approach.

I settle Henry in for his afternoon nap and take one of the two tests in the package. It's negative. I'm not sure if I'm relieved or disappointed at first—it's a little too soon; the timing isn't right. Still, by the time John returns home from work, I know. Definitely disappointed.

The next few weeks are a whirlwind of holiday decorating and baking, stopping in to see family members, attending preschool parties and pageants. My in-laws visit us on Christmas Eve, and the kids behave like perfect angels. I'm grateful because this schedule comes after weeks of negotiation. My in-laws have a tradition of a five o'clock dinner on Christmas Day, followed by gift-giving and the usual festivities. They are night-owls, and this schedule works for them. I'm not a night-owl, but before the kids came along, John and I conformed. We visited with extended family on Christmas Eve. Then we drove to my parents' house early on Christmas Day, so that we were available to be at my in-laws on time in the evening. We continued to do this for a couple of years after Danielle and Henry were born, though my parents began traveling to us on Christmas Day, rather than the other way around, once Henry arrived.

As Henry grew and his dependence on routines and structure emerged, not to mention my own need for consistency, this schedule became more difficult. Last year I was not feeling well, run-down from all the holiday tasks, so John took the kids to his parents' house alone. Not surprisingly, the kids were also exhausted and cranky. They didn't behave well at my in-laws, had trouble settling once they got home, and in turn were tired and irritable the next day, too. After that experience, John said, "Never again. I'm done with this." I agreed. So this year we offer up multiple other options, none of which are acceptable to either my parents-in-law or John's sisters. John's family is deeply resistant to any change in their customs, but we weren't aware of this until the evolution of our own lives required some alterations to the status quo.

A simmering resentment toward John and I already exists, because we asked his family to stop smoking cigarettes around the kids—a request they deemed insulting. This animosity is now further exacerbated by our request to rethink the holiday traditions. Recently, some of John's family members have become openly hostile to us, but especially toward me, publicly undermining my parental role in front of extended family and my own children. This behavior begins with relatively mild, dismissive comments to my young daughter like, "Oh, don't listen to your mother," but quickly escalates to acrimonious actions such as intentionally ignoring me at family gatherings. My sister-in-law walks into a room and greets everyone but me; if she's taking food or beverage requests, she skips over me, asking the person to the right and left of me for their preferences.

Ours are the only kids on either side of the immediate family—the only nieces or nephews of both John's sisters and my brother, and the only grandchildren of John's parents and mine. But both my parents come from larger families, and there were always numerous other kids around when I was growing up. John's upbringing was more nuclear, so I try to have some empathy for the changes my growing family brings to my in-laws' lives. I know they love our children, but the lack of support is disappointing to John and me. And unexpected. We thought they would ask, "How can we help? What do you need?" But John's family members are disinterested in learning how to care for our children by twenty-first-century standards. The nap and meal schedules we maintain seem unnecessary to them, and they say so. When I offer to demonstrate how to properly install a car seat, my mother-in-law says, "We never used car seats with our kids and they were fine." No one in John's family counters these statements, and I feel chastised for acknowledging progress and expecting them to as well.

Of course, I imagine my in-laws view John and me as the uncooperative ones, but engaging them in any open, honest discussion seems impossible. John maintains that these skills—functional communication and compromise—were never modeled in his household growing up. There was no constructive arguing, he says. Disagreement was not viewed as a normal aspect of healthy relationships. He learned how to navigate conflict on his own through professional activities and personal counseling. But he had to identify that knowledge gap at some point in order to rectify it, and many of us who were raised with this sort of dysfunction are well into adulthood before we reach that level of self-reflection, if we ever do.

In a scene in *Mom Rage*, author Minna Dubin tells her young son (who is neurodivergent) that screen time is over. She explains to readers that she'd come to understand how long he could watch videos on the laptop before she needed to transition him to another activity, in order to prevent major meltdowns. In the scene, her son protests, and Dubin's husband

Paul undermines her decision by calling from down the hall that he thinks another fifteen minutes would be okay. This causes more arguing with Minna's son, and drives a wedge between the couple. Dubin writes,

"Co-parenting was often harder than solo parenting. Weekends felt challenging to the point of dread. The eating and naptime routines I'd implemented through an exhaustive process of trial and error were golden structures that helped me survive the long weekdays when I was in charge and Paul was at work. At best, Paul saw these routines as optional. He chalked up my frustration (which often presented as rage) to my being fearful and controlling. I felt I was having a legitimate reaction to the hard work of mothering while being unseen, unappreciated, and then undermined."

I experience similar feelings as my husband also works long days and is often gone for entire weeks at a time on business travel. When he's home with the kids on the weekends, he wants to enjoy them, have fun, and not be tied to a rigid nap or meal schedule. But these schedules keep the kids well rested and fed at regular intervals, helping to avoid unnecessary tantrums. They are essential to maintaining my sanity during the workweek when he's gone. In *Mom Rage*, Dubin discusses how gendered perceptions of motherhood, fatherhood, and anger contribute to domestic labor disparities and exacerbate parental stress and relationship discord. John comes to understand this, but my in-laws never seem to. They call me too "high-strung" or "uptight." I just need to relax, they say. I'm still insecure in my own motherhood, and these comments wound.

They are also unfair. Neither of my sisters-in-law have children. They've never been up all night breastfeeding an insatiable infant. They can use the bathroom and shower without children in the room with them. They don't know what it's like to grocery shop with an infant and a toddler, or to keep small children entertained in medical waiting rooms for an hour or more. They can go out to dinner or a movie whenever they choose; they don't have to spend a half hour loading up a double stroller with diapers, snacks, and sippy cups just to go for a walk and breathe some fresh air. And yet the women in my husband's family feel entitled to comment on my parenting style at what feels like every opportunity.

The implication and sometimes literal messaging from my in-laws is always, "This is how we do things. The kids (and by consequence, you) need to adapt." This "dictatorship not democracy" parenting philosophy is not an uncommon one, particularly among our parents' generation, and plenty of people still subscribe to it. As misguided as I believe it to be, I recognize that it's difficult for my mother-in-law to put this concept aside, and I know that she's relented to a Christmas Eve visit this year only because she and my father-in-law want to see the kids at the holidays and be a part of their lives. For this reason, I breathe a sigh of relief when Danielle gushes over each gift they give to her with hugs and kisses of gratitude, and when Henry smiles sweetly as he gingerly opens packages. I'm annoyed by all the drama surrounding it, but I truly do want my in-laws to have a wonderful holiday experience with their grandchildren.

However, Christmas Day is a different story altogether. Shortly after the kids wake, John tries to lead Danielle and Henry toward the basement to see if Santa has left anything in the playroom. Henry starts shaking, then screaming. The reaction is so violent, so jarring, it's like he's staring into the eyes of a demon that's invisible to the rest of us.

"The lights. The lights!" I yell, but it's too late.

* * *

The lights fixation is a new quirk. Henry had become consistently irritable in the mornings as fall approached. I thought maybe his sleep cycle was changing, or maybe he was going through a growth spurt and needed to sleep more than our busy schedule would allow. Some days, he was absolutely irate when I carried him downstairs for breakfast. One morning in early November, just a week or two before I bought that pregnancy test at the grocery store, I emerged from my bedroom a few minutes later than usual to find that Henry had dragged the stepstool out of the bathroom and into the hallway. He'd climbed up on it and was dangerously teetering above the stairwell. He appeared to be reaching for the hall light switch. I scooped him up, gently scolded him, and made a mental note to place a temporary baby gate at his bedroom doorway that night, in addition to the one permanently installed at the top of the stairs. But early the next morning he scaled the new barrier, and I again found him attempting the same risky climb to the hall light switch.

The hall light was on and he seemed to want it off. I couldn't imagine why, but he was risking life and limb to do it. So on the third day, instead of whisking him into my arms mid-climb, I let him continue while I positioned myself within catching distance should he tumble. With the stair gate unlatched, I watched as he turned off the upstairs hall light, stepped away from the stool, and scooted down the dark stairs on his rear-end. When he reached the bottom, he toddled over to the living room switch that controls a timer-activated lamp by the couch. A few months ago we'd set the timer to turn the lamp on around dusk and turn it off around dawn. When the switch is in the "on" position, so is the lamp, between those hours. Henry pulled up his mini *Blue's Clues* "thinking chair," then climbed up and turned that switch off, too. He crawled back up the stairs, got on the bathroom stool once again, and turned the hall light on. He scooted back down, repeated the previous process, and switched on the living room light. When Henry moved out of sight, I descended the stairs and caught him dragging one of our dining chairs toward the chain that controls the overhead kitchen light.

After following Henry's process a couple of mornings in a row, I learned that the acceptable order for our home's illumination is upstairs hall light first, then living room lamp, then overhead kitchen light. Once he's made sure that these three lights are on, he opens the basement door (it has to be closed when he reaches it) and turns to me with raised arms—a signal to lift him up so he can switch on the basement light himself. He cannot go on with his day if this order isn't followed. He will sit in place, scream and cry, then eventually regroup, shut off all the lights, climb back up the stairs, and begin again.

I hadn't initially connected his new morning crankiness with the days getting shorter and the mornings growing darker. It didn't occur to me that with this came another change—some of the lights being switched on in the house before Henry awoke, lights that had remained off during the summer months when the days were longer and daylight flooded through our front windows from very early in the morning until after Henry's bedtime. Thanks to Henry's lack of language skills, this is yet another of his idiosyncratic patterns that I discovered the hard way that year, like how I found out his shoes need to go on left before right.

The shoe lesson was learned back in September. Henry had been suffering from a cold and been up most of the night congested. An hour after I finally dozed off in the well-worn rocking chair, Henry's sweaty and feverish body nestled in my arms, I heard the buzz of my bedroom alarm clock. John was traveling for work, so I rose from the chair, one tiny movement at a time, then gently lay Henry down in his crib. He murmured and I froze, barely breathing, desperate not to wake him. I watched as he shifted, turned to his side, and drifted back to sleep.

I tiptoed toward the door. The too-bright blue, eco-friendly, zero-VOC paint that I'd slathered on the walls of the nursery before Henry was born was now pleasantly muted in the dim light of daybreak. I carefully closed the door behind me and walked the few steps to my bedroom. It took all the will I could muster to bypass my bed, which I would have given anything to collapse on. I turned off the alarm clock on the nightstand and forced myself into a quick shower before Danielle woke up.

As the hot water streamed down my back, I silently blamed Danielle's first weeks of preschool for my difficult night. Maybe not so silently, as I'd recently taken to talking out loud to myself in the shower and elsewhere in the absence of any other adult human to speak with during the day. Danielle's exposure to other kids increased ten-fold that month and, as it turns out, not all parents comply with the preschool's illness policy. They need a break and that two-and-a-half-hour, twice-a-week respite is sacred, so they give their kids a dose of a children's cough and cold medicine and hope they won't sneeze or sniffle in front of the teacher and get sent home. I was probably one of only a few parents who didn't engage in this deceit, not because I was above trying to sneak my sick kid in but because getting out the door was such an ordeal with Henry lately that I was almost grateful for a reason to call it off.

There was no canceling on that day, though. Despite Henry's illness and my utter exhaustion, Danielle was feeling fine and eager to go to school. It took monumental effort to remain calm while she protested against the only available breakfast options—plain Cheerios or toast with butter. I didn't have it in me to go to the grocery store that week with a toddler who hated leaving the house even on a good day, and who now was also ill. We were down to our last few diapers, sorely lacking in any sort of grown-up food, and out of wine in the house (I'd eat chicken nuggets and apple sauce for dinner three nights in a row so long as they were accompanied by a glass of decent cabernet, the "decent" part being negotiable depending on the day's circumstances).

Bathing was a personal victory that morning but finding time to conceal the dark circles under my eyes or otherwise make myself presentable was too much work. Henry started to fuss before Danielle finished eating, so I gathered my damp hair in a ponytail and dragged myself up the stairs to get him. When I returned to the kitchen, I plopped Henry down in his highchair and set a small plastic bowl of Cheerios in front of him. He immediately dumped the bowl of cereal onto his tray and sorted the oat circles into equal piles. I prayed to any god who would listen. *Please, please let the rest of this morning go smoothly.* My head ached from lack of sleep and caffeine withdrawal, but coffee would wait until I could get to a drive-thru because I'd used the last of the grounds at the bottom of the bag the day before.

After breakfast, I pulled a pair of Henry's elastic-waist pants and a loose t-shirt from the yet-to-be-folded mound of laundry on top of the dryer. I got them on him with little difficulty, but he screamed and kicked when I tried to put on his sneakers. It took me all of ninety seconds to admit defeat. Discouraged, I threw his shoes on the floor and sank into a sobbing mess. This isn't how I'd imagined second-time motherhood two and half years earlier when the pregnancy test showed double blue lines. Nowhere close.

Danielle pleaded that it was time to go, so I tried talking myself off the ledge. *Okay, Amy, get it together. He's a two-year-old. You're an adult woman. You can handle this,* I told myself, as I took a deep breath and picked up the shoe closest to me. It was the left one. I reached across Henry's little legs and attempted to put it on. He suddenly calmed down and allowed me to wrangle it onto his foot. The about-face was startling. *Henry must have tired himself out,* I thought, *has no more fight left in him, same as me.*

"There we are," I encouraged. "That's my boy." He neither smiled nor frowned but rather looked at me blankly. I put on the right shoe, slipped on his jacket, and off we went.

The following Tuesday, I again sat Henry on the kitchen bench as we prepared to leave for Danielle's preschool. His tiny right ankle fit completely within the width of my grasp. I held it steady while I picked up a little blue sneaker with my other hand. But before I even brought the shoe to his foot, Henry's face became flushed, adrenaline flowing, readying for combat. I picked up speed hoping that if I got the shoes on in under five seconds, swept Henry up and out the door, and quickly strapped him in the car seat with a toy, I could avoid this scene that almost every trip outside of the house now incited. As I ripped open the sneaker's Velcro closure, Henry kicked violently, the first strike landing squarely in the middle of my ribs atop an existing tender bruise I'd incurred during our previous showdown. I winced and pulled back, dropping the shoe to the floor.

"Why, Henry?" I demanded in a raised voice. We were face to face—he on the bench and I kneeling on the floor—his big blue eyes filled with indignation.

"We have to leave the house sometimes, Henry," I said, as Danielle pulled on her pink windbreaker. I picked up a shoe and hesitantly brought it toward Henry's foot. He didn't flinch, didn't flush, didn't kick. I slid it on and closed the Velcro. Baffled but grateful, I picked up the right shoe.

Wait....

I took off his left shoe, set it on the floor, and picked up the right one. Henry tensed up. His shoulders hunched, legs stiffened. I put it back down, and the tension fled from Henry's expression so fast, it was like some supernatural force waved its magic wand and instantly drained all unease, exactly like the abrupt turnaround he'd made after I dropped his sneakers in overwhelmed dismay the previous Thursday.

"It's the order of the shoes. Isn't it, Henry?" I pointed to his left foot. "It's this shoe first." I slipped a sneaker onto his left foot with no resistance. Then I pointed to his right foot. "Then that one. Right?" And I slid the other sneaker on. Again, no resistance. It wasn't that Henry hated leaving the house or even that he hated wearing shoes. It was the *order* of the shoes. I paused to absorb this small but important revelation, then exclaimed, "That's it! It's the order of the shoes!"

Henry looked toward me with such wide-eyed relief in that moment, such pure deliverance, that I felt ashamed I hadn't figured it out sooner. Just as in his arrangement of toy cars or blocks or Danielle's dollhouse furniture, he needed strict order in this—some internal rule that Henry felt compelled to follow. I didn't know where it came from, what caused it, or how long it would last, but it was clear to me that it wasn't a choice. Henry could no more ignore this instinct than he could ignore the need to eat or drink or sleep.

I gathered him in my arms, rocked him gently, and ran my fingers through his dark curls that refused to be tamed by comb or conditioner.

"I'm so sorry, sweetie. I didn't know."

Henry rested his head against my neck. It was as if I held a ragdoll to me, every ounce of discomfort released from his body. He was quiet on the way to the preschool, calm and content.

As incompetent as I felt—*a better parent would not have waited weeks to try reversing the order of the shoes*, I chided myself—this incident also bolstered my belief that these altercations would soon pass. I viewed his strict routines as a symptom of his communication problems. It's normal for kids this age to try and assert some control over their environment. But the way Henry did that looked different from the tantrums other two-year-olds might have because of his developmental delays and lack of age-appropriate vocabulary. No one in our sphere had suggested any different. Until Henry could tell me what he needed or what was bothering him, I'd have to get more skilled at reading his cues, view his behavior with new eyes, and implore our family to be more patient. As far as I was concerned, these communication breakdowns were as much my problem as they were his. He tried to tell me using the only tools he has; I just hadn't been interpreting properly.

This is the mindset I'm operating under as we stand there on Christmas morning with the basement door ajar and the light already on. But Danielle isn't having it. Not today. She isn't going to wait for Henry to start over before she sees what Santa brought. She runs down the basement stairs, and Henry crumbles into a wailing heap.

Henry recovers later in the morning after some new-toy distractions, and I desperately hope the remainder of the day goes well. But I know that's too much to hope for as soon as Danielle's nose starts dripping—a sure sign of a cold coming on. She's tired and petulant by the time my parents and brother show up. After dinner, my mother hands her a gift. Danielle tears off the paper, opens the box and, realizing it's a dress rather than a toy, throws it on the floor and walks away. I want to crawl under the coffee table.

Five days after Christmas, both kids are miserable with full-blown head colds. I fumble through the linen closet looking for more tissues, see a box of tampons, and realize my period is still late. When both kids fall asleep on the couch, I take the second pregnancy test from the box I'd bought earlier. No disappointment this time.

"Seriously?" John asks when I share the news.

"Yep, no mistaking this result. Maybe the universe just wanted to remind us how dicey parenthood can get before giving us this little gift. You know, have a good laugh at our expense."

"No kidding," John says. "Timing is everything."

* * *

The connection between obsessive-compulsive disorder (OCD) and neurological disorders is a complicated one that researchers are still trying to untangle. OCD is considered a type of chronic mental health disorder that typically starts in adolescence or young adulthood, but research shows that children can develop it, too. The National Health Library describes OCD as "an impairing condition associated with a specific set of distressing symptoms incorporating repetitive, intrusive thoughts (obsessions) and distressing, time-consuming rituals (compulsions)." If a child under eight years old is diagnosed, it's called "early onset OCD." It's very rare in toddlers, and what few studies have been done with young children looked at kids ages four and older.

Though OCD is currently categorized as a mental illness, disorders that fall under the "neurodivergent" umbrella, like autism, attention deficit hyperactivity disorder (ADHD), and dyslexia, are not. But neurodivergent people have a higher incidence of psychiatric or mental health conditions, such as OCD, depression, and anxiety, that may exist alongside their neurological differences or disabilities. To further complicate matters, children with OCD tend to have more autistic traits, while people with autism often exhibit repetitive behaviors that mimic both OCD and tic disorders, such as Tourette syndrome. Twenty years ago, when Henry was a toddler, we knew far less about these complex connections than we do today, but we still have a long way to go before we fully understand how all of these disorders and neurological differences intersect.

PART II
LOST IN TRANSLATION

LESSON 8

Answers are Elusive

"Let's go, let's go, let's go!" I say as soon as my father arrives. He recently retired and is now perpetually late. I'd asked him to stay with Danielle so John and I could give Henry's evaluation process as much time as it needs without feeling anxious or rushed, as well as give ourselves the time necessary to get through Boston's rush-hour traffic. John is a heavy footed, impatient driver on a good day, and it's that much worse if we're paying a babysitter by the hour or have a hard deadline for child pick-up.

At the hospital, the lead doctor for the developmental medicine program gives Henry a physical exam. She's friendly, gentle, and soft spoken. He lets her listen to his heart and lungs, look in his ears, and check his reflexes with no fuss. Then her assistant leads John and me into a bland beige room. We answer her questions and fill out surveys about Henry's behavior and physical health. Some of the boxes have been pre-filled by the staff. "Patient: age 2 years, 10 months; atypical speech and motor development; referred to Early Intervention by pediatrician at age 15 months. Mother: age 34; married; 20 weeks pregnant; two previous unremarkable deliveries." *Unremarkable?* Maybe to them. "Father: age 33; married; occupation: Manager." I chuckle. Reading that first sheet quickly, you might conclude that we, Henry's parents, were married to other people rather than to each other, which would make our current shared pregnancy awkward.

Henry is led into a separate area where the doctor will ask him to perform tasks like those in the Early Intervention evaluation, only with added gross motor tests like hopping on one foot, riding a tricycle, and bouncing a basketball. I plow through the paperwork, tense and jumpy. I always feel this way when anyone unfamiliar takes Henry out of my sight. John puts his hand on my thigh and squeezes—a subtle encouragement to settle down.

I find several of the questions difficult to answer. I know the exact age Henry was when he first crawled, walked, and threw a ball, because I've been asked for those dates so many times by this point that they're now ingrained in my memory. But when exactly did he stop nursing altogether? When did he first drink from a sippy cup or munch on finger foods? At what age did he first sleep at night for six hours or more without waking? Those things were gradual and happened in the midst of significant growth and milestones for Danielle as well. For all I know, Danielle gave Henry a handful of her morning cereal long before I ever introduced him to a cookie or a slice of cheese. I was in survival mode that first year and exhausted most of the time.

A light goes on in the room adjacent to ours. There is a one-way window like you see on those TV police procedurals, where other interested parties gather to covertly watch a super-skilled detective interrogate a suspect. John and I can see in, but whoever is in there cannot see out. Two women clinicians select toys and games from a cabinet and arrange them on a kid-height table. Henry's gross motor testing is over, and the doctor brings him into the room and introduces him to the clinicians. The space they're in is much brighter and cheerier than ours. The walls are painted in primary colors and decorated with framed posters of playgrounds, sandy beaches, and baby animals.

The clinicians test Henry's fine motor skills and his cognitive ability with puzzles, memory games, and role playing. He does fine for the first thirty minutes or so, until they start introducing activities that he can't complete. One of the women briefly shows him a picture, gives him a couple of crayons, then asks him to recreate the image from memory. He pushes the paper away and says, "Nah, tank yah." Then he pulls one of the puzzles back over. This is his standard response to requests that frustrate him. He still doesn't have a lot of words and he can't produce the "th" sound in "thank" or the "oo" sound in "you," but this phrase otherwise works for him most of the time. Not here, though.

"We'd like you to try, Henry. It's okay if you can't make the whole picture. Just try to remember what it looked like," the clinician says. I suspect his aversion to this task isn't about remembering; he's already showing signs of possessing a phenomenal memory. But he doesn't like to draw. He has trouble translating anything onto paper, whether it's from his own mind or simply replicating an image he's seen on TV or in a book. We don't have rudimentary scribbles and finger paintings of Henry's posted to our refrigerator door the way we did with Danielle.

As the testing continues, I see Henry disengage. His shoulders fold in; his eyes droop. I'm grateful when the lead clinician says, "Are you getting tired, Henry? How about we do just two more?"

As Henry and the clinicians clean up the toys, the doctor opens the door of our room. "What a wonderful little boy Henry is," she says, "so helpful and polite."

I'm not surprised by her observations. He's often frustrated, and has quirky behaviors that seem almost instinctual, involuntary. But he never appears willfully disobedient.

"He struggled a bit with a few things, but we expected that," she says. "The team will review Henry's results and write up a full report. I'll give you a call to discuss our recommendations."

We walk out to the reception area just as Henry is entering it with the clinicians. The doctor shakes our hands then turns to Henry. "So nice to meet you today, Henry. I hope to see you again." He doesn't reply.

Henry drifts off in the car before we're even out of the parking garage. We'd been at the hospital a little over four hours, and we're all tired. I'm also slightly discouraged. We were told at the outset that we wouldn't receive any immediate feedback. Today was all about diagnostics and evaluation; interpretation would come later. Still, I thought I'd glean something from the doctor's reactions. But she was a polished professional and her tone revealed nothing. *That report can't come soon enough*, I think. I'm eager for answers, for any direction or guidance.

"I just want to know," I say to John as he merges the spaceship onto the expressway. "If there's something wrong, I want to know what it is, so I can do something about it."

"Exactly," John says. "Just tell us what we're dealing with."

We're naïve enough to think this is it. We'll get the results, act upon them as necessary, and everything will get better from here. But when the results finally come via a thick envelope stuffed into our mailbox, we have more questions than answers.

* * *

The mail is delivered while I'm picking up Danielle at preschool. I don't wait for John. I make the kids lunch, settle Henry down for his afternoon nap, and sit at the kitchen table with the bulky brown envelope from the developmental medicine center. I flip through the pages looking for a conclusion or diagnosis, like an impatient reader who just can't help herself from taking a premature peek at the ending of a novel.

There are plenty of statistics throughout. Henry's "Expressive Articulation" is in the twenty-fifth percentile, far below average. But his "Performance IQ" is in the ninety-eighth percentile, the "very superior" range. He couldn't tell the clinicians what he was doing, but he could perform almost any non-language based intellectual task they asked him to—things like showing him a model or formation and asking him to recreate it with small blocks. His gross motor skills are in the third percentile. *Third.* Ninety-seven percent of children his age have better agility than he does. I know he's behind—he can't pedal a tricycle, hop on one foot, or use a pair of kid-safe scissors—but that number is shocking to me. Furthermore, a "significant discrepancy" exists between his "intellectual capacity" and his "adaptive behavior," whatever that means.

The report mentions something called "hyperlexia"; the hallmark of that condition is the ability to read at an abnormally young age coupled with significant difficulty using spoken language. I'm confused; Henry certainly can't read yet. But the condition is listed only as "possible," not definitive. Later the report notes that, although hyperlexia is often associated with autism, Henry's profile "does not meet the criteria for a diagnosis of autism spectrum disorder."

At that time, in 2004, five to six children per 1,000 were being diagnosed with autism. The possibility had briefly crossed John's and my mind, but we associated autism with a severe level of disability, as most people did then. The few media representations of autism depicted autistic savants—people with some sort of extraordinary gift for music or math but who otherwise had disabilities that profoundly impacted their ability to function in day-to-day life. Henry didn't fit.

Finally, on page nine, I find something that resembles a synopsis: "Communication Disorder, Not Otherwise Specified, with atypical features." What the hell does that mean? Also listed at the end of the eleven-page report is "Motor Coordination Disorder" and a notation that Henry is "at risk for future learning difficulties." Okay, so he doesn't communicate well for his age. We know that. And he's clumsy. No surprise there. At risk for future learning difficulties? Exactly why we had him evaluated in the first place. We learn what we already knew: Henry isn't developing on a normal trajectory. They can describe that in official terms, but they can't tell us why. I feel like we're back where we started. We wanted black and white; we got gray.

Still, the recommendations of the developmental team are of some help. They prescribe a diagnostic language evaluation by an independent speech pathologist, as well as an occupational therapy assessment. Both are completed just a few weeks later. The speech pathologist determines that Henry's speech therapy should be increased to at least three times per week and should be paired with occupational therapy sessions. Thank goodness for health insurance. The copays alone for these services will consume a good chunk of our monthly budget, but we'd be destined for bankruptcy if John's benefits plan didn't cover the rest. I vow to start searching for more free-lance work that I can do when Henry is napping or otherwise occupied.

Aside from suggesting those evaluations, the developmental team recommends that once Henry turns three he be transitioned to a "structured, therapeutic, supportive setting" on a full-day, full-year basis. "He'll require individualized and small group instruction by a special educator with specific training in developmental delays," they write.

By the time I'm done reading, I desperately want a cup of coffee, or better yet, a glass of wine. But since I gave up both caffeine and alcohol when I discovered I was pregnant, I settle for a cup of herbal tea. It's woefully inadequate.

* * *

I show the report to Rose on her next visit. "Where do I find a facility like this?" I ask, referring to that "therapeutic supportive setting."

"Every district has a separate special needs preschool or pre-K classroom. I'll make a referral, and then they'll set up an evaluation of their own," she says.

How many evaluations does this poor kid have to endure? An initial assessment was conducted by Early Intervention, then one by the private speech therapist, and another after Henry had been working with Rose for a year. The one by the hospital's developmental medicine team came next, followed by the two assessments they'd recommended, and yet another exit evaluation scheduled at the completion of Early Intervention services. Not to mention the medical appointment where I watched Henry scream and writhe as one phlebotomist held him down and another drew vials of blood to check for elevated lead levels, thyroid dysfunction, and Fragile X syndrome as possible explanations for his developmental delays. Now the preschool needs to do their own assessment? I have a foot-high stack of paper on my desk with results from these individual analyses. I thought the full developmental evaluation would bring them together, provide a connective center or define an encompassing condition that magically made sense of them all. I was wrong.

Rose goes on, "The special needs preschool will determine what services to offer based on that evaluation, but I can guarantee it won't be five days a week, year-round. They have limited resources, and the most disabled kids get the bulk of them. Because Henry's diagnosis is vague, it gives them a lot of leeway."

The preschool performs their evaluation in late June and offers Henry two half-days of classroom time for the upcoming school year with one speech therapy session per week incorporated within that. Rose tells me that I have two choices: either hire an advocate and demand that the school more closely meet the hospital's recommendations—a process that can end up in the legal system—or try and make up the gap through private therapy and working with Henry at home. With no money left in our family budget for advocate services or attorney fees, particularly for a case that we have no assurance of winning, I choose option two. Rose promises to show me specific activities I can do with Henry to help him overcome some of his challenges and master the skills a full-day preschool program would have worked on. Armed with Henry's most recent language diagnostic results, the private speech therapist we're currently working with can further customize his sessions to address the areas where progress is still stagnant.

A week later, Henry ages out of Early Intervention. The program holds a graduation ceremony at the group center. I don't think Henry understands what's happening, but I sure do. A few tears roll down my cheek as the group facilitator presents Henry with a certificate of completion. But those tears aren't shed for this specific milestone or for the bittersweet realization that my little boy is growing up and moving on to preschool. Rather, my emotional response comes from the recognition that in saying goodbye to Rose, I'm losing the only person who has given me any real, tangible, comprehensive support for Henry's "disability." That's what we're calling it now, a "disability," because he has to be officially disabled to qualify for any services beyond this point.

I'd wanted a label when we left the developmental medicine center a little over two months before. I wanted something to call this. But "disabled"? No. I wanted a specific diagnosis, a "difference" that I could pinpoint and help Henry overcome or at least cope with. But all we got was "not otherwise specified." I wonder if any of the other children at Henry's new preschool will fall into this same ambiguous category and how the teachers and therapists there will help them in a classroom setting as compared to the individualized, one-on-one assistance of Early Intervention. When I think about the hours upon hours that Rose, along with the Early Intervention group facilitator, spent just getting Henry to make the sign for "cracker," I can't imagine how a single teacher in a classroom of a dozen or more special-needs kids will manage it.

Later I'll find myself wondering how dedicated Early Intervention therapists like Rose must feel when they put so much time, effort, and compassion into helping children like

Henry only to release them to various public education systems that don't always have the resources and/or motivation to give those kids the full suite of services they need.

LESSON 9

Hope Springs Eternal

In the last weeks of summer, I bring Henry to his new preschool to meet his teacher and get accustomed to the classroom. I park near the old brick schoolhouse nestled in a residential area, a relic from the days when our community still educated its children within their own neighborhoods. The other public schools in the district are now located within a quarter mile of one another in a campus-like arrangement—one building for kids in kindergarten through second grade, another for third through fifth, a middle school and a high school across the street. Each grade has 350 to 400 kids. The roads surrounding the area are gridlocked for a mile in every direction at drop-off and pick-up times. Compared to that utilitarian complex, this old two-story schoolhouse, with its fenced-in patch of asphalt stocked with ride-on toys and playground balls, feels homey and nostalgic.

Henry's new teacher, Miss Coleman, however, exudes no warmth. She says hello to Henry and directs him to a corner where he can play. No kneeling to his level to speak with him the way Rose always did. Henry explores, and I wedge my nine-months-pregnant self into a kid-size chair at a kid-size table at the other end of the room. Miss Coleman shows me worksheets she'll be using in class. They are filled with pictures

that the kids have to match up with their associated companion items—a helmet goes with the bike, a sandwich goes with
the lunch plate, and so on. Not an inspiring or motivating lesson plan for a classroom full of kids reluctant or unable to
communicate. She doesn't explain her goals with enthusiasm.
She's young and new to the school, and I guess that she's a bit
overwhelmed.

In Miss Coleman's classroom children will work at round
tables on art projects, count with small blocks, and complete
those worksheets. There is a plastic bin of toys meant for
sensory stimulation—soft plastic spheres with small spikes
to grasp, kaleidoscopes with rubber grips, shape sorters, and
nested boxes. One large box is full of oversized nuts and bolts
that the kids can connect, disassemble, and reconnect in multiple ways. Next to that is a large rack filled with wooden puzzles. Henry is enthralled. I'm sure that I'll have no problem
getting him out the door for his first day of "real" school a few
weeks later if I remind him of this cornucopia. I leave the visit
feeling not thrilled by this new environment for Henry, but
not totally discouraged either.

* * *

On September 10—four days before Henry's first day of
school—I wake with a start at four-thirty in the morning. A
wave of pain follows. *Like the ocean swooping in, the cold water
washes over your feet, causing your knees to shake. Then the swell
retreats back to let you catch your breath. Soon, the tide will come
in, those waves more persistent, crashing against the sea wall, telling you it's time.* I'd read that description in a brochure for a
new-age birthing center and I thought it was a nice visual for
first-time mothers who may be afraid of labor and delivery. Of

course, it's also total bullshit. Contractions are more like an iron-hot dagger plunged into your abdomen, then pulled out, then plunged back in at ever-more-frequent intervals. When it's "time," the knife twists and turns until your innards feel as if they've been turned inside out. Or at least that's how it felt for me. Both Danielle and Henry were born within four hours of my first contraction. There was no time to watch the tide roll in. That first wave had a shark in it, with a full set of teeth.

I take a shower, get my bag together, and call my mom. I nudge John, still sleeping soundly. "Wake up, honey. I think we're having a baby this morning." By the time my parents arrive to watch Danielle and Henry, I'm in full labor. The birth takes a little longer this time, but John is still calling home by 11 a.m. to announce the arrival of our new baby boy.

We name him "Finn" after I veto John's idea to call him "Elvis." John wants something a little rebellious, which, it turns out, would have fit. A pound and a half heavier than either Danielle or Henry were at birth, Finn is pink and round and vigorous, with a shadow of carrot-colored hair atop his fair head, and clear blue eyes. Unlike Henry, whose hands had stayed clenched for days, Finn is grabbing at the sides of the bassinet, and the nurse's smock, within hours of his birth. From day one he seems ready for whatever the world will bring. I'm relieved. I'd kept any concerns to myself, but I wasn't sure I could handle another child like Henry. I feared that I could not be an effective parent to two kids with developmental delays. There are no guarantees at this early stage of course, but Finn already appears more interested in his environment than Henry ever was.

I had no evidence for my concerns during my pregnancy; just my own self-doubt and feelings of inadequacy.

But twelve years after Finn's birth, a Kaiser Permanente study would find that the risk of younger siblings developing an autism spectrum disorder (ASD) was fourteen times higher if an older sibling had autism. Specifically, kids who had older siblings with ASD had an autism rate of 11.3 percent compared to 0.92 percent for those who had only neurotypical older siblings. Younger boys were much more likely to be affected, with younger male siblings having an ASD rate of 15 percent versus 7 percent for younger female siblings. But these numbers could be skewed by the diagnostic gender bias that existed then and continues now—girls are less likely to be referred for neurological assessment and are more likely to be misdiagnosed than boys are. This gender disparity in diagnosis has resulted in many girls not receiving essential interventions. It also has important implications for further research on familial inheritance of ASD and for the development of improved diagnostic criteria—a study published in 2020 found that the sibling rate of autism was about 50 percent more for children who have an older sister with ASD as compared to having an older brother with it.

* * *

Finn and I come home from the hospital on Sunday, September 12, 2004. On Monday, Henry gives Danielle a big hug and watches as she marches up the steps of the bright yellow bus that will take her to her first day of kindergarten at the big school downtown. I push aside a few tears as the bus pulls away, but Danielle is eager for this next adventure and excited for the new independence. Just like on her first day of preschool, she never looks back.

The following day, Henry climbs out of the backseat of

the spaceship and waves goodbye to his baby brother. He takes a teacher's aide by the hand and steps into his first day of preschool—his first real separation from me. He doesn't have the big, determined grin on his face that Danielle had as she left for kindergarten, but he's not visibly upset either. I spend most of the morning anxiously pacing around the house with newborn Finn snuggled in my arms. That afternoon, I'm thirty minutes early to pick Henry up, half-expecting that he's had a meltdown or endured some calamity and will be searching for me by school's end. But he emerges from the building smiling.

Both Danielle and Henry seem to adjust well to their new schools. By the end of September we're maintaining a semblance of a routine. It feels like a new chapter. Henry comes out of school two days a week holding tight to an aide's hand, often with at least the beginnings of a smile. He's gotten used to the drive to private therapy the other three weekdays, using the quiet time in the car to flip through a favorite book. He likes the pattern—knowing what will happen on which days.

Finn is a happy, easy baby. As long as someone is paying attention to him, he'll coo and cuddle all day long. His face lights up whenever Danielle or Henry enters the room, and his obvious pleasure spurs them to talk to him, tickle him, or gently push him in the baby swing. This third kid is destined to be a charmer.

We decide that Finn will be our last child, and John schedules a vasectomy at the end of October. Danielle is doing great; Henry is making progress; and all signs show Finn to be a healthy baby boy. Parenting three young children is challenging, but it will only get easier from here as they grow and become increasingly self-sufficient—or so I think.

LESSON 10

Paper and Practice Collide

November brings the first snowstorm of the season and Finn's first giggles. By mid-month he's sleeping from 10 p.m. until 4 a.m. Those six hours of uninterrupted rest are critical for both him and me, because we're busy. Almost every weekend, Danielle has invites to playdates or birthday parties. Not so for Henry, though. The special needs preschool enrolls some typically developing students as "peer models," but the majority of Henry's classmates have various challenges that make group outings complicated. Like us, their families have therapy visits to attend and sensory issues to accommodate alongside busy work and family schedules. At least that's what I tell myself.

At our first parent-teacher conference before Thanksgiving break, Miss Coleman says that Henry is very well-behaved, but he prefers to play by himself. The only trouble arises when Henry is working on a puzzle or building with blocks and another child wants to play with the same toy. Henry pulls the toy back and, if the other child doesn't move on, he'll bang his fists on the floor and yell out. Henry isn't great at sharing but that is expected at his age, Miss Coleman says. They'll continue to work on it.

But in mid-December I get my first "discipline" phone call

from the school. When I see the number on the caller ID, I panic. "Is Henry okay?"

"Oh, yes. He's fine," Miss Coleman replies. "But he got quite agitated today and we couldn't completely calm him down. I didn't want you to get here and find him upset without a heads-up."

"Agitated?" I ask. She explains that it was Henry's turn to pass out snack, and after they ate, the kids headed outside for a short recess. Henry didn't want to go for some reason. He refused to leave his chair and cried when she tried to put on his coat and urge him toward the door. When it was clear he wouldn't budge, she carried him to Ms. Jenson's room. He was supervised there and the rest of the class went out to play.

I visualize Henry being forcibly carried into another classroom. My cheeks flush with anger, but I say nothing. I don't know what to make of his behavior; I wasn't there to see it.

Miss Coleman says, "The kids will start packing up their things for dismissal soon. I just wanted you to know that he's not quite himself."

"Thank you," I say. "I appreciate the call."

I know the goal is to get Henry to act appropriately in a classroom setting, to learn to cooperate and use words to communicate, but I feel a wave of protective instinct sweep over me. I put Finn in the infant carrier and warm up the car, determined to be first in line at preschool pick-up.

Henry walks out of the brick building with one of the aides, as always. I get out of the car and she guides him into the back seat. (It's always a "she"—there's not one male teacher, therapist, or aide in the entire school.)

"How's he doing?" I ask.

"Fine, I think," she says, seemingly unaware of the earlier

drama. I look at Henry. He isn't crying, but his face is damp and blotchy.

"Hi, baby," I say, buckling him into his booster seat. No response.

As we get closer to home, I broach the subject. "Henry, Miss Coleman says you got upset at school today. Can you tell me why?" Henry still has little language, but he often uses gestures now. He'll bring items out from other rooms in our house to try and express himself. He might find a plastic cookie in the toy kitchen and drop it at my feet to tell me he wants a sweet treat, or he might mean he wants to bake cookies with me, or he might be sharing that he had a cookie at snack time that day. It can sometimes take a half hour or more to complete a game of his communication charades and I want to get the ball rolling, get him thinking about what tools to use.

"No," he says.

"You don't want to tell me?"

"No. No, no, no!"

"Alright, sweetie."

Parked in our driveway, I unbuckle Henry, grab his backpack, and help him out of the car. I'll come back for Finn once I get Henry safely into the house.

"No, no, no!"

I take Henry's hand. "Okay, Henry. I heard you the first time. Let's go inside."

He lets go of me, steps to the side of the driveway, and plunges his hands into the pile of shoveled snow that has accumulated along the edge of our front yard. "No, no, no! Sssss-nooooo!"

"Snow? Snow, Henry?"

Henry nods his head. He runs through the snowbank and

points to the snowman that John and Danielle built over the weekend. "Sssss-nooooo mmuunnnn!"

"Snowman? Yes, Henry, that's the snowman Daddy and Dani built."

"No, no, no!" He yells. "Mmmm Mmmiii Ssss-noooo mmuunnn!"

I'm confused. He hadn't helped build that snowman. He was playing in his room when Danielle and John ventured outside on Sunday afternoon. Maybe he was building a snowman at school? But that doesn't make sense, either. He didn't go outside today; he was kept in for recess. *He must have seen the other kids working on one,* I think, *and is angry that he didn't get the chance to participate.*

"Did you want to build a snowman, too?"

Henry nods and then his eyes droop. His expression glazes over, as if it took every bit of mental energy he had to try and share this one message.

I pick him up, carry him inside, and tell him to stay put until I can get him a pair of dry pants and socks. When he's at the table eating his lunch and Finn has settled down for a nap, I call the school hoping Miss Coleman hasn't left for the day. The receptionist catches her.

"Hi, Miss Coleman. I talked to Henry about the incident in the classroom, and he mentioned something about a snowman. Were the kids building a snowman outside today?"

"No. Hmmm," she pauses. "They were making paper snowmen today. Before snack. That's the only snowman I can think of."

"Did Henry make one?"

Miss Coleman explains that because Henry was the snack helper today, he wasn't able to finish his snowman. "I put it in his backpack," she says. "He can finish it at home and bring it back in when he's done if he likes. The other kids hung theirs up in the classroom."

The other kids got to finish their snowmen and hang them up, I think, *while Henry passed out snack. Then, when he sat back down to finish his project, you told him it was time for recess.* I picture the clothesline that runs from end to end on the far wall of the classroom, the kids pinching together the ends of their designated clothespins with one hand and sliding their snowmen into the open clasps with the other—no small task for many of them. I imagine an array of proud young children stepping back to admire their work.

I thank Miss Coleman for the information and hang up the phone, fuming. Henry needs to finish a project once he starts it. Not wants. Needs: a compulsion to finish something once he's begun it. It occurs to me that the "lack of sharing" mentioned in his progress report could be linked to this same compulsion.

Though I know Henry must learn to be more flexible, I don't think he should be forced to put away his project without advance notice or preparation. He's a child who requires a warning when things are going to change, schedules are rearranged, or environments altered. It says so right in his Individual Education Program (IEP) that John and I were required to sign off on, and agreed to abide by, as a roadmap for how to help Henry. He needed Miss Coleman to say, *Alright, Henry, it's your turn to be snack-helper. That means you won't be able to finish your snowman in class today. But that's okay. We'll put it in a folder in your backpack, with all the pieces you need, and you can finish it at home. When you bring it back tomorrow, you can hang it on the line with the others. How does that sound, Henry?* But she didn't. She neither considered his obsessive-compulsive need to finish what he started nor his need to be apprised of a change in plans and, as a mostly non-verbal three-year-old, he couldn't advocate for himself.

The Individuals with Disabilities Education Act (IDEA), a law passed in 1975 and revised and recertified by Congress multiple times since, mandates a free appropriate public education to eligible children with disabilities and ensures special education and related services for those children. The law requires that these services be delivered by individual school districts with oversight by each state's department of education. But what I am beginning to understand is that "appropriate" and "eligible" are key words here, because the school system not only delivers the services but also decides who is "eligible," what is "appropriate," and which accommodations will or will not be offered. Schools are not required to accept or implement recommendations of medical professionals who may be treating a child. The Early Intervention program that Henry benefitted from before transitioning to preschool was created through one of the revisions to IDEA in 1986—only fifteen years before Henry's birth. Public responsibility for the education of people with disabilities is still a relatively new concept in American culture.

As Henry finishes his lunch, I open his backpack and pull out a piece of blue construction paper and three white foam circles. I find no other pieces. Riffling through a bin of art supplies in our basement, I pluck out two googly eyes, a few buttons, and a light brown pipe cleaner. The latter will serve as a corn cob. I braid bits of yarn to make a miniature scarf. *This will be the best goddamned snowman on the classroom wall,* I mutter. I put Henry's dish in the sink and lay out the supplies on the table. "I get it now, Henry. Let's finish this snowman you started. Then you can hang it with all the others tomorrow."

Henry looks at me and flashes a smile. It's full of relief, not for the craft supplies, but for the understanding. A basic human exchange—something other parents and children take for granted a hundred times a day. I wonder how often Henry attempts this at school and how often his efforts are ignored. In that moment I have no compassion or respect for Miss Coleman. She's on the front lines between Henry and "the system," one of only a few people who are in a position to guide him through his challenges, build on his strengths, and prevent him from becoming a statistic. I want a four-star general for this job, not a private who's still in bootcamp.

That evening, I talk with John and draft a note to Miss Coleman, explaining that I believe Henry may not have understood that he would not be able to finish what he started and suggesting that she could give him advance notice the next time a similar situation arises. I keep my tone flat and unemotional, almost clinical, trying not to put her on the defensive. I am aware that she and her colleagues aren't expected to go above and beyond the usual effort to help Henry, and that their input and assessments decide what services he will or will not receive. I also don't want the school to label me as a troublemaker or a problem parent; this would only make things harder for him.

Winter break comes and goes, and I've received no more calls from the school about Henry's behavior. I don't know whether this is due to a lack of troubling incidents or better management by the teachers when Henry does have a meltdown. Frankly, with a kindergartener, a preschooler, and an infant at home, I'm too exhausted to question it. A stretch of relative calm evokes nothing but gratitude. But one day in early spring Henry has a blotchy, damp face again when I pick him up from school.

"Did something happen today, Henry?" I ask, glancing in the rearview mirror.

"No cah," he says.

"No car?"

"No caahhhh!" he shouts, banging his fist against the armrest of the booster seat.

"You don't want to ride in the car today?" I ask.

"No, no, no, no, no," he says, shaking his head.

"I'm sorry, Buddy, but that's not an option."

Henry's limited communication skills have progressed from long games of charades to a more efficient system we invented together—a blend of American Sign Language and our own made-up gestures—but I still struggle to understand with so little context. Did he see a picture or hear a story about a car that frightened him in some way? He doesn't usually have a problem riding in our car. Or is he talking about something else altogether, like a toy or an altercation with another child?

At home he calms down. I ask, "Why didn't you want to ride in the car today, Henry?"

"No, no, no, no."

He walks over to the little fire engine ride-on toy that he often cruises around the kitchen in. He shoves and knocks it over. "No cah."

I'm at a loss. I call the school.

"Henry's really out of sorts this afternoon," I tell Miss Coleman. "Do you know if anything happened at school today that might've upset him?"

"Oh, darn," she says. "I meant to send home a quick note.

Henry was held back from recess today."

Again?

He wouldn't let the recess monitor zip up his jacket before going outside, she explains. I'm surprised; that isn't like him.

Henry has issues with tags in clothes and rough fabrics against his skin, but he'd worn the jacket he brought that day several times previously. It's made of soft fleece and I'd long since cut the tags out.

Miss Coleman says that Henry kept pulling the zipper out of the monitor's hands.

We hang up, and I sit next to Henry on the living room floor where he's playing with a Fisher Price farm set. He's lining up the animals by size—an activity that relaxes him.

"Henry, why wouldn't you let the teacher zip your jacket today?"

"No zzzipppp. No cah."

"Right," I say. "No car at recess."

He nods. The school has ride-on toys for the kids to play with on the asphalt behind the building, and Henry likes the green plastic car best. He sits in it whenever he's outside there.

"But why didn't you let the teacher zip your jacket, so you could play with the car?" I ask.

Henry lets go of the little plastic horse he has in his hand and pats his chest. "I zzzzziiiiipppp. Beh Boh."

"Oh, sweetie." I sigh as my heart sinks.

I finally understand. For the past several weeks I've been working with Henry on how to operate a zipper. I encourage him, telling him that he's a "big boy" and he can do it himself. That's what he'd been trying to tell the recess monitor and his teacher when he pushed their hands away, and why he became frustrated when they didn't understand. He was kept in from recess because he wanted to try zipping up his jacket on his own. This attempt at self-care represents huge progress for Henry. But the adults couldn't decipher his cryptic communication. I try to sympathize with them, be more forgiving than I'd been about the snowman incident, remind myself that Miss Coleman has at least a dozen kids in her charge. On any given day, there are four classes of preschoolers out on the blacktop at recess who need to be supervised. Maybe she's doing the best she can with the resources she has.

Maybe I am, too. Sometimes I still have trouble understanding Henry.

But I'm not a trained special education teacher. I don't work with multiple kids like Henry every day. I'm still angry. I wonder how many notes never got written, how many times similar situations transpired that I don't know about because Henry wasn't visibly upset at dismissal time.

I share my frustration with John later that night. I'm concerned about systemic problems within the school system and the possibility that things won't improve. But he believes these miscommunications are the result of one inexperienced teacher who doesn't fully grasp her students' individual challenges, not a prelude to how Henry's education will be handled going forward. It seems a plausible explanation. Nonetheless, I spend the latter part of April researching private preschools just in case things don't improve or, as much as I hate to think about it, get worse. But no conventional preschool I contact will take a child with any type of developmental delay or disability.

One independent special-needs preschool operates in our area, but it accepts children only by referral from the school district. When I inquire about this option, the IEP advisor assigned to Henry tells me that they only refer kids to that school who have disabilities that can't be adequately addressed at the public preschool. Henry doesn't meet the criteria—criteria based on the school's own evaluations and standards, not those of his pediatrician, the developmental medicine team at the children's hospital, or any other outside clinician. They have determined that Henry's challenges are not significant enough. As Rose had warned me earlier, if we want to dispute that, then it may become a legal matter that John and I will need a professional advocate or attorney to help navigate.

I believe I have no other options, so I sign the paperwork for Henry to attend the district preschool again the following year and hope for a more experienced teacher. Shortly after I submit it, Henry has a follow-up with the developmental medicine team who performed his full evaluation previously. The results are not reassuring. Their report notes that transitions between activities are difficult for him, and when presented with an unfamiliar task he simply refuses to engage. He repeats phrases multiple times and answers questions in a robotic manner. He shows low energy, and his eye contact seems reduced in comparison to his last visit. He cannot catch a ball. The evaluators say he's experiencing "developmental regression." Although his verbal skills and vocabulary have improved, he tests in the "low" or "moderately low" range in every other area.

We still have no useful diagnosis, but given Henry's sluggish progress the team recommends an intensification of services. They say that he should receive occupational therapy to work on fine motor, sensory, and adaptive skills. Preschool should be five half-days a week to boost his pragmatic language and social competence. A behavioral plan must be written into his IEP, providing tools to ease some of his anxiety and elevate his ability to self-regulate. The specialists order lab tests to check for abnormal levels of acids and compounds I'd never heard of: pyruvate, lactate, and carnitine. An EEG is recommended to rule out seizures as a cause for the episodes when Henry gets very still and stares into space.

I present these updated recommendations to Henry's IEP advisor. She promises to share them with the school's leadership team and says that they'll send me a draft of a revised IEP soon.

I receive that draft two weeks later. Nothing—*nothing*—has changed. The district deems all the new recommendations unnecessary. Henry is offered the standard three half-days per week of preschool for a second-year student, with a twenty-minute speech therapy session incorporated into two of those mornings.

I'm in the same predicament as last year. Again I determine we don't have the resources to fight the school's decision. John and I decide that I'll continue to take Henry to private speech therapy when he isn't at preschool. But we can't find a private occupational therapist or a behaviorist who will take our health insurance and their standard hourly fees are out of the question. I hope that the developmental medicine team is being overly cautious and that maybe Henry isn't all that different from other kids his age; that's why the district denied him these services. But I also can't avoid the nagging thought that this kind of rationalization is exactly how those false narratives that both my mother and John's mother hold about their own parenting experiences got started. Maybe we let go of the responsibility at some point because it becomes too daunting; it exceeds our own personal ability to carry it.

Still, the disagreement between the developmental team's

recommendations and the IEP team's conclusions further sours my opinion of our special-needs preschool. I'm not feeling optimistic when Henry and I return to the school in August to meet his second-year teacher.

Mrs. Matthews is at least twenty years older than Miss Coleman. She's not only more experienced, but kinder and warmer. She sits down to color with Henry, handing him crayons and pointing out geometric shapes on the paper. He seems comfortable with her—he doesn't cringe or pull away when she leans in next to him. *Maybe this year will be different after all*, I think.

Henry is also assigned to a different speech therapist for the year. I've had no complaints about the previous year's therapist, but Debra is fantastic—enthusiastic and patient. Before school starts, I bring Henry to his first speech therapy session. Someone had made a mistake with the dates on the IEP, and speech therapy was designated to begin a week and half before the actual start of school. Debra is providing summer services to a few kids and she's told me that she can see Henry in between those other students. This saves all of us paperwork and allows Henry to become reacclimated to the school before the entire student body arrives.

I sit in the hallway outside Debra's office during one of these first few visits, bouncing Finn on my lap and letting him play with my keys to keep him amused. Debra leaves the door ajar. I hear her praising Henry, speaking brightly and gently, helping him connect a funny picture with his own environment. "Look, Henry. The boy in the photo has a red jacket just like you!" The minute I detect fatigue seeping into Henry's limited speech, Debra says, "Okay, Henry. That's enough for today. Let's go find your mom!"

With Debra, everything becomes an adventure. I admire the excitement and joy she brings to her sessions with Henry. She motivates him without pushing so hard that he's discouraged into silence. She also communicates often with Mrs. Matthews so that Henry has opportunities to practice his specific speech exercises in the classroom. Henry may not be getting the fullest range of services, at least according to the children's hospital developmental medicine team, but Debra and Mrs. Matthews give me hope.

* * *

Many families have to fight for this level of care, and COVID-19 worsened the situation. School shutdowns were devastating for many special education students and their families. Some parents requested and eventually sued for compensatory services in order to help make up for the lost time and get their kids back to where they should have been, cognitively and socially. But even before the pandemic caused a temporary stop to in-person, therapeutic, tactile services for kids who need them, many parents were battling their school systems in court over special education. In 2018 alone, the San Diego Unified School District paid $2 million to settle 128 "due process" cases filed by parents. Due process filings seek reimbursement or direct payments for special education services that parents believe should have been offered to their children by the school district but were not.

These cases are controversial: school districts pay out hundreds of thousands of dollars to support a small minority of students—money that schools could better apply toward programs accessible to *all* students. But would they? In a 2021 NPR story on special education, Therese Yanan, Executive

Director of the Native American Disability Law Center, describes a pre-pandemic conversation she had with a school attorney who was arguing against paying for a student's special education services: "I said to him, 'What are we really fighting about here? You know this student needs these services.' And he said to me, 'Therese, if the school provides this student with these services, the football team won't get new uniforms this year.'"

Obvious and pervasive problems with educational priorities doesn't mean schools aren't also faced with difficult decisions about how to spend their budgets. In a 2018 report titled *Broken Promises: The Underfunding of IDEA*, the National Council on Disability analyzed historical and current funding levels for all parts of IDEA. The legislation was passed in 1975 and was originally called the "Education of Handicapped Children Act." In it, the Federal Government committed to pay 40 percent of the average per pupil cost of educating a child with disabilities. Since this first iteration of IDEA, Congress has never fulfilled its funding promise, which has shifted the burden mostly onto individual states and school districts. In 2023, funding was less than 13 percent, according to a bill introduced by Senator Chris Van Hollen of Maryland and co-sponsored by an additional twenty-four Senators from around the country.

Due process cases are expensive, time-consuming, and contentious, with no guarantee of a positive outcome for the child. In 2015, a study of 280 due process cases over an eight-year period in the state of Massachusetts found that the state prevailed over 60 percent of the time. The odds are not in the child's favor and most families consider lawsuits a last resort. In late 2023, after multiple advocacy groups and school personnel raised concerns, the U.S. Department of Education launched an inquiry into whether Massachusetts is adequately protecting the rights of disabled students and providing necessary monitoring to ensure local districts are complying with federal law.

I'm not sure where I would have landed on this due-process debate before becoming a parent myself. But now that I have years of experience with both special education and mainstream school systems, I support these parents in their fight to ensure their children get appropriate assistance. Henry unmistakably regressed when he was denied some of the services that the medical professionals recommended. Had I not been home during the day to work with him myself, this backsliding would have continued and been devastating to his progress.

LESSON 11

One Child's Symptoms are Another Child's Strategies

Henry is obsessed. Four Australian men known as The Wiggles have danced into his life and cast a spell. He likes watching Blue solve simple puzzles on *Blue's Clues* and Dora tackle challenges on *Dora the Explorer*. And he still holds a sweet affinity for Elmo. But his fixation on The Wiggles is of another order. Henry's day is no longer complete without the TV show that features these four singers and their friends: Captain Feathersword, Dorothy the Dinosaur, Henry the Octopus, and Wags the Dog. From the very first episode that we stumbled upon one morning, Henry's been enthralled by the 22-minute interactive musical performances this crew of characters puts on. Jeff, the lethargic Wiggle who is always falling asleep, routinely needs waking up during the show. His three friends implore viewers to help them yell, "Wake up, Jeff!" And Henry does. He's so engaged it's as if they are talking only to him. I start recording episodes to play later, should we miss their regular airtime.

I want to buy a Wiggles-related gift for Henry's upcoming birthday but soon realize this won't be easy. *Sesame Street*, *Blue's Clues*, and *Dora the Explorer* merchandise is abundant in the stores, but Wiggles merchandise is hard to find. On the internet I discover there are dolls for the four members of The Wiggles, as well as their pirate sidekick. Not typical action figures; they're large, poseable, accurate representations, about fifteen inches tall—big enough for Henry to carry around or cuddle the way many kids do with stuffed animals. I find a full set for sale on an online auction site that's been growing in popularity—eBay.

The day the box shows up on our doorstep, I don't have the heart to hide the dolls away until his birthday.

"Henry!" I call. "A package was delivered for you."

Henry trots out from the living room, a puzzled look on his face. I push the large brown box in front of him. I've sliced open the packing tape and he has no trouble lifting the cardboard flaps. Each of the dolls is wrapped in brown paper; he slowly unwraps the first: Anthony. Henry's face lights up the moment he sees the familiar blue shirt that this character always wears. He removes the paper from the next doll at double the pace. This one has a yellow shirt: Greg. Then comes Jeff, Murray, and finally Captain Feathersword, the friendly pirate.

The Wiggles' animal friends are at the bottom of the box; they're smaller, beanbag-like toys. Henry arranges them with the pirate on a living room chair and gathers up the four singers in his arms. The next thing I know, the dolls are moving around our house as if they have lives of their own. I go to bed with the dolls standing upright against a wall in Henry's room and I wake up to find them sitting on the shelf of his changing table—he's relocated them during the night. One day Henry moves the dolls from a chair in the living room to the stairs of the basement, carefully posing them as if they are climbing down the banister. I open the door, laundry basket in hand, and jump back, the miniature men's painted plastic smiles leering up at me. But I love how Henry's enjoying these toys. On their show, The Wiggles sing and dance, but they also tackle riddles. Maybe Henry's imagining these puzzles when he moves the four dolls around the house—perhaps he's setting up mysteries or conundrums for them that only he understands. Puzzles he can solve. Questions that have conclusive, definitive answers. Maybe he's using the basic riddles presented on this show, and others like it, as a first step to more advanced problem-solving. The extent of his focus and the deliberate way he moves these dolls around suggests something beyond typical play to me. Some of our family and friends view Henry's intense attachment to The Wiggles as odd, but I don't.

I imagine Henry's mind as a congested city at rush hour, and none of the traffic lights are working—a mayhem of information that cannot be easily sorted out. A mess of lights and sounds and irritated, impatient people yelling and beeping and demanding attention. He can't easily figure out a path through. Arranging his stacking cups over and over as a toddler, lining up his Matchbox cars, rapt as Elmo asks questions and finds answers on *Sesame Street*, and now creating and solving The Wiggles' mysteries—these activities help create order in the chaos. With his obsessions, he boards a train that bars distractions, that cuts a route through the confusion. Without them, his environment swallows him—he'll never make it out of the depot and into the next stage of his journey.

I don't yet see that the rigid routines I've created for myself, not just as a parent but throughout my life, serve the same purpose.

* * *

It's summer 2005 and we're at a new pediatrician's office for Henry's four-year checkup—I switched to a doctor closer to home after Finn was born. Henry is not using the potty at all and is still in diapers. He continues to struggle with motor skills. He's finally learned to pedal a tricycle, but he can't button his clothes or tie a basic knot. He's become even more sensitive to loud noises and intolerant of chaotic environments. But what worries me the most is an entirely new behavior.

A few weeks before, I was working on a freelance job while Henry watched an episode of *The Wiggles*. The program ended and I heard him walk into the kitchen. I looked up to see what he needed and spotted a red trail across the floor. At first I thought he got hold of a juice box from the fridge and had spilled it. But as I got closer, I could see the liquid was too dense, too opaque.

I raced toward the cupboard he was shuffling through and turned him around. A crimson stream flowed down his forearm.

"Did you cut yourself, honey?" I asked, as I dabbed at his arm with a paper towel.

He looked at the blood as if noticing it for the first time, then turned back toward the cabinet and grabbed a box of graham crackers.

I guided him toward a kitchen chair and opened the box. He munched on a cracker with one hand and I held his other arm flat to the table and gently cleaned the cut with a peroxide-soaked cotton ball. The wound was small and round, about the size of a pencil eraser, with a crescent-shaped flap of skin still covering half of it, like a tiny red eclipse. I figured he must have nicked it on the corner of the coffee table or TV stand. I squeezed a bit of antibiotic cream on it and covered it with a Band-Aid. The bright purple racecar-themed bandage stood out like a tattoo on his pale skin.

The next afternoon, when Henry's allotted hour of television was over, I went into the living room and spotted a small dark stain on the new beige carpet we'd recently installed. As I got closer, I could see blood dripping down Henry's left arm— the one without the Band-Aid. He was scratching at it, picking at the skin.

The wound was self-inflicted.

"Henry, don't do that!" I scolded him and cleaned and covered this cut with a Band-Aid, too.

By the end of the week, a dozen brightly colored miniature racecars adorned Henry's arms and legs. I made him wear long sleeves and long pants, even though it was late June. I was grateful school was out for the summer so I didn't have to explain this to his teacher. Who's to say whether she would have believed me or chose to contact the Department of Children & Families instead.

I called the pediatrician's office, but Henry's regular checkup was scheduled for three weeks later, and they couldn't see us before then. The doctor advised me to keep the spots covered and to cut Henry's nails down as short as possible. "It's not that uncommon with kids like Henry," he said. "We'll talk more when I see him next month." *Kids like Henry?* I've never met another kid like Henry.

"How is it that a child whose skin is so sensitive that he needs every tag in his clothing removed can then turn around and pick at himself until he bleeds, and not even feel it?" I ask John that night. "He won't go near any textured or rough fabric, won't wear anything remotely confining—not a turtleneck or a scarf or even a button-collared shirt—but he doesn't notice the blood dripping down his limbs?" I don't expect John to have an answer; he doesn't know any more than I do.

The day of the appointment Henry sits on my lap in the waiting room, not interested in playing with the other children there. The twice-weekly private speech therapy sessions in conjunction with the school's services have improved Henry's verbal language skills. Words have replaced many of the gestures he once made to get what he needs—a drink, a snack, a toy. But he rarely uses language to interact with others beyond that. He sometimes repeats questions that John or Danielle or I ask, but he never asks his own. "Echolalia," his speech therapist calls it. He makes no spontaneous declarations. Rather than articulate what he wants to do, he just does it. That morning in the waiting room, another small child might announce, "Mommy, I get book." But Henry climbs down from my lap, walks over to a shelf affixed to the wall, finds a book and brings it to me, without any prior notification.

I read a few sentences to Henry. Soon I'm distracted by a toddler having a temper tantrum on the floor. I smile sympathetically at the child's frazzled mother as she scoops the baby up. I look down again and Henry has turned the page of the book. "Henry, don't you want me to finish that page?" I ask. I go to turn it back. Henry presses his hand firmly on the book to stop me, never looking up. His mouth is moving but the sound he makes is soft, barely a whisper; he's talking to himself. I lean over and try to lift the book to see the title on the cover. Henry pushes it back to my lap. At home we read our books over and over, and I'm sure he's memorized every word. But we don't own this one. Henry isn't yet visiting others' houses without me, so he's not being read to by relatives or friends. Maybe he's heard this story at preschool. But Mrs. Matthews reads a new book to her class every week, not the same one repeatedly.

"Henry, do you know this story?"

Henry shakes his head, dismissing me. He's enthralled by the book and annoyed by my interruption. He must be making up a narrative to go along with the pictures. I want to hear it.

"Henry? Can you read me the story, too?"

Henry speaks, still softly.

"A little louder, please. I can't hear you."

He raises his voice, "Ta boy..."

Henry reads me the rest of the story. His articulation is still poor—he's unable to make the "th" sound and struggles with several others, like "v" and "z"—but I can decipher enough to know nothing is fabricated. He's reading every word of the simple sentences that are printed on the page. I want to scream but I try to remain calm so the other parents and the office staff don't think I've lost my mind.

"Why don't you go over to the table and get another book, Henry? I'd like to hear another story," I say, practically hyperventilating.

He does. I've never been so happy to wait forty-five minutes at the pediatrician's office. Henry reads to me until they call us in.

"I've reviewed Henry's previous evaluations," Dr. Ballister starts.

Yeah, yeah, yeah, who cares? My kid can read!

"Kids who struggle with developmental delays sometimes experience anxiety. He's previously exhibited obsessive-compulsive behaviors and an extreme need for control over his environment; this picking at his skin is probably an extension of that," the doctor says. "Continue to keep any wounds clean and bandaged so they don't get infected. I suspect Henry will outgrow this once his language and other skills improve."

I don't tell the doctor about the reading; I'm sure he won't believe me. I try to remember the questions I have about Henry not using the toilet and his continued difficulty in performing everyday tasks like washing his hands. But my mind is racing. I absorb what advice I can from the doctor, remember to get the signed form confirming Henry is up to date on vaccinations and otherwise able to attend school, and hurry out.

Once we're both back in the spaceship, I turn toward him. He's secured in his black and red high-back booster seat that looks very much at home in our NASA-inspired minivan. "Henry?" I ask. "How did you learn to read?"

He tilts his head and looks at me, puzzled.

"The books, Henry! How did you know what the books say?"

"Iggls," he says.

"The Wiggles?"

"Iggls," he confirms.

That morning my mom and dad have been watching Finn. They're both retired now and I'm leaning on them more often when one of the kids has an appointment. I'd joined a weekly meetup of new mothers and their kids when Danielle was just a toddler. We were going to help each other out as our families grew, create a babysitting co-op. One of the moms in the group watched Danielle once when Henry was sick in the hospital, and I watched her daughter once so she and her husband could attend an evening event. But the group stopped getting together not long after that. We all had second children by then, and I thought everyone was too busy, but I later discovered that the gatherings resumed without me. I and my kids were no longer invited. So, grandparents are now my only babysitting option on weekdays.

I don't share Henry's reading revelation with my parents. They love the kids immensely, but their attitudes around Henry's challenges, as with my in-laws' ideas, haven't changed. They still believe I'm an anxious parent who's overreacting to his developmental delays. I'm not ready to explain or defend the importance of this moment to them.

Later that afternoon, Henry retreats to our basement. He slides down the stairs on his rear-end, step by step, to the portion that John and I cordoned off into a play area the previous winter. We installed drywall and cheap carpeting ourselves, then added shelves and plastic storage boxes for toys. There's a CD boombox on the floor, with oversized buttons that John taught Henry how to operate. Henry will often listen to The Wiggles CDs there all afternoon.

I creep down the stairs shortly after to find Henry sitting against the interior wall, his back to me, boombox in front of him. His small hands are wrapped around one of the booklets of song lyrics. I settle on an upper step and watch as Henry starts the CD over from the beginning. His head toggles from left to right as if following the printed text. I lean closer. I've seen him in this position many times, listening to the music and holding the booklets, and have always assumed that he was looking at the photographs of the characters interspersed throughout the pages. I never considered that he might be following along. After several minutes, I move farther down the stairs until I see Henry's jaw moving, mouthing the words.

"Oh my God," I say aloud. Henry has listened to those CDs over and over again for months, booklets in hand, focusing not on the photos but on the printed lyrics. He's made the connection between the sounds and the corresponding letters that represent them. He identified the patterns that combine those individual letters into words. The countless episodes of *The Wiggles* that he watched—the characters singing those songs and acting them out—must have helped him attach meaning to the language.

The Wiggles had taught Henry to read. Rather, he'd taught himself to read using The Wiggles' voices, words, and movements. Without my noticing. Without anyone noticing.

I always know what's going on with Danielle. She waves aloft her latest worksheet, story, or drawing as soon as she returns home from school. I share in her joy and praise her achievements. It's different with Henry; he doesn't seem to experience that glee. He's happy sitting in a corner sorting his toy cars or putting together a puzzle, but these activities seem less about having fun and more about finding peace and making sense of an otherwise stressful, uncomfortable existence.

Sometimes I worry that Henry will never partake in anything that isn't necessary to his daily functioning. He doesn't exhibit the curiosity that other children do. His instinct is to withdraw from the world rather than explore it. But reading will open up new possibilities. He was intrigued by those new books at the doctor's office, a little excited even. Most kids learn with time-honored, traditional instruction—worksheets and classroom lessons and mimicking the other people around them. Henry doesn't appear interested in any of that. But he clearly *is* motivated to learn so, at least in this case, he found a way, on his terms and his schedule. Who am I to say if one method is better than another? Who is anyone to say? I laugh to myself and wonder if, when Henry does finally start talking fluently, he'll speak in an Aussie accent.

It's Tough to Face Reality

During February school vacation, less than four months before the end of Henry's last year of preschool, John takes a couple days off from work so we can spend some time together as a family. We plan a few kid-friendly outings, including a community theater production I've reserved tickets for. As we're getting ready to go, John brings a pair of socks down from Henry's dresser. Henry flies into a rage. Apparently he wants to get the socks himself, or wants a different pair, or a different color. It's impossible to know. Regardless, he will not put the socks on or allow anyone else to put them on for him. I explain to him that if he doesn't put socks and shoes on, or let us put them on, he won't be able to go to the show.

I point to the clock. "See, Henry. The clock says 9:38. The show starts at 10. We need to leave now." I'm hoping his recent fixation on time will play into our favor. He's become obsessed with the clocks in the house, specifically having them all perfectly synced. The numbers on the bedroom clocks, the oven range, the microwave, and the grandmother clock in the living room have to match. Henry also must witness the arrival of certain times. One minute past seven is the most important. At seven o'clock every morning and evening, Henry stands in the kitchen where he can watch the digital oven and microwave clock roll from 7:00 to 7:01. He listens to the grandmother clock chime seven times, then cease. If we're out and I forget to call attention to this changeover on the car radio's clock or other timepiece, Henry has a meltdown.

My effort to bring our time restriction into this current situation doesn't help, though. I try to slip on the socks one more time, and Henry pulls them from his feet and throws them on the floor with a scream that quickly turns to wailing.

"Just go," John says, exasperated. "I'll stay here with him."

A few hours later I return from the theater with Danielle and eighteen-month-old Finn. John informs me that Henry eventually calmed down by sitting alone in his bedroom and urgently flipping through his books. I go up to see him and tell him I'm sorry he didn't come to the show with us. "I go laaatr, Mommee," he says. Of course, there is no "later;" the show's over. And it doesn't matter anyway, because I know Henry doesn't care. This phrase is meant to appease me, and it implies *Maybe next time, Mommy;* "maybe" being the operative word. I know this interpretation is correct, but I don't know what to do with the knowledge.

Both John and I are becoming more confused and frustrated with Henry's behavior. We're not sure what we should or shouldn't discipline him for, what is intentional "acting out" versus behaviors that are not within his control. We don't feel enlightened by the many medical assessments we've received, so when the developmental medicine unit at the general hospital calls to say they are taking on new patients, I make an appointment. I hate dragging Henry through these evaluations, but my magical thinking prevails: the next professional opinion might be the *right* one, and we'll find the specialist who knows what to do and can give us a guide.

Keeping Henry's day structured and stable enough for him is becoming increasingly difficult. John and I both put on a happy face and make a big deal of each major milestone. "Henry, when you go to kindergarten, you'll get to ride the big-kid school bus like Dani!" But the truth is we're worried. About the bus ride he'll take every morning and afternoon. About a new class that's twice the size of what he's accustomed to. About a much larger school building and a much higher staff-to-student ratio. We won't know about any problems that arise during the hours he's gone unless they're noticed by a staff member at the school, or reported to one. The likelihood of that recognition seems small. No monitors watch on the school buses or in the hallways. A scant one or two teachers survey dozens of children on the playground at a time. There's no aide in the classroom to help the lead teacher manage thirty six-year-olds.

I'm hesitant about Henry starting kindergarten for all these reasons but remain hopeful that it will go smoothly. Maybe the perspective of a new team of doctors from the general hospital can offer me more than hope. I've been driving Henry to and from preschool three days a week, driving a half hour each way the other two days to private therapy, and trying to involve him in a mommy-and-me music or art class one afternoon a week. Finn is a happy, social toddler who loves attention. So far he's exhibited none of the quirks Henry has and is much easier to travel with. But it's exhausting to drag him everywhere we go. I'm ready for a break.

"This will be good for you," John says. "Now Henry will be at school five half-days a week, and he'll be pulled out of class for occupational and speech therapy. No more thirty-minute drives to the Speech and Language Center. You'll have a little time to yourself in the mornings." It's true. I'm annoyed that the evaluation team at the elementary school followed the preschool's example and offered Henry therapy sessions only twice per week, rather than every day as the doctor suggested. But at least he'll finally get the five days of school and the occupational therapy that the developmental specialists have been recommending for over two years. And, yes, I'll get a break.

At our initial meeting, a therapist on Henry's new IEP team echoes what others at the school have continuously asserted: "Henry attending class with typically developing children his own age will be a therapy of its own. He'll naturally try to mimic their behavior and attempt to communicate on their level. You'll be surprised at how quickly he progresses."

Danielle is going into second grade, so she'll ride the same bus as Henry in the morning. This eases some of my apprehension. Henry turned five just two weeks before the kindergarten age cutoff and is therefore the youngest kid in his class. His developmental delays make him appear even younger. Danielle is acutely aware of this. That first day when the bus arrives, Danielle makes sure she's right behind him, guiding him onto the bus and into an empty seat. I learn later that she'd insisted on walking him to his classroom that morning, despite a teacher meeting all the new students at the entrance. On the way, Dani showed Henry the bathrooms and demonstrated how to hang his jacket on one of the hooks in the hallway. Before she left for her own class, she explained how to get to the nurse's office—a place he could go to if he felt scared or nervous. Henry is still not fully toilet trained, so this is also where he'll go if he has an "accident."

Danielle is a big girl, strong and sturdy and taller than

most of the boys her age. By the time she gets to middle school, she'll be plagued with the same self-doubt and puberty-fueled angst most tweens deal with, but at the tender age of seven, she's confident, determined, and fiercely protective of her brothers. That Halloween she'll dress up as Kim Possible. It's not a stretch—she and the character share thick auburn hair and a get-out-of-my-way attitude.

Many flyers come home in Henry's backpack during the first weeks of kindergarten advertising one or another opportunity to volunteer, but I never sign up. Finn is as active and busy a toddler as I've ever seen. Henry was just beginning to walk with certitude at two years old, but Finn can run like a leopard at twenty-one months. He's quick and curious. A parent volunteer may bring a younger child into class as long as that child remains seated in a stroller the entire time. That's not happening with Finn.

I haven't observed Henry in the classroom, so I'm relieved when Henry's first progress report indicates that he's doing fine in kindergarten. He's never a behavioral problem and always completes work on time. But the report says nothing about his social behavior. Just as in preschool, at home Henry never mentions the other kids and he receives no invitations to birthday parties or classmate get-togethers on the weekends. He may not be fitting in as well as I'd hoped.

One day in October, when my mom is watching Finn so I can attend a routine doctor's appointment, I decide to drop by the school on my way home. I sign in at the office and explain that I want to pick up a few of my son's art projects so he doesn't have to carry them home on the bus. The secretary doesn't question, and I wander down the hall toward Henry's classroom, a bright green visitor's pass clipped to my jacket.

I hear Ms. Bates laughing. She's a stout, cheerful woman, who—when we'd met her at the school's open house in late summer—seemed as comfortable sitting on a floor pillow as she was in the teacher's chair. I'm not surprised to see her on the area rug now, playing a game with a few of her kindergarteners. The other kids are gathered around her, waiting for their turn at the large cardboard spinner that sits in the center of the group. I don't see Henry anywhere. I scan the room and catch sight of his dark curls. Two rogue strands dart out from the top of his head like a Martian from a retro *Star Trek* or *Twilight Zone* episode. He's in the back corner of the classroom in front of a short bookshelf. He has set a puzzle on top of it. His back is to me, and I watch as he puts the chunky pieces into place, then dumps them all out onto the top of the shelf and completes the puzzle again. Unnoticed, I stand in the doorway for almost fifteen minutes, watching him. He appears uninterested in the group that's gathered around their teacher. He doesn't turn to look when one child lets out a high-pitched squeal of delight or another loudly yelps, "Can I spin it now? Can I?"

It's as if he's all alone in the room.

I drop by the classroom twice more that fall during "open choice" times. I see the same thing on both occasions—children interacting with Ms. Bates, laughing and playing or working on some project, and Henry in the corner completing a puzzle over and over.

At our first parent-teacher conference on December 1st, I ask how Henry is integrating socially into the class. Ms. Bates hesitates. I'm there alone because John is working, and I wonder if she's sizing me up, deciding whether I can handle the truth, or at least a portion of it. I already know the truth, of course. I've seen it. But I say nothing. Maybe I'm hoping that what I witnessed is not representative of Henry's overall experience, or maybe I'm testing her willingness to acknowledge the problem. After our time at the special-needs preschool, I've come to believe that teachers are expected to strike a difficult balance: they should provide pertinent information to parents while ensuring they don't say anything that might imply their school is not in compliance with IDEA. If a teacher feels a child needs additional services and verbalizes that, a parent will likely ask for a meeting to revisit their child's IEP. More services require more money and more staff—two things that schools are constantly deficient in.

To Ms. Bates's credit, she errs on the side of frankness. "Henry is usually on the fringes of any activity or discussion in class. He becomes anxious and easily flustered when anything goes wrong, and it can take a great deal of time and reassurance to bring him back from that state." *Don't I know it.* She goes on to say that he struggles with clear articulation. His speech is monotone, nasally and robotic, and his classmates often have difficulty understanding him. Henry also seems to have trouble managing social situations and frequently withdraws into a corner. If the classroom gets really loud or chaotic, she'll occasionally find Henry crouched underneath her desk, overwhelmed, covering his ears.

Ms. Bates explains how story recall and the proper sequence of events seem to escape Henry. But I'm still stuck on the image of him cowering under her L-shaped metal desk.

"He can't correctly answer these types of questions without visual cues." *Wait, what types of questions?* I've fallen behind in the conversation. I feel as overwhelmed as Henry. "If he doesn't know how to respond, he reverts to what he does know and will make an unrelated statement, like 'I like *The Wiggles*' or 'My favorite color is red.'"

I wish I could get away with that strategy now. I want to change the subject, too.

Ms. Bates pauses. "But his vocabulary and reading ability are off the charts. He prefers reading to conversation. He doesn't often make eye contact with people, even when speaking directly to them."

I wanted honesty, and I got it. But this is a whole lot of truth at once. Ms. Bates then offers what is possibly the most useful advice I've received up to that point, maybe the most useful advice I will ever receive regarding my son's education. "I've been an elementary-school educator for nineteen years," she says, "and I don't believe any curriculum can 'correct' these behaviors. His language skills will surely improve over time. But I think you should focus on helping him develop coping strategies for social situations and educational settings, rather than trying to teach him to respond like other children do in these environments."

Henry is extremely intelligent academically, Ms. Bates says. But he doesn't seem to understand basic jokes or silliness. She cautions that this gap is going to become a problem as he progresses through school. My mind jumps to a recent dinner party that John and I attended where the host made an offhand remark that caused everyone to erupt in laughter. I smiled and pretended to get the quip, but I'd lost the thread. It's a common occurrence for me in social settings, and a lousy feeling. I attribute it to my relative lack of education and experiences among the people in our current circle.

I want better for Henry. I want him to fit in. I want him to get the joke.

"I suggest you request a meeting with his IEP team regarding his placement next year. A full school day, with unstructured times like lunch and recess, is going to be an extraordinary challenge for Henry," Ms. Bates says.

I leave the classroom and walk through the school's double doors and out to the parking lot at an accelerated pace. I keep my head down and look only at the pavement; I don't want to make eye contact with anyone on the walkway. I drop myself into the driver's seat of the minivan, cover my face with my hands, and cry. An odd mix of discouragement and relief washes over me, similar to the way I felt at the Early Intervention center when Henry finally made the sign for "cracker." Henry spent a year and a half in that Early Intervention program, followed by two years at the special-needs preschool, supplemented by hours and hours of private therapy sessions. But this is his first time in a class full of "typical" peers and the first time someone essentially tells me straight-up, with no equivocation or medical jargon, that he isn't like other children and that the future will likely be more difficult for him, not less. This isn't something we can fix.

I now drive a new Toyota Sienna. We'd traded the spaceship in after it broke down one too many times and I'd had enough of its quirkiness. Searching through the Sienna's glove compartment for a tissue, I suddenly miss the spaceship. This Toyota is practical, ordinary, reliable transportation that blends in with the dozens of other late-model minivans parked in the school lot, at the grocery store, or in the local shopping mall's garage on any given day. When we first purchased it I was excited that my vehicle would no longer stick out in the crowd. But now it feels like a charade, and I yearn to be sitting in that old peculiar van that was so uniquely mine.

As I pull myself together, I watch parents walk out of the school and get into their own vehicles, smiling. They're no doubt happy with their little ones' progress, maybe even feeling a bit smug about their ability to raise children who are adapting to "big kid" school so flawlessly—the same way I felt after Danielle's first parent-teacher conference. Today's discussion provides a different sort of affirmation for me. I'm not an anxious, hypervigilant, overprotective parent; I'm not exaggerating Henry's odd behaviors or the impact they have on his and our family's day-to-day life. He *is* different. He doesn't behave or adapt like other children. He doesn't have fun with or find joy in the activities that most other kids do. I reflect on all the times I've been accused of being a "worrier" during conversations with family, friends, and even some educators. How my concerns were brushed off as unwarranted, dismissed as "nonsense." Those people were wrong, *are* wrong. I feel sad, but also validated. And then guilty, because what kind of mother feels liberated after hearing such news?

LESSON 13

Diagnoses Can Help and Hurt

Two weeks before Christmas, I call John at work. "I can't do this anymore," I say. "I just can't. And my tooth hurts."

I sound like an incoherent wreck because I *am* an incoherent wreck. The week after Henry started kindergarten, Finn had his two-year checkup. The pediatrician suspected a speech delay and referred us for an evaluation. Only weeks after Henry's private therapy transitioned to the public school, I found myself driving Finn a half hour each way to the same independent speech and language center that I'd been taking Henry to. Finn also gets a weekly home visit from an Early Intervention therapist. The "time to myself" that John had touted as a benefit of Henry starting kindergarten was short-lived.

Speech issues clearly run in our family. All three of our kids will now have had speech therapy before they even started preschool. The pediatrician observed no other developmental problems in Finn's behavior and assured me that this was likely just a standard speech delay that would resolve with minor intervention, just like Danielle's had. "He'll be fine," the doctor says. Finn is certainly far more outgoing and engaged than Henry was at this age, but that can change. Kids can lose speech, lose skills, in toddlerhood. I try not to worry, but the possibility creeps into my mind every time Finn throws a minor, otherwise very age-appropriate tantrum, or pulls off his socks, or seems even remotely interested in the time on any clock.

And now my toothache. Searing pain radiates through my jaw. I ignore it for a week amidst holiday events at the school that require baking and gift-wrapping and concert-attending. I hate going to the dentist; the thought of sitting in that chair incites panic in me. But I can't even drink a glass of room-temperature water without discomfort, despite taking ibuprofen every four hours.

John calls in sick to work that Friday so I can go to the dentist. I need a root canal. I don't respond well to Novocain and when I tell the dentist that I can feel him poking at the tooth, he doesn't believe me. He says I'm feeling pressure, not pain. He starts to drill, hits the nerve, and my entire body jumps from the pain. My shoulder bumps his hand—the one holding the drill—and he slices into my tongue. Blood spews everywhere. The dentist stitches me up and sends me home with a temporary filling and a referral for a specialist to finish the job. I sit in the car for twenty minutes, my body involuntarily shaking, before I feel safe to drive.

John has to be in Detroit on Monday for work, so he spends Sunday afternoon setting up a toddler bed for Finn, who's been protesting the crib and demanding a "big-boy bed" like his brother has. John's trying to help but apparently this is a "grass is always greener on the other side" scenario, because the following night Finn refuses to sleep in the bed John assembled. I have fresh stitches in my mouth and am in no mood to argue, so I put the crib back together. *Adjustment issues.* I push the thought out of my mind. Two days later I discover that a nasty ear infection is what's making Finn so ornery.

My mouth pain eventually subsides but the overwhelming feeling that I'm falling apart, that I can't keep going on like this, does not.

"You're just tired," John says.

* * *

Henry finally has his initial assessment with the new developmental team at the general hospital in late December. It pretty much mirrors the one he had at the children's hospital two and a half years before, with one major difference. This time, we're asked to bring him back a week later for another entire afternoon of testing at an offsite unit of the hospital that specializes in developmental delays and neurological disorders, specifically autism.

The neurodevelopmental center is west of Boston, twenty miles from its parent hospital, in a nondescript industrial park. It looks more like a corporate office than a medical center, except all doors are locked; we're buzzed into every hallway. John, Henry, and I sit in the reception area, and I study the other children waiting to be called. I've never seen another child like Henry, never witnessed any kid sort or stack or classify items with such meticulous determination or avoid social contact and group activities so consistently. I'm seeking kindred spirits. But I find none here, at least I don't think so. A couple of children are independently busy with books, as Henry is. One child is focused on a handheld video game, and another is playing with a small toy kitchen positioned in the corner. All boys. The kids don't notice my scrutiny, but I get caught staring by two adults sitting across the room. They both smile warmly at me in return, the way I do when I encounter a parent with an uncontrollable toddler at the pediatrician's office, as if they'd once been where I am now.

Because Henry's earlier evaluation at the children's hospital noted that he did not meet the criteria for an autism spectrum disorder, we'd ruled that out at the time. But the possibility continued to cross my mind when some new study or article got traction in the news. Hyperlexia was mentioned by the specialists with a bit more conviction then, but Henry was never definitively diagnosed with it. And Henry's obsessions have become more pronounced over the last year and a half. He's become more intolerant of schedule changes. More withdrawn. The gap between his intellectual ability and his social/emotional awareness has grown wider, as his kindergarten teacher predicted. I've read that a child can be hyperlexic without being autistic, but I can't attribute Henry's current behaviors to a single communication disorder or learning disability—his challenges are too complex and disjointed.

* * *

A month later I'm back at the neurodevelopmental center for a third appointment, alone, so the doctor can go over the results of the prior two visits without Henry present. I'm hoping for answers.

"Henry qualifies for an autism spectrum disorder diagnosis," the doctor says. Her choice of words makes it sound like we've won a grand sweepstakes. "But maybe you knew that?" she asks.

Maybe I did.

I ask why the previous developmental specialists ruled it out.

"Pervasive Developmental Disorder Not Otherwise

Specified, or PDD-NOS, is the specific diagnosis," she says. "It falls under the autism spectrum umbrella, and it means that Henry displays many of the symptoms of autism but has some symptoms that don't exactly fit." She says this kind of case is difficult to diagnose before the age of six or seven. We discuss the obsessive-compulsive behaviors Henry exhibits and his need for rigid routines. "There are therapies that can help," she says. "You'll receive a full written report in six weeks or so with a list of recommendations to present to Henry's school."

A local college student has been watching Finn for me that afternoon (my parents are now "snowbirds," having inherited my grandfather's little house in Central Florida, and won't be back until spring). Once the babysitter leaves, I call John at work and tell him the news. He sighs—not out of disappointment, but relief. Many parents fear an autism diagnosis, but at this point we almost welcome it. We need a locus, a point from which to get help. I don't know a lot about autism, but during our conversation the doctor explained that people with the disorder fall on a wide spectrum that includes those with severe coexisting intellectual and physical challenges all the way to those who are very "high functioning" and who struggle only with social interactions and relatively minor compulsions or quirks. She warned that much of the public is still ignorant of the intricacies of autism. We may need help in advocating for Henry.

At the time this conversation took place, the term "autism" was well known outside the medical community. But the condition itself was not. Three years after we got this diagnosis, NBC debuted *Parenthood*—a prime-time family drama that tackled several issues rarely addressed on network TV and included a prominent child character with Asperger syndrome.

The show follows how both the child and his family are affected by it. Some contemporary critics believe the depiction fell short and even the show's creator, Jason Katims, who has a child on the autism spectrum, feels the representation was flawed. But whatever deficiencies the portrayal may have had, it was a significant improvement on what had been available.

Before *Parenthood*, the character of Raymond Babbitt, an autistic savant from the 1988 movie *Rain Man*, was the only point of reference many people had for autism. In 2017, this savant-based vision of autism also appeared in ABC's *The Good Doctor*, albeit in a more measured way. There was virtually no representation of mild to moderate autism in media when Henry was diagnosed. Adults on the autism spectrum who had been labeled as socially awkward, quirky, eccentric, or "slow" when they were young, and who struggled to thrive in school or in the workplace, would not have recognized themselves as neurodivergent. That idea and terminology weren't introduced until the late 1990s by sociologist Judy Singer, and they didn't become part of the vernacular until well into the 2000s. What are now known to be disabilities and/or thought by some to be manifestations of naturally occurring human neurodiversity were then described as character flaws—deficits that consequently affected one's career trajectory, socioeconomic status, and personal relationships.

* * *

The full report arrives on a sunny day in late February. Snow and ice glisten on the front lawn as I cross the street to the mailbox. Later when Finn goes down for an afternoon nap, I sit at the kitchen table and read slowly through the report, not skipping ahead like I'd done with previous evaluations. It's strange to expect that a team of doctors who have spent all of two afternoons with your child will be able to tell you who he really is, that thirteen pages of type could confirm or deny what you, as his parent, see with your own eyes every day. But I do expect that. I still don't completely trust my own observations and intuition. I pore over that report like it's introducing my son to me for the first time.

The clinicians had asked Henry about friends, but Henry couldn't explain what a friend is. He referenced a couple of children from his class that he thought were nice and said that those two kids often played together at recess. When asked if he ever joined them, Henry said, "No. They play games for two people. I play puzzles because that's just for one." This is a consistent theme throughout the pages. Henry's responses all seem to reflect a flat acceptance of his place outside the social circle, like he's resolved that he'll always be alone.

"Henry's developmental profile is complex," the report states. "He meets the criteria for a Pervasive Developmental Disorder, but not a typical one, as he presents with a severe receptive language delay not usually associated with PDD-NOS."

Pervasive Developmental Disorder Not Otherwise Specified. I've done hours of research since meeting with the doctor in January and now feel like an expert on the term. It's a subtype of autism, used for people with "atypical presentation," and is often given to children whose symptoms fall somewhere between the high-functioning variety known as Asperger syndrome and a more disabling form called "classic autism." These individuals can have some moderate to severe attributes of autism paired with mild or missing symptoms that doctors would otherwise expect to see.

The doctors who review and revise the Diagnostic and Statistical Manual of Mental Disorders ("DSM")—the definitive resource that clinicians use to diagnose a host of developmental and mental health issues—determined that Asperger syndrome does not include a speech delay. So if a person exhibits all other signs of Asperger's but as a child had delayed speech or had other verbal challenges, he or she cannot be diagnosed with Asperger's. Henry exhibits every symptom of Asperger syndrome, but because of his speech issues, they can't diagnose him with it.

A person might take this as evidence that a diagnosis of a disorder that is neither fully understood, nor that consistently manifests itself in the same way from person to person, is not reliable. It's reasonable to question the usefulness of it. The fact that the diagnoses of both PDD-NOS and Asperger syndrome were eliminated in the subsequent edition of the DSM, only six years after Henry's diagnosis, supports this notion. You cannot identify or define these disorders with a simple blood test or biopsy. A diagnostic label is far less meaningful than a multi-page report outlining an individual's specific challenges and strengths. But the public special education system in our country is built on diagnoses that "negatively impact educational performance," within IDEA's guidelines. Autism is one of the eligible disability categories under IDEA, and "Autism Spectrum Disorder" will now define every one of Henry's IEPs going forward. It will define *him*, at least on paper, for the rest of his time in public school.

LESSON 14

The Extremes are Both Exhausting and Exhilarating

In March I write an email to Henry's IEP administrator to request a meeting. I attach a copy of the general hospital developmental team's report, with their recommendations highlighted in neon yellow marker.

"You think it'll do any good?" John asks as I hit send.

"It better. What else can we do?"

The lead developmental doctor wants Henry in a full-day kindergarten program for the remainder of the school year. If that isn't available (it isn't), she says his speech and occupational therapy services should take place before or after the school day so he gets the full benefit of the classroom environment for the half-day he's in it. Henry needs summer services to avoid a regression of skills, the report also states. He should have speech and language therapy at least three times per week, and two of those sessions should be with a pragmatic language group so he can work on conversation and learn how to appropriately talk with and respond to his peers. Finally, he needs an educational aide to help him access the curriculum. The doctor wants a paraprofessional in the classroom to encourage and help him participate in group activities (so he's not in a back corner making the same puzzle repeatedly while the rest of the class plays a game, for example). The report specifies that Henry should not share this aide with more than one other child.

All these recommendations make perfect sense to me; this is the ideal formula for helping Henry progress, if not flourish. "Social relationships must be closely monitored," my email notes, "as kids like Henry are often vulnerable to the actions of more aggressive children." That's my addition, not the doctor's. I've read this troubling fact over and over in my research.

What happens next shouldn't have been a surprise. We receive an invitation to attend an IEP meeting; the school has scheduled it for five weeks later. On the day of the meeting John and I arrive fifteen minutes early, a copy of my previously sent email in hand. We're ushered into a bare interior office—no personal items, no photos or plants. The singular source of light in the room comes from an industrial-style overhead fluorescent. The administrator—a woman who's been assigned to be the spokesperson for the IEP team—sits behind a gray metal desk that has nothing on its surface but a file folder and a pen. I wonder what else this office is used for. It's as if we're about to be interrogated. The woman stands up, offers us a formal "good morning," and directs us to take a seat in the two generic reception chairs opposite her. I know from that two-word greeting that Henry isn't going to get what he needs. She has spoken in the strained tone of a negotiator who can't comply with an opposing party's demands.

The woman presents us with a proposal for the following year. The IEP team suggests that Henry continue with speech therapy twice a week and occupational therapy once a week for the remainder of kindergarten. He'll be pulled out of the classroom for those sessions, as there are no services available before school starts. After morning kindergarten session ends, the therapists are too busy with the afternoon group to add another child to their roster. Henry will not receive summer services of any kind. He will not receive an educational aide. These recommendations are based on the most recent educational evaluation that the school has conducted, the administrator says.

"Henry tested in the average to above-average range on many of the educational assessments," she says. It's a preemptive strike. We haven't fully absorbed the previous information. I already know about his scores. His inarticulate speech and his difficulty in holding a pencil or a pair of scissors have nothing to do with his academic ability. But, as Ms. Bates had pointed out to me at that first parent-teacher conference, Henry's level of competence in writing a letter of the alphabet neatly between two lines, cutting a square out of construction paper, or exercising his intellect aren't the problems that are interfering with his ability to thrive at school.

I ask the administrator if a social competency assessment was done. She says this is not something the school offers. Even if it were, she adds, no formal social skills programming exists in the school to help Henry better relate to the other kids; we'll have to seek outside help for those issues.

"Did you even read the report from the developmental team?" John asks. John is far more confrontational than I am in these settings with school administrators, teachers, or medical staff. It makes me uncomfortable; I was raised to be submissive and polite to people with authority. Later I complain about them in private—one of the few lessons from my parents that stuck.

"Our conclusions don't match those of the hospital's," the administrator says.

I interject before John can respond, hoping to keep this interaction from becoming too antagonistic. "Will there at least be protocols in place to make sure Henry is doing okay socially—to catch any bullying or exclusion before it becomes a serious problem?"

"The school encourages a supportive environment; if there are any issues the principal will promptly address them," she says.

"So, the answer is no," John says, looking at me. I cringe, embarrassed by his blunt comment and angry that this disappointing meeting warrants it.

We receive a draft IEP in the mail a week later with bright red sticky notes marking the areas where we're supposed to sign.

In the end, nothing changes. Henry receives no additional services, no summer services, no educational aide for the remainder of that school year or the next. He's placed in the first grade class of a middle-aged woman who is new to teaching. She's strict. Henry appreciates the structure but shows no progress. At our first conference, the teacher seems unaware of Henry's social aptitude, one way or the other. I inquire about free time and recess, and she admits that she hasn't noticed who is friends with whom.

First grade would have been forgettable had it not been for the school bus.

Henry didn't like the bus in kindergarten. He said it was too loud. But Danielle rode with him in the morning and helped to mitigate the madness, whether it was ushering him to a quieter seat or telling the rowdy kids to settle down. There were only kindergartners on the bus ride home at noon, so that trip was less raucous. A full busload of kids, both to and from school, proves to be a different situation altogether, especially without his big sister to help him cope.

For the first few months Henry seems to manage the ride okay. But shortly after winter break he begins getting off the bus visibly upset, day after day. I ask him what's going on, but he ignores me and finds a quiet corner of the living room or basement playroom to settle into. Then he starts going straight to his room after school. "What's wrong, Henry?" Danielle asks, but he doesn't answer her either.

When it's clear this behavior isn't going to resolve quickly, I call the school. Henry's teacher says she's walking the kids back and forth to the bus each morning and afternoon, same as always. She insists nothing has changed in the classroom and that Henry seems fine during the day.

Beth is the only other child who gets off the bus at our stop. She and Danielle had socialized on their daily rides until Danielle moved on to the bigger school, leaving Beth, who's a year younger, behind. The bus stops at the front right corner of our property, so I generally just watch for it from our front door. But a few weeks into Henry's troubling behavior, I decide to wait outside. When the bus arrives, Henry is the first one off. He storms past me toward our house without a word. Beth steps off immediately after him.

"Beth? Can I talk to you for a second?" She stops and turns toward me. "Have you noticed anything different with Henry? Has anything changed on the bus?"

She looks down at her feet, and I know I'm on to something. "Beth, what is it?"

"You can't say I told," she says, "because then he'll pick on me, too."

"Who? Who'll pick on you?"

"Eric. He lives on Wentworth Road. He sits with Henry on the bus."

"I thought Henry was sitting with Justin from Pine Street?" That was his seat partner when I'd seen him off in the first few weeks of school.

"No," Beth says. "After winter break, the driver changed our seats."

At first Henry says nothing when I confront him in his room later that afternoon. He's afraid, like Beth. I tell him that I can't make it better if I don't know what's going on.

"Eric kicks my legs on the ride home," he murmurs.

I know that Henry keeps to himself and reads a book on the bus to avoid interaction. His speech has improved some but he often still sounds as if he has a mouth full of marbles, and other people continue to have difficulty understanding him. He's also intolerant of people touching him and protective of his personal space, so for all I know Eric just has a nervous tic—taps his foot or bounces his leg in a way that brushes against Henry. But Beth's intel indicated something more serious.

"Anything else?" I ask.

"He squeezes my arms and flicks his fingers at my face."

Okay—no nervous tic.

"What do you do when this happens?"

"Nothing."

"You ignore him?"

"I look out the window. But…."

"But what, Henry?"

"Sometimes he dumps my backpack out on the floor, and

then I have to pick up all my stuff. That makes me really mad."

"Really mad" doesn't quite capture my own emotional response. I'm enraged, ready to march out to the bus tomorrow morning and grab this Eric by his collar. A better parent might want to talk to the aggressor, get to the bottom of his behavior in a mature manner, but I have no such adult-like motivations in this moment. I have empathy only for Henry and Beth. I've run into enough bullies in my own life to know their fears are valid.

That night I devise a plan that's guaranteed not to make things worse for Henry or Beth, a scheme that will in no way suggest that they'd told on Eric. I write a note to the bus driver explaining that Henry is getting carsick on the ride home from school and that he'll do much better at the front of the bus. I request his assigned seat be moved. *No driver wants to deal with a kid throwing up on the bus*, I tell myself. I seal the note in an envelope and hand it to the bus driver the next morning, pleased with my ingenuity. My son will be moved to a seat in full view of the driver and he can blame this reorganization on his weak stomach or the long ride home, but not on the bully.

"How'd it go today?" I ask as soon as Henry comes through the door that afternoon. He marches past me in the brusque manner that has become his new norm.

"The driver didn't move me," he mumbles on the way to his room.

"What? He didn't change your seat?"

I envision Henry hesitating at the top of the bus steps that afternoon, waiting for the driver to direct him to a new spot at the front, and the driver ignoring his pleading gaze. I now want to strangle not only the kid who's bullying my son but also the driver for not putting an end to it. I'm so tired of the adults in Henry's life not doing right by him—from his first therapist to his first preschool teacher to his IEP team, and now this bus driver.

That night the kids go to bed and I vent my anger at John for an hour. "Why wouldn't the driver respect my request? What does it matter to him where Henry sits?"

"I don't know," John says. "I think you've got to talk to him tomorrow morning."

"What's that going to do? He must know what's going on. Why wouldn't he have stopped it already if he cared at all?"

"You've got to talk to him or call the school," John insists.

"The school should have bus monitors if their bus drivers can't keep the kids under control!"

"Tell them that," John says.

Sleep doesn't curb my anger, and I resume my rant the next morning.

"Don't say anything, Mom," Henry pleads. "It'll make things worse."

I promise Henry I won't make a fuss, but I only half-keep my word. I don't say anything to the driver but once the bus is on its way, I call the school and ask for the principal. She's unavailable, so I leave a voicemail saying that my son will no longer be taking the bus and to please have Henry leave the school with the walkers that afternoon. She calls me back an hour later. I intend to tell her that it's just a personal choice based on our schedule, but I can't help myself. I blurt out that my son has been bullied on the bus for weeks and no one seems to notice or do anything about it. And when I discreetly asked for his seat to be changed, the request was ignored. She vows to look into the matter and get back to me.

The principal calls later that afternoon to tell me that

she's spoken to the bus driver. He chose Henry to sit with Eric because he thought Henry would be a "good influence" on him. *It's not my first grader's responsibility to fix your misbehaving student*, I want to yell. *That's your goddamned job!* But I don't. Instead, I tell her that I understand, but this pairing is too stressful for my child so I'll be driving him to and from school from now on. She says she's going to call both Henry and Eric into her office the following day to talk. *Great*, I think. *I may have just set my kid up to be ridiculed for the rest of the year.*

I lose a good part of my mornings and afternoons driving Henry to school, while the principal continues her mediation sessions with Henry and Eric. Henry likes being driven and is in no rush to get back on the bus, but it's a serious inconvenience for me because Danielle's and Finn's schedules don't align with the elementary school's drop-off and pick-up times. So, when the principal calls three weeks later to say that both boys have agreed that Henry can go back on the bus without issue, I encourage Henry to try again. I don't know why it took so long to work out, but the principal says that Henry will be allowed to sit alone at the front of the bus (what he originally asked for), and Eric will sit farther down with a promise to be respectful and not bother Henry in any way.

This agreement works through the end of the school year. But the following September, Henry is again paired with Eric on the bus seating plan. A lack of communication and fluctuating staff is a recurring problem in our school system (and in many others across the country, I imagine). With each new academic year, no one seems to know Henry. It feels as if we have to start all over again. But I don't have to call the principal this time. Due to some confusion that results in a couple of kids waiting for a school bus that never arrives, the routes are shuffled around for day two, and ours gets a new driver—a weathered-looking gruff man named Joe who's recently retired from his job as a public transit driver in Boston. He sees everything that transpires on that bus. "Like eyes in the back of his head," Henry says, mimicking some other child's use of the idiom.

By the end of the week, Joe has assessed his charges and rewritten the seating plan, moving Eric to a spot where he can keep an eye on him in the rearview mirror and assigning Henry the very front seat opposite the driver's. Henry and Joe start chatting a bit along the ride and before long Henry walks through the door in the afternoons sharing information like, "Mom, did you know that Joe's been to Asia?" and "Joe's kids threw him a big birthday party on Saturday; he was really happy to see them all because some of them live in different states." By the end of October, Joe and Henry are fast friends.

Second grade is special in other ways, too. Henry's latest obsession is American presidential history. Every Saturday, when John takes the kids to the public library, Henry comes back with nothing but biographies of American presidents. By December, he's read everything our library has to offer and his holiday wish list consists of numerous additional books on the subject.

Henry's new teacher embraces this obsession. Mrs. Santoro is one of those educators who loves her job and genuinely enjoys children. Finn is in preschool a couple of days a week now, so I volunteer in Henry's classroom as much as I can. Not once do I see Mrs. Santoro get annoyed or aggravated with her students. She's a short, round, jovial woman, with a mop of curly white hair and perpetually rosy cheeks. Put a red dress and a white ruffled apron on her and she could pass for

Mrs. Claus. She's kind and tolerant, but like Joe, she has a firm grip on what happens under her watch and what her students are up to when she turns her back.

Henry still withdraws into a corner with a puzzle or a book during less structured parts of the school day, the way I'd witnessed him do in kindergarten. But Mrs. Santoro draws him out by giving him desirable tasks or errands. One day he's delivering a message to the main office; another he's picking up a project at the copy machine. The first time she sends him to the mail room, Henry is ecstatic. "Mom!" he says, before he's even put his backpack down by the kitchen door. "Mrs. Santoro sent me to the mailroom today. I got to sort all the letters by name and put them in the right box!"

Henry's enthusiasm is infectious. Some of his classmates start asking, "Mrs. Santoro! Mrs. Santoro! Can I go with Henry?" They assume something incredibly fun must occur on these excursions if Henry returns from them so happy.

Despite having worked in the system for decades and already eligible for retirement, Mrs. Santoro is one of only a few teachers in the school who still takes the time to put together a class play. This year's will be a historical montage. We'll meet Pilgrims, Native Americans, Founding Fathers, and Abraham Lincoln, all in the same story. Henry continues to struggle socially, but he's the most engaged he's ever been. His speech now falls at the lower end of normal on age-level guidelines; if he chooses to speak, most people can understand him. Still, when Mrs. Santoro announces that Henry will be playing the lead in their production—Abraham Lincoln himself—I'm aghast. "He can do it," she reassures me.

An Amtrak promotion appears in our mailbox that spring, and I come up with the idea to use that, along with John's soon-to-expire hotel points, to visit Washington, D.C., with Henry. I'll have to take him out of school for a few days to make it work.

I know that Henry hates to miss school. He needs his routines. I tread carefully.

"Henry, how would you like to go to Washington and see some of the places you've been reading about in your library books?" I ask him after school one day in late March.

He sits with his daily snack of peanut butter toast and contemplates the idea. Travel is daunting for many people on the autism spectrum, with its unpredictability, noise, and crowds, and Henry is no different. He's also terrified of boats and planes—distrustful of the physics that these modes of transportation rely on or, maybe more accurately, distrustful of humans' ability to competently employ those physics. And he staunchly objects to sleeping anywhere but in his own bed. This will be an experiment for him and me.

"We'll ride on a train, just like Abraham Lincoln did," I add. "And we can walk to the White House from our hotel."

Just as I hoped, the lure of these wonders outweighs his fears and after a good bit of silence he replies, "I think I'd like that."

I book the trip. Henry and I will go alone, making an extra-long weekend of it, while John stays home with Danielle and Finn.

Mrs. Santoro is completely accommodating when I tell her that Henry will miss a few days of school to travel to Washington. "What a wonderful learning experience for him!" she says with her Mrs. Claus smile.

We choose to leave from Providence, Rhode Island—it's ten miles closer and much less crowded than Boston's South

Station. On the day of our departure a month later, John parks the car and walks us into the station. At six-thirty in the morning, there are just a few passengers waiting to board. Henry sits on a bench by himself while John and I say our goodbyes and confirm logistical details for the next few days. We glance over at Henry, who's intertwining his fingers over and over—his newest tic—and patting his backpack about every three seconds, as if to ensure that it's still there.

"Good luck," John whispers.

Our train's arrival is announced and we approach the escalator that leads down to the platform.

"Have a great time, Henry!" John calls out, but Henry doesn't reply. He's focused on processing this new experience and anticipating what will come next.

"Watch your step, sweetie," I say, referring to the space between the platform and the train car's vestibule. He steps over the gap cautiously. I've been on the commuter rail into Boston plenty of times, but I've never taken a long-distance train like this one. Growing up, my family's preferred mode of vacation transportation was my mom's little hatchback, but only when my dad was behind the wheel—she wouldn't drive much beyond the county limits herself. She was a nervous driver, unlike my father who would venture anywhere without hesitation.

When I was a little older than Henry is now, my mother decided that she and I would visit my dad in Tennessee. He was there for a few weeks of training with the Air Force Reserve—a part-time branch of the military he'd joined after leaving active duty. She bought us tickets on a discount bus line. That trip was my first foray into long-range public transportation, and I was excited; I kept a journal documenting every phase of the trip. I pulled it out recently from a basement bin and glanced through it. What stood out most to my ten-year-old self on that journey were the provocatively dressed ladies who loitered around the sides of the bus stations where we stopped to pick up new passengers or use the restroom, and the older men who slept draped across the molded plastic chairs that were bolted to the cement floors inside the depots. I was a curious kid and I wanted to know their stories. When my mother and I reached our destination two days later, everything we'd brought with us smelled of cigarette smoke and diesel exhaust.

I assume that this train ride to D.C. will be a significant improvement over that, if a bit less intriguing. I wonder what aspects of this trek might imprint themselves on Henry's young mind.

The conductor shows us where to leave our luggage at the front of the train car.

"Where would you like to sit, Henry?" I ask. He walks toward the middle of the car and chooses a row with no one seated in front of or behind it. This is a regional route with several stops, not the more expensive, high-speed direct train, and I know these seats will fill in as we make our way down the Northeast Corridor. By then, I hope, Henry will be more comfortable.

Henry tugs the straps of his backpack off his shoulders. It's a generic green and black satchel that we purchased specifically for this trip, because his school backpack wouldn't hold all the books he wanted to bring. He climbs into the window seat and positions the backpack between us. The seats have pull-down tray tables, so I suggest that he take out his notebook. Together we'll create an itinerary. I suspect that this activity might relieve some of his anxiety, and I'm right.

"Definitely the Capitol Building, Mommy. And the Washington Monument." By the time we're through, it looks more like the schedule for a visiting diplomat than a seven-year-old's wish list. Destinations like the National Zoo and the Museum of Natural History—the places most children would choose first—are not even on the agenda until I add them. Once our schedule for the next few days is complete, Henry spends the remainder of the eight-hour train ride reading. He asks for nothing and agrees to walk to the café car only when I remind him it's time for lunch. He could not be a better traveling companion, at least for someone like me who also prefers reading over talking or socializing with fellow passengers.

As we approach D.C. I warn Henry that Union Station is a lot bigger than the Amtrak station in Providence but that we'll stick together and be fine. When we arrive, it *is* overwhelming, but Henry is taken with the architecture, which distracts him from the seemingly infinite mass of people surrounding us. We get in a cab parked outside the station and the driver starts up a conversation. He recognizes Henry's interest in the city and offers up a brief history of each landmark that we pass. Henry leans in, enthralled, as this lifelong D.C. resident shares his love for "the District."

The driver wishes us a great visit before he pulls away from the entrance to the Marriott. When I traveled with my own parents as a kid, we stayed in places where roaches went scurrying into the woodwork as soon as someone turned the lights on. It occurs to me that Henry might be spoiled by this upscale hotel with its sparkling clean interior and attentive concierge, but I'm grateful for the luxury. I have enough to worry about traveling alone with him for the first time. That cab driver started things off on a positive note, and Henry seems more excited than anxious as we eat a light dinner in the hotel restaurant and then settle into our room. For a kid who usually refuses to sleep anywhere outside of his own bedroom, he snuggles into the oversized hotel bed with no problem and promptly drifts off to sleep. I can hardly believe it. I expected him to be unsettled the first couple of days and not get much rest.

The next morning we tour the Old Post Office Clock Tower then walk to the Museum of Natural History. That museum, with its dinosaur skeletons, giant insects, and ancient Egyptian artifacts, is the most popular attraction for families and therefore the most crowded, but Henry looks at a few fossils and doesn't care to see much else. We're out of there in less than an hour and on to our next stop—the National Museum of American History. Henry spends a long time in the Abraham Lincoln exhibit, curated to commemorate the 200th anniversary of Lincoln's birth. The exhibition explores who Lincoln was as an individual, dissecting the man from the myth. Henry reads every plaque and examines every artifact. He spends another solid hour in the American Presidency exhibit. My parents gave him some spending money and we wrap up our visit in the gift shop, where he selects three new presidential history books.

On day two Henry doesn't slow down. We walk to the Washington Monument, Ford's Theatre, and the National Portrait Gallery. He listens attentively as a park ranger gives us the history of the Washington Monument, but he's a bit bored at Ford's Theatre—he's studied so much about Lincoln that the tour guide is unable to offer him anything new. He does enjoy looking at the exhibits and artifacts on display there though.

By the time we reach the National Portrait Gallery, it feels like we've walked a dozen miles or more across the city and I'm exhausted. I collapse onto a bench that has a view of the gallery space, while Henry peruses the collection on foot. He stops in front of a portrait of John F. Kennedy and lingers there. The painting is a bit abstract, brush strokes blending into others so that there are few solid borders. Henry studies it with intense focus, as if it's a puzzle and he's separating each blurred stroke from the whole and putting it back together again. He stands there, motionless, for thirty minutes, so mesmerized that he doesn't hear me when I tell him it's time to go. The museum is closing.

On the way back to the hotel, I ask Henry what he found so interesting about that painting of J.F.K. He says he doesn't know, and I believe him. It seemed to me that he was drawn to it by instinct. It spoke to him in the way I imagine any of his obsessions do; it isn't a choice.

The next day we walk by the White House, tour the Capitol Building, and visit the Library of Congress. In the late afternoon, we head back to the hotel. I order a couple of sandwiches from room service and we get ready for our Monuments by Moonlight bus tour. Henry is very much looking forward to seeing all the memorials lit up in the dark. He's normally in bed so early that just being out this late at night will be an adventure.

The bus picks us up at the designated stop and provides a drive-by tour of some of the landmarks, including the White House, the Supreme Court building, and the Capitol Dome, which are even more impressive lit up at night. The driver is also the tour guide. He's a burly, boisterous fellow—knowledgeable and friendly. He has the deep forehead lines of a person who's seen a lot of life, both good and bad. "This is America's city," he says as he describes the sights we pass and the complicated history behind them. The night sky is clear of clouds and we enjoy great views of everything.

Henry is the youngest person on the tour bus by several decades. In my late thirties, I'm the only person sitting between his seven years of age and the rest of the group who all appear to be sixty-five plus. After our first stop, the elderly lady seated behind us taps my shoulder. "Your son is doing so well on the tour," she says. Before I can respond, Henry turns around and tells her that he can recite all the U.S. Presidents in order, their term years, which ones died in office, how they died, and other little-known facts.

With the voice projection of a drill sergeant, the woman stands up and announces this to everyone on the bus. The passengers quiet. She turns to Henry and says, "Go ahead young man. Show us what you've got." Henry looks at me. I nod and smile. He gets on his knees in the bus seat so he can see over the backrest and proceeds to spout off his knowledge, President by President. The whole bus cheers and applauds when he's through. Henry beams. The usual hunch of his shoulders relaxes a bit; his clenched fists open. A rare wide and genuine grin overtakes his cautious expression. This knowledge of American history does not win him any friends among his peers, but he's a king in this group of senior citizens. The driver/tour guide jokes that Henry can have his job when he's ready to retire.

We stop and get out at the Jefferson Memorial. I fall behind as Henry charges up the steps. He gazes in awe at this spectacular homage to one of America's founding fathers.

Given everything he's read about Jefferson, I expect Henry understands both the human fortitude and flaws this larger-than-life memorial represents—as much as any young kid could. I catch up to him at the barrier and hear him say, "I can't believe I'm here. I can't believe I'm here." Some children dream of going to Disneyland. For Henry, this place is more magical.

Our last stop is near the Vietnam Veterans Memorial, located past the Korean War and Lincoln Memorials on the National Mall. The driver directs us to explore these three monuments on our own and meet the bus back at this same spot in ninety minutes—no later than ten-thirty. Henry's knowledge of and interest in Vietnam and Korea at this point are superficial and limited to how the wars there intersected with key moments of specific presidential terms, so he's focused on getting to the Lincoln Memorial. He pulls my hand to pick up the pace, and we walk along the massive Vietnam Memorial Wall, where the thousands upon thousands of names in the black granite are softly illuminated by lights embedded in the cobblestone walk. The branches of surrounding trees, eight of which were planted in honor of the American servicewomen who lost their lives in that war, cast shadows all around us.

Henry explores the Lincoln Memorial then asks if we can go see the Franklin Delano Roosevelt Memorial. A National Park Service employee points us in the right direction. The Roosevelt Memorial is designed differently from the others— it has large separate outdoor rooms, and Henry is compelled to survey each one. The site is massive, and I start hurrying Henry along, worried that we'll be late for the bus. Finally I persuade him to head back. I look at my watch. We've got ten minutes to get to the meeting spot, but it's darker now and I'm disoriented. I can't remember which side of this massive park we entered from. I make a guess, an incorrect one, and I have no idea where we are. We turn around and keep walking.

The Lincoln Memorial comes into view, and we hurry in that direction. There's no one around. The park ranger who showed us the way to the Roosevelt Memorial earlier is gone. So are the other tourists. I see a bus stop that looks exactly like the one we were originally dropped off at, but this one is too close to the Lincoln Memorial; it can't be the one where we're supposed to be. Henry and I rush ahead to find another bus stop, then another. They all look the same—the same benches, the same snack carts (which are now closed up and secured with large padlocks), the same plantings, the same walkways—and no one else is waiting at any of them. Not one tour bus has passed us. It's after eleven now—more than thirty minutes past when we were supposed to meet our tour bus—and frightening scenarios begin playing out in my mind.

Everything is closed, and there isn't an employee or ranger in sight.

I direct Henry to sit down on a bench as I try to get my bearings. Smartphones are a new technological advancement, and I don't own one. I have no way of contacting anyone unless I can find a pay phone somewhere. Henry starts interlocking his fingers repeatedly and tapping his feet at double speed. "Will they leave us here?" he asks. "How will we get back to the hotel?" I assure him that we'll return safe and sound one way or another, though I haven't seen a cab or city bus drive by in a while.

I chastise myself. *I should've had a better plan, made mental notes or marked a map where we were supposed to meet the bus—I know how easily I can get confused in unfamiliar environments. My negligence has put us both at risk.* I sit on the bench with

Henry, alone in the dark, not sure what else to do. My old Girl Scout training sets in, telling me to stay put when lost, let someone find you rather than make yourself a moving target. But who would be looking for us? People are free to leave these bus tours at any point in the evening and find their own way home; the driver has no responsibility to wait for us or anyone else.

I try to appear calm because Henry's anxiety is building. But I'm panicking, too. My feet are tapping the ground almost as fast as his. It's getting cold and Henry curls in close to me, an unnatural move for him.

"Let's wait here for a little while," I say. "See if a taxi comes by, or a police car."

"What if it doesn't?" Henry asks.

"I guess we'll start walking again." I'm grateful he doesn't ask in what direction we'd go or if I know which way our hotel is, because I have no idea.

We sit there for twenty minutes or so, minutes that feel like hours. Headlights approach. Big headlights. *A bus.* I nudge Henry aside and get up, ready to flag down this vehicle. I'll jump in front of it if I have to. Then I recognize the sign in the window: "Monuments by Moonlight." It's *our* bus! The driver pulls up in front of our bench and the hinged doors fold open, the gates of heaven welcoming us in.

As Henry and I climb the steps onto the coach, the group greets us with thunderous applause. Many of our new white-haired friends stand while they clap, like they're giving us an ovation, as if we had anything to do with finding our way back to them. I wonder about the conversations that might have taken place between the driver and the other passengers when Henry and I were deemed missing. My cheeks flush with embarrassment.

"The bus driver has been circling around looking for you," says the woman who was sitting behind us earlier. "He drove from stop to stop several times over," she says, "until we spotted you on that bench!" She doesn't reveal even a hint of irritation and seems invigorated by all the excitement. I thank the driver profusely and apologize to him and my fellow passengers, but none of them seem legitimately annoyed. "What else would we do?" the driver asks. "You think I'm going to leave a woman and her kid out on the National Mall all night? If I didn't find you in the next few minutes, I was calling in the cavalry." It isn't clear to me if "the calvary" means D.C. cops, U.S. Park Service, or some legion of dedicated tour bus drivers, but I sense that many of my fellow passengers would have enjoyed finding out.

I relish the warmth of the bus and the soft upholstery against my body, so contrary to the cold bench that Henry and I had huddled on. Shortly after we settle back on the bus, he's asleep in the seat next to me. I've never seen him do this; he never even sleeps in our minivan. I remember driving back from New Jersey in the spaceship when he was just a toddler. We got stuck in bad traffic for hours. Danielle snoozed away for the entire last leg of that trip, but Henry never fell asleep until he got into his own bed that night.

Our designated stop is outside a hotel two blocks away from the Marriott, but the tour bus driver asks where we're staying and takes us to the door. I struggle to carry sleeping Henry up to our room and tuck him into bed.

The next day we'd planned to take a metro bus to the National Zoo, but Henry begs me to go back to the National Gallery instead. I'm disappointed; it's our last full day in D.C.

and I want to see the giant pandas. But this trip is for him, not me.

Henry lingers over that J.F.K. portrait a while more and then explores the other galleries before we leave to see the rowhouse where a wounded President Lincoln succumbed to his injuries. The house had been closed by the time we got out of Ford's Theatre two days prior, and I'd promised Henry we'd get back over to see it. This humble space seems to impress Henry more than the theatre. He stares at the replica of the bed Lincoln died in as if he were looking at a ghost. Like the J.F.K. portrait, I wonder what he sees, if his mind creates images that are inaccessible to my own imagination.

On the train ride back to Rhode Island, Henry dives into the books we purchased at various museum gift shops over the previous few days. For a kid who's frequently out of tune with the rest of the world, his ease in D.C. was remarkable. I hope he's pleased with himself for navigating this unfamiliar territory, even if he can't articulate that feeling to me. I'm proud of both of us. And grateful. I'd spent an entire five days not working on speech and occupational therapy, or social competency skills, but enjoying my son and watching him enjoy the world in his own particular way.

* * *

Henry practices his lines, and *all* the lines, for the school play, with no expression or intonation. He's routinely prompted to modulate his tone of voice during conversations in speech therapy sessions, but he's so focused on the play's dialogue that modulation goes out the window. I think he believes that the only way he'll survive this task is to obsessively control it, as he did with so many other new, uncomfortable experiences when he was small. He'll memorize every word, his and everyone else's, so there will be no surprises, no mistakes.

On the day of the play, I draw a beard on Henry with stage makeup. He tolerates my sketching out and filling in Lincoln's chinstrap facial hair, and I'm pleased with the results. He wears black pants, an oversized button-down shirt, an old black suit jacket of John's that almost reaches his knees, and a top hat that Mrs. Santoro has supplied. Henry's uncomfortable and lost in the clothing, but he accepts his fate. I drive him to school that morning, so he doesn't have to ride the bus in his costume. "You're pretending to be someone else," Mrs. Santoro reminds him when we walk into the classroom.

Henry makes it through his lines but looks disoriented on stage, unnerved. As the production comes to an end, the kids take a bow. Henry's top hat falls off his head, bounces off the front edge of the stage, and falls into the audience below. A few of the children chuckle, as do some of the parents. Henry looks out at the audience, rattled. His shoulders pull inward. His eyes widen with panic. This isn't in the script. This is wrong, a mistake. I look at John and he stares back at me with the same urgent expression. Henry's going to implode. He's going to fall apart in front of all these people over something that, to other children, is silly and warrants laughter.

At that moment the little girl on Henry's left—in a long white petticoat, English apron, and Pilgrim's bonnet—looks toward the top hat that now rests on the floor below the stage and then looks at Henry. She reaches and grabs his hand, holds it in hers, and whispers something to him. He holds on, anchors himself to her, and they take a second bow.

The class separates into groups and exits the stage. Henry walks close behind the little girl. The two children, dressed as characters some two hundred years apart in history, still holding hands, disappear into the adjoining hallway. Tears wet my face.

Amidst all the detached clinical assessments Henry has endured and the many maddening educational negotiations John and I have engaged in, we've also experienced several acts of kindness. But the compassion offered by this little girl—a child who had nothing to gain by helping Henry—will forever stand out. Henry can empathize with others at this point, but I don't believe he's yet capable of being a true friend to someone; he can't advocate for himself, much less anyone else. In that moment, an eight-year-old girl demonstrated how to do it, with intuition and grace.

My first seven years as Henry's mother have been punctuated by extremes—soaring highs and abysmal lows. The anger is sharp and biting; the frustration makes me want to scream. But the joys, too, are acute. Loving someone who acts and thinks differently than most exaggerates who you already are. Your positive attributes and those of the people around you become more pronounced, and so do the flaws. My anger at even the slightest mistreatment of Henry can magnify into rage, but a joyful moment, the smallest act of kindness, can feel transcendent. I crave a more consistent, temperate experience for Henry and our family, but I wonder if the beauty might lessen along with the anguish. There's no one to ask; Henry and I are both, in many ways, still alone. I've yet to find another mother, another family, who is navigating similar issues. Neither Henry nor I have anyone to share our specific experiences with.

PART III
TEARS AND T-SHIRTS

LESSON 15

Systemic Obstacles Abound

On September 3, 2009, we take a tour of the bigger school where Henry will start third grade the following week. Once again, he and Danielle will be on the same bus, and both his and my mind are eased by this prospect. His new teacher was friendly and receptive to the letter I'd sent explaining Henry's challenges. Henry's IEP now lists autism as his primary diagnosis, but I've been reading up on Asperger syndrome, the condition that most closely describes his behaviors. This specific subcategory is not an option on the school's list of disabilities that qualify for services, but article after article reports that kids who are on this higher functioning end of the autism spectrum experience more difficulty as they get older. This aligns with my own observations of Henry. He has stopped picking at his skin until it bleeds, but he's developed a new, more obvious tic—he rubs his hands on his thighs when he's anxious, which is often. In any new or uncomfortable situation, he makes this repetitive motion with enough force that his whole body rocks back and forth.

Younger children have often ignored Henry's unconventional behaviors or innocently inquired about them, but as Henry and his peers reach their tweens these odd quirks are sure to make him a target of derision. Every article I read warns of it. The school counselor as well as the district's therapists and administrators reassure me that their schools are tolerant and welcoming places where teasing (they never use the word "bullying") is not a problem. Their descriptions make it sound like our town's mostly middle- to upper-class demographic is somehow immune to this common human cruelty and that Henry's previous bullying experience on the bus was a rare, isolated incident.

Our schools are large suburban enclaves with social hierarchies built on popularity and physical prowess. Not much has changed since I was Henry's age, except for the introduction of social media and cell phones. There's no escaping the torment for vulnerable kids now, even when they make it home at the end of the day and lock the door behind them, as I once did. Henry doesn't have a cell phone. He has no social media accounts. He uses my email address to access educational websites or games and does not yet need his own computer to complete his schoolwork. He's off the grid, at least by modern standards. I hope to keep it that way as long as possible.

Despite my concerns, Henry's first year at the new school starts off relatively well. One student in his class calls him names, but it turns out that this child is feeling left out at home and has no real malevolence toward Henry. The quietest, most passive kid in class (Henry) is a natural mark for this student's misdirected frustration. The teacher gets to the root of the problem quickly.

Henry joins a new weekly lunch group led by the school's adjustment counselor. The kids in the group talk about challenges at school, and the counselor offers advice and helps them brainstorm ways to cope with or improve these situations in the future. At my first parent conference Henry's teacher reports that the group seems to be helping Henry socially; he's playing with other kids at recess. I'm thrilled. That night at dinner I ask Henry what games he and his friends play. "Tag," he says, "and I'm always it."

I park at the school the following week at lunchtime and discreetly walk along the outside perimeter of the playground. I see Henry's thick mop of dark, loose curls flying across the blacktop. He doesn't like to be touched at all, but especially not on his head, so his hair is always at least an inch too long and perpetually disheveled. He finds getting a haircut traumatic and those appointments have become fewer and farther between. His lanky build and that wild hair, coupled with the round, metal-framed glasses that constantly slide down his nose, make Henry look like a small eccentric scientist.

Sure enough, he and some of the other kids are playing tag. And Henry *is* "it." I watch the other boys run by him and around him as he tries to chase them in his awkward, uncoordinated stride. The boys know he can't catch them, and they laugh as Henry exhausts himself. He gets within an arm's length of one of them, just for that boy to turn and dart out of his reach.

My heart sinks. They're humiliating him. As socially inept as Henry can be, he must sense this too. But he wants to fit in somewhere, to have friends. He just doesn't know how. I drive away wondering how I'll explain to the adjustment counselor that Henry isn't playing with his peers on the playground, as she and his teacher perceive, but is being taking advantage of. I never get the chance. Not long after my playground observation, the school's counselor takes a leave of absence and Henry's school and the middle school across the street begin sharing one counselor between them. Henry's lunch group goes from once a week to once a month, then stops altogether. Eventually the boys on the playground tire of their "game." When I make another impromptu stop at recess time later that school year, I spot Henry sitting under a large shade tree by himself, reading a book. I don't intervene or encourage him to play with the other kids. He looks too content within the jagged shadow of that tree's imposing branches.

* * *

A 2017 study showed that people with autism spectrum disorder, including those who require a lower level of practical or clinical support, experience a higher incidence of loneliness and social isolation. The study also found that their neurotypical peers are less willing to interact with them based on "thin slice judgments," a clinical term for first impressions made about a person based on very limited information. To combat this within educational systems, the Child Mind Institute advises that "schools need to be proactive about creating layers of social scaffolding to support those kids."

The Institute notes that neurodivergent kids need social support during chaotic activities like lunchtime and recess. Schools might facilitate, for example, "lunch bunches," which was the counselor's term for the helpful group Henry was participating in. Henry looked forward to that group and was negatively impacted by its elimination. The loss was exacerbated by his school's failure to offer other proactive interventions that the Child Mind Institute recommends, such as mentoring programs.

Henry is one of many kids who pay the price for this lack of programming. In 2012 researchers from the Kennedy Krieger Institute and Johns Hopkins University found that 63 percent of school kids ages six to fifteen with an autism spectrum disorder had been bullied. According to a 2018 study, this amounts to children with ASD being bullied at three to four times the rate of their neurotypical peers. Another study, published in 2022, concluded that, among all neurodevelopmental disorders, autism is at the top of the list for risk of bullying. This same study found that children ages twelve and older with ASD were more likely to be bullied than younger children with ASD, a contrast not found for their neurotypical peers. Bullying can destroy a child's vulnerable self-esteem and many kids act out, sometimes in the form of self-harm.

This absence of system-wide, meaningful interventions for neurodivergent kids, combined with a dearth of awareness initiatives for their neurotypical peers and the school staff they interact with, cause harm. Staffing problems worsen things further. If a school can't provide a student with a service listed on their IEP due to personnel shortages, as in Henry's case, the district is required to make up the services later. They can also contract with education staffing agencies to fill the gaps, but I never saw that happen in our schools. There is a nationwide shortage of special education professionals; as of May 2024, more than 20 percent of American schools were understaffed in special education. At the start of the 2024-2025 school year, there were a total of thirty open positions across my suburban district, from kindergarten through high school; fifteen of them were vacancies for special education teachers and paraprofessionals. Dozens of kids are missing out on the services they are legally entitled to, the interventions they need to succeed academically and socially. Existing teachers are stretched too thin and experiencing burnout. The problem requires a radical rethinking of the entire system.

When Henry's school finally secures a substitute for the absent adjustment counselor toward the end of the school year, they stack these group sessions, formerly "lunch bunches," to try and make up for all the ones Henry and other participants missed. The counselor holds the sessions three or four times a week, instead of once, and more children are included in each group. This defeats the original purpose of these meetings— to provide special education students opportunities to build trusting relationships with their peers while working on their social skills, in a small-group setting, over time. The session length is also doubled, so the kids are eating their lunches in the counselor's office *and* going right through recess. These strategies are not successful, at least not for Henry. The damage has been done. He's had no support at these unstructured times for months, and the crowding of group sessions in the last few weeks of school disrupts Henry's schedule even more and causes additional unnecessary stress. These make-up sessions may have helped the school meet its obligations on paper, but they didn't help Henry.

LESSON 16

Some Rules Should be Broken

Henry is assigned to Mr. Colby's fourth grade class. Mr. Colby and Mr. Danforth are two of only three male teachers in a school of approximately eleven hundred students. Their classrooms are situated right next to each other with an adjoining door in between. Halfway through the school day, they have their students swap rooms, so the kids can have a change of scenery and experience a different instruction style. This is remarkable to me; I didn't see this kind of creativity in any of Danielle's classes when she attended this school.

Mr. Danforth is a large man, well over six feet tall with the build of an NFL wide receiver. Mr. Colby is equally fit, but short and wide, built more like a guy you might see bouncing rowdy patrons out of a local bar. They are both involved in school athletics. John and I have encountered plenty of stereotypical machismo in town, especially among some of the parents who regularly attend local sports games. I'm worried when we initially receive this class assignment, as Henry does not fit the idea of a "typical" boy that so many of these school and community members hold dear. My worry doesn't last long, though. Both teachers are indeed well versed in sports, a popular topic among many of the kids in their respective classes and a knowledge that commands a different level of respect among some of the male student population (or their parents), in particular. But that's where the comparisons end. Mr. Colby and Mr. Danforth are two of the most competent, caring teachers I've ever met. This starts to look like an ideal fit for Henry, not only because his latest obsession is baseball (studying it, not playing it), but also because both teachers have zero tolerance for any teasing or nastiness from the students in their charge.

Maybe it's this unusual control of the standard classroom chaos that gives Henry the confidence to sign up for the spring play, albeit hesitantly. Danielle participated in this annual event back when she attended this school, and though theater isn't a particular passion of hers, several of her friends have continued with it into middle school and beyond. Theater seems to be a refuge as much as an outlet for these kids, and I fantasize that it might serve as a haven for Henry, too. His first role as Abraham Lincoln in second grade didn't exactly soar, but I wonder if Mrs. Santoro sparked an interest that can now be nurtured. So when Henry tells me he's joining the cast, I say, "That's fantastic, Henry. You'll do great!" But I know better than to leave this significant step to chance. I write a note to the theater director explaining that Henry is on the autism spectrum and needs specific instructions about when and where to do things. "Don't assume he understands implied directions," I advise, "spell everything out." I figure this should be an easy task for a theater teacher accustomed to directing young children, and something she's likely already doing with all her students. But better to be proactive.

The first after-school meeting for that year's production—*You're a Good Man, Charlie Brown*—goes well as far as I can tell. I pick Henry up afterwards and he appears happy enough.

I think, I hope, that maybe this is it; he's found his niche and theater will be his way to connect with the world. But as soon as I spot Henry exiting the school's main entrance after the second meeting, just a week later, I can see something has drastically changed. He wears a deep frown and walks toward our minivan fast and purposeful. His eyes are fixed on the pavement in front of him, laser-like in their refusal to fall upon anything else. His torso leans forward at about sixty degrees, and his arms lie stiff and rigid, as if glued to his sides. This is the awkward gait he always assumes when he's anxious. The stance that alerts me to a problem. The posture that tells otherwise unknowing bystanders that something about Henry is a little "off."

He opens the sliding side door, throws his backpack in, then slumps onto the seat.

I glance at him in the rearview mirror. "What's wrong?"

He doesn't reply.

"Talk to me, Henry. What happened?"

I get no response. Not a word from the backseat.

When we get home, he storms up the stairs to his bedroom and slams the door with a force that rattles the walls of our aging house.

I take a deep breath and follow him. I knock on his door and when there's no answer, I let myself in. He's sitting on his bed, staring at his Star Wars comforter.

"What's going on, Henry?"

"I hate my life!" he shouts.

"Sounds like you had a really bad day. Want to talk about it?"

He glares at me.

"Well, we all have bad days. It's okay. I'm sure tomorrow

will be better."

"No. It won't," he says.

He gazes out his bedroom window, almost calm again, as if admitting defeat. Then, in a voice so soft that he may be talking only to himself, he says, "It never gets better. Every day is worse than the one before."

Henry's shoulders curl inward, his neck bends chin to chest, and his knees pull up, as if a drawstring is cinching his limbs together. His body closes in on itself. He begins to sob. I've never seen such sorrow in him before. No nine-year-old child should feel such anguish.

Physical contact stresses Henry, so I try using words. I tell him he'll be okay, remind him of an upcoming minor league baseball game we have tickets to, and of his tenth birthday only a few months away. His eyes are blank. My attempts at encouragement evaporate into this fog of melancholy before they can reach him.

"Leave me alone," he says, catching his breath between snivels. "Please."

I leave his bedroom, walk down the stairs, and collapse onto the living room sofa. I'm overcome with an unfamiliar terror. I worried about bumps on the head, broken bones, and vicious stomach bugs when the kids were small, so I'd obsessively childproofed our house, stayed within arm's reach when they climbed play structures, and doused their hands with antibacterial gel the minute we left a public place. When Henry was diagnosed with developmental delays, I learned to communicate with him using our own hybrid of sign language and charades until the words came, and I taught my husband and daughter to do the same. I took Henry to therapy multiple times a week for speech and social competency training, and when we were at home I reinforced what those thera-pists taught him. Both John and I sought out opportunities for Henry to interact with other kids his age as he grew, and I communicated with his teachers and visited his school when-ever I could. It wasn't enough.

As difficult and exhausting as those early years of parent-ing often were, I now long for them. Threats that can be mit-igated with extra pillows beneath the crib, baby gates at the stairways, booster seats, and bicycle helmets now seem ridic-ulously manageable. Problems that can be fixed with a kiss and a Band-aid, or a trip to the ice cream shop, are long gone. I wish for the time when I still believed that a regimen of therapies would result in Henry "fitting in." But longing and wishing aren't going to change anything and I'm at a complete loss for what to do next.

Later in the evening I carefully prod and pry until I dis-cover that Henry had forgotten to bring a pencil to theater practice that day. His part was not rehearsing, though all actors were required to attend, so he'd planned to do his homework during the wait. But he couldn't, because he didn't have a writ-ing utensil. So he just sat there for the ninety-minute rehearsal, silently calculating the additional time he'd have to stay awake that night in order to complete his assignments and, with every passing minute, became increasingly more frustrated at the circumstances that created this situation.

Most kids would have asked to borrow a pencil from another student but I'm not surprised that Henry didn't. This is the most difficult aspect of his experience to explain to peo-ple who don't know him well. He's not comfortable with most of his peers and he will not ask them for anything or other-wise approach them unless specifically told to do so. It's not a natural option for him. I remember being in similar situations as a child, and even as an adult—inconveniencing myself in order to avoid interaction. I attributed it to being a serious introvert in an extroverted world. It seems so counterproductive, but sometimes the reaching out feels more difficult than solving the problem, especially at the end of a long day during which you've been forced to engage with people more than you'd like and are socially and mentally exhausted.

In the end it doesn't matter what, precisely, occurred. It could've been anything, or nothing. The things that other kids shrug off, both big and small, disproportionately upset Henry. That day's episode may have had little to do with a pencil and everything to do with multiple mounting incidents, a series of slight but poignant moments of confusion when Henry didn't understand his or others' behavior and didn't know how to express or process that.

In a 2020 article for *Spectrum* magazine, Dr. Connor Kerns, who leads the Anxiety Stress and Autism Program at the University of British Columbia, says, "There's a kind of chronic potential trauma of being in a world where you understand 50 percent of what's going on most of the time because you're missing all these social cues, so you're feeling constantly out of the loop and having chronic stress around that." I didn't think of it in these terms when Henry was a fourth grader, but this explanation describes the way I've moved through the world for most of my life, too. That chronic potential trauma and stress is why, as a child, I hid in the back of my bedroom closet when my parents had company over. It's why, as an adult, I ducked into an office restroom for extended periods of time when my boss wouldn't leave me alone or there'd been too many meetings to attend. I regret that I may have passed this trait on to Henry, as it has severely affected my ability to build and maintain personal relationships and has impeded my potential for professional success.

Despite Mr. Colby's consistent attempts to engage Henry and forge common ground between him and his classmates, Henry continues to shrink behind his desk at the back of the classroom and meld into its bland beige plastic. It seems to me that he's living his young life under a crushing weight of anxiety fueled by a constant expectation to be someone he cannot be, and it's impacting every interaction between him and the outside world. His outburst turned capitulation after today's theater rehearsal reminded me of when he was a toddler— those days when he couldn't tell me that his shoes had to be put on the left foot before right, and that the lights had to be turned on one at a time each morning, from second floor to basement. But now there's no order or solution for me to figure out. I have the sinking feeling that Henry has crossed some sort of threshold. This isn't the common tween angst that his older sister is going through. And it isn't plain bitterness resulting from the name-calling and exclusion that has become all too prevalent in Henry's life. His demeanor is flat, resolved, final, as if he's finished with it all. Tired of the loneliness. Tired of the frustration. Worn out from constantly trying to find his place—in school, in extracurricular activities, and in our community—with little success.

Henry doesn't say much to me or anyone else for several days. He continues with the spring play, neither happy nor unhappy about it. He simply does what he's told and, as always, takes comfort in following the rules and whatever structure they offer. I wait for him to bounce back but it feels like something has shifted. Henry has never been a gregarious child, but he's always enjoyed reading, acquiring deep levels of knowledge on topics that interest him, solving puzzles. He doesn't seem as energized by those activities now. He's shrouded in a sort of apathy that I haven't seen from him before.

A few weeks later Danielle comes home from school somber and teary-eyed. There was a school assembly that day—the father of a thirteen-year-old boy who'd died by suicide talked about kids who are different, kids who have trouble finding their place at school or in the larger world, and the impact bullying and, alternatively, kindness can have on them.

"The man talked a lot about his son," Danielle says, "and it was like he was describing Henry. I'm afraid Henry might try to hurt himself like that boy did."

I reassure her that Henry will be fine, but I'm lying. That evening after the kids are in bed, I find that father's website and read all about his son.

* * *

On opening night of *You're a Good Man, Charlie Brown*, I iron Henry's costume while he practices his lines. He's been cast as part of a group of extras—"people on the street" who will perform call-and-response scenes and participate in a group dance at the end. He's nervous but also excited, and I'm encouraged to see him show any emotion at all. The performances will take place at the middle school because the elementary school does not have a proper auditorium. The theater director walked the kids over there for the last few rehearsals, so the space isn't entirely unfamiliar to Henry, which I'm grateful for.

John and I decide to split the performances. I'll attend opening night alone; he'll attend the second night alone;

and Danielle and some of her friends will go to the Sunday matinee. Finn is still too young to sit through a play, but this way Henry will have one of us there at every show regardless. When the time is right, I drop Henry at the door of the middle school auditorium where a handwritten sign reads "actors enter here." Then I get a cup of coffee and sit in the parking lot until the doors are opened for the audience.

Henry does well. His movements and speech are somewhat robotic, as usual, but he doesn't freeze with stage fright, doesn't forget his lines or choreography. He even smiles once. After the play is over, all the children who participated in the production rush through the auditorium's main entrance to find their parents. I stand across from the double doors in full view of the crowd so Henry won't miss me, and I wait. And wait.

The crowd slowly dissipates, but still no Henry. I walk back into the auditorium; it's empty. I don't see the theater teacher anywhere. I start to panic and begin searching the school. I don't think Henry would have ventured up to the darkened second or third floors alone, so I focus on the maze of convoluted hallways on the first level. I poke my head into classroom after classroom as well as into the modular units that jut out the back of the school like sewed-on appendages—they've been added one-by-one as the population of our town's children steadily outgrows the original school building.

I stumble upon an older student who's putting sound and lighting equipment in a storage closet. I ask him if he knows of anywhere a kid from the play might have gone after the show, other than out the front doors.

"The kids gathered in the cafeteria after rehearsals," he says. "Maybe your son left some stuff in there that he had to get?"

The school is cleared out. If Henry had things to pick up, he would've returned long before now. Still, I follow the student's directions to the back door of the cafeteria.

A small shadow cast in the thin stream of a single fluorescent light bulb is the only indication that a human being sits in the otherwise dark cafeteria. Henry is seated at the one table that hasn't been folded up and pushed against the back wall. His shoulders sway forward and back as he scratches his fingers up and down his thighs. If he wasn't wearing thick jersey pants, there would be perfectly parallel streams of blood striping his legs. When I get to him, he's frightened, confused.

"Hi, Henry," I say. "Thought I'd lost you there for a minute!" I force a reassuring smile and pick up his backpack. I lead him down the hallway, back toward the auditorium, and through the only door not yet locked for the night. My heartbeat slows back to a normal rhythm. The anxious sweat on my forehead dries in the cool night air.

Later I learn that at the conclusion of all the previous rehearsals the kids waited in the cafeteria and were not allowed to leave until the theater teacher formally dismissed them. Henry did not differentiate between rehearsals and the performance, and no one—not the theater teacher, not another student, not one of the parent volunteers—thought to explain it. So after the performance, Henry had walked to the cafeteria. He followed the rules.

* * *

A 2020 study found that the suicide rate among people ages ten years or older with a diagnosed autism spectrum disorder was more than three times that of their neurotypical peers. We need to minimize the social isolation that so many neurodivergent children and adults experience.

Henry is a concrete thinker, as many people on the autism spectrum are to varying degrees. He uses and interprets speech literally. I am also a concrete thinker so I understand that he needs clear, consistent communication. I've experienced decades of negative social consequences around this difference and have worked at improving my ability to decipher the information I need from the imprecise language of others. Still, I'm often disheartened to realize that I've yet again misinterpreted the sarcasm in someone's written language or in casual conversations. It's why I wrote that note to the theater director; I knew that the school play situation would be ripe for these misunderstandings—the line between what was pretend or "performance" language and "real" communication would be blurred. Someone explaining that the opening night's performance was different and that Henry should leave the auditorium directly after the show through the front doors would have taken ten seconds. Not explaining it causes repercussions for days or weeks, the full consequences of which are difficult to measure. These experiences provide further evidence to Henry that he doesn't belong.

New research emphasizes the need to educate neurotypical people about these nuances in communication. Up until recently, therapy and interventions focused on modifying the behavior of people with autism to appear more "normal." Autism is a lifelong condition and engaging in this type of assimilation—what some in the neurodivergent community call "masking"—is mentally exhausting. Dr. Bernadette Grosjean, a practicing psychiatrist with thirty years of experience who was diagnosed with autism herself later in life, presented at the

2023 Stanford University School of Medicine's Neurodiversity Summit. Discussing neurodiversity in the workplace, she posed the question, "Would a near-sighted person be asked to remove her glasses to make her coworkers more comfortable?" Of course not. Yet we ask neurodivergent people to hide their differences and avoid the tools that help them manage their daily challenges because those tools and strategies may seem socially atypical. This is how we expect them to avoid discrimination and exclusion at school and work.

Perhaps it isn't fair to compare a mild to moderate visual impairment that can be easily corrected with a pair of glasses to a complex neurodevelopmental condition that manifests itself in multiple ways and affects both verbal and nonverbal communication. But in terms of social acceptance, I like Dr. Grosjean's example. If a child is called upon in class, and they say they don't know the answer because they can't see the board, the teacher will likely notify the parents and suggest that the child's vision be tested. If a neurodivergent child is called upon and doesn't have the answer because they can't understand the information on the board as written, they're more likely to be viewed as not paying proper attention. The child with a visual impairment is not blamed for their disability, and the tool they need to fully access the curriculum (glasses) is socially acceptable. For the neurodivergent child to fully participate, the necessary tool might be as simple as providing the information in a different format, but investigating this is not the default. It wasn't when I was a kid; it wasn't when my children were kids; and though it's slowly getting better, it still isn't now. We see the consequences of this in recent studies that find children with autism and/or other learning disabilities experience in-school discipline at a higher rate than their peers, are suspended more often, and have significantly higher drop-out rates.

These disparities and discriminatory practices carry into the workforce, making neurodivergent people reluctant to disclose their diagnosis, if they even have one. Psychologists who are experienced with adult autism and other neurodivergent conditions are rare; help is hard to find. But this expertise is critical. Despite increased focus around diversity, equity, and inclusion, most employers will not make reasonable accommodations for their employees without a documented disability, just like in public education. It often isn't enough for an employee to say, for example, "I process information better in writing, so let me review my notes from the meeting and get a response to you by end of day." Or "I focus better in a quiet, predictable environment, so I'll be present in the office for important meetings but otherwise would like to do my daily work from home or another location." Without a formal diagnosis, employees may be viewed as "difficult" or deemed to be "complainers." So neurodivergent employees try to conform to their organizations' expectations, often with poor results.

A 2022 study investigated this and noted, "Participants expressed being caught in a double bind, recognizing that both disclosure and failure to disclose resulted in negative consequences." The study further observes, "Participants discussed navigating these double binds, in terms of access to support, versus stigma. The weight of stigma appeared to outweigh the perceived benefits of disclosure, resulting in concealment." Research in this area is still in its early stages, but there is already clear evidence that this concealment, or masking, has substantial negative effects on the mental health of neurodivergent people who suppress aspects of their identity due to social constructs.

Individual Kindness Isn't a Substitute for Institutional Reform

For the first time in a dozen years, all three of my children are in school all day. The organization I've been working for as a weekend receptionist offers me a part-time administrative position during the week. I take it. I'll still accept the occasional freelance assignment that comes my way but this new job has a better pay rate, gives me weekends off, and provides the opportunity to work "mother's hours," so I can be home in time for the school bus. Maybe we can finally plan that family vacation to Disney World.

Due to my new job, all three kids will have to go to camp this summer. After reviewing the options with them, Danielle and Finn want to attend a place that's a twenty-minute drive east of us and focuses on outdoor activities. Campers row boats in a pond, take swim lessons in a pool, play sports, make arts and crafts, and climb an indoor rock wall. Henry wants no part of all that. I find an academic camp on a college campus another fifteen minutes to the north, where he can learn computer animation, experiment with basic chemistry, and play chess in quiet, air-conditioned classrooms. I'll spend my entire paycheck and then some on these camps, and getting the kids to and from them will add an hour to both my morning and afternoon commutes. But these temporary inconveniences allow me to keep my new job during the rest of the year.

Danielle and Finn both have okay experiences their first week—don't love it, don't hate it—but Henry thrives at his camp. His posture is usually round-shouldered, but he stands as straight and tall as I've ever seen him while he waits for me in the designated pick-up area. "Bye, Henry!" a couple of kids call out when we walk toward the minivan on Thursday. I think they're talking to another kid with the same name. But Henry replies in his usual monotone, "Bye."

"Are those friends of yours?" I ask, half expecting that these kids are mocking him in some way. I have developed a deep cynicism in every situation involving Henry now—no one gets the benefit of the doubt.

"Yeah," Henry responds. "We sit together at lunch and play *Magic*."

Magic: the Gathering is a role-playing card game popular among the geeky set. Unlike when I was a kid, "geek" is no longer a derogatory term in pre-teen circles. Geeks invented Windows, the iPhone, and video platforms like YouTube. The geeks are millionaires. Henry isn't completely tuned in to the details of the digital revolution yet, but he knows this much.

"I wish school could be like camp," he repeats several times during those summer weeks. He attends camp from 8 a.m. to 4 p.m. Monday through Friday, taking classes in structured periods throughout the day and eating lunch in a large institutional cafeteria. It looks exactly like school to an outsider. But the classes are ones *he* chose, courses that attracted other kids with similar interests who *wanted* to sit with him at lunch and whom he also mutually wanted to be around. The scenario is more typical of a college freshman's experience than a soon-to-be fifth grader's.

Henry echoes this sentiment into the fall, despite his having the good fortune of being assigned to Mr. Danforth's class—a teacher and a classroom he is comfortable with. Like Mr. Colby, Mr. Danforth has no tolerance for bullying or exclusion. But Henry remains on the fringes, not integrated the way the rest of the kids are. I don't recognize this until six weeks into the new academic year, when Henry starts asking to have pasta and sauce packed in a thermos for lunch every day. He doesn't like sandwiches, but he doesn't want to buy a hot lunch at school anymore. At first I think this is another one of his repetitive quirks. He eats the same cereal for breakfast every day, at the same time, in the same bowl. Maybe our rotating family dinners are all the variety he can stand and he wants his midday meal to be predictable. I eat the same thing for breakfast and lunch almost every day, too—it's one less thing to worry about among the hundred other daily decisions to be made. But one day when I give him money and tell him he has to buy lunch because we're out of pasta and sauce and pretty much everything else, he says, "I can't. I can't. I can't."

"You can still have pasta and sauce in the cafeteria, Henry. I just can't pack it for you today."

"It's not the pasta," he says.

It continues to be an exhausting effort to pull any explanation or details out of Henry, especially about something that conjures negative feelings. But I eventually get to the root of his agitation. The one child he sat with at lunch moved tables in the second month of school and didn't invite Henry to join him. After Henry waits in the long lunch line, there are few empty seats left. When he had no choice but to sit down at a populated table the kids there told him to leave.

"I try to find a seat where I can be by myself," he says, "but it's really hard."

Sometimes he just throws his lunch away and stands by the door until it's time for recess, but then he's hungry the rest of the afternoon. Bringing lunch from home allows him to find a seat before they're all filled and not go hungry. Though he doesn't say it, I assume it also gives him the additional reassurance that he won't have to deal with the kids who are unkind.

I leave a voicemail message for Mr. Danforth that night, explaining the situation. The next day he watches from the hall as Henry emerges from the lunch line with his tray. Mr. Danforth calls me later that afternoon and reports that Henry stood at the front of the expansive cafeteria scanning the space for a seat where he could separate himself from the others. There were none. When it looked as though Henry might give up, Mr. Danforth called to him and ushered him back to the classroom, where the two of them ate their lunches together and talked baseball. After that, Mr. Danforth directed Henry to leave for lunch five minutes before the bell, five minutes before the rest of the class, on days when he was buying lunch. Henry could be first in the lunch line and have first pick of available seats. That was the end of his demand for daily thermos meals.

Mr. Danforth proves to be an expert at off-the-record interventions. Adding a new accommodation to Henry's IEP can take weeks or months. Mr. Danforth skips the bureaucracy. When Henry is having bathroom accidents because he can't align his personal biology with the designated classroom breaks, Mr. Danforth gives him permission to go to the restroom whenever he wants to—no need to raise his hand or wait for a scheduled break. When recess is not appealing to Henry or becomes too overwhelming, Mr. Danforth gives him a special project he can work on in one of the classrooms instead. And on Red Sox opening day that spring, Mr. Danforth asks Henry to go up to the board and write out what the starting lineup would be if he were manager of the team. Henry lists every position on the field, his preferred batting order, the starting pitcher, the closer. Mr. Danforth prompts him to explain his choices and Henry goes on to provide a half hour lecture on individual player statistics, injury and rehab reports, the opposing team's strengths and weaknesses, and how the remainder of that week's schedule affects the rotation. His classmates are dumbfounded. Mr. Danforth finds a place where Henry can shine and for the first time since that second grade trip to Washington D.C., Henry feels competent and proud to share his knowledge publicly.

As wondrous as these moments are, they are still outnumbered by the unpredictable challenges that never disappear but only evolve. One day in early June, the phone rings as I'm heading out the door for work. It's the main office at Henry's school. Henry has worn his pajama top that day. He put on regular pants in the morning but forgot to change from his pajama top into a t-shirt after breakfast. He was tired because I'd let him stay up past his bedtime the night before to watch the end of a Red Sox game. When he got to class and removed his jacket, he discovered his mistake and panicked.

Danielle and Finn would have joked about a mishap like this and proudly worn the top throughout the entire school day. Not Henry. He's now in the office, too distraught to go to class, says the school secretary over the phone with an edge of irritation. I understand. She has hundreds upon hundreds of children to deal with. I can get annoyed with Henry's unreasonable reactions myself. I tell her that I'll be right down with a new shirt for him.

Arriving at the office, I see Henry sitting in one of the waiting area's chairs, quietly sobbing. Mr. Danforth is sitting next to him. The teacher looks at me with a compassionate but defeated expression that implies *I don't know what to do; I don't know what to say.* I smile. *You did just fine.* The gratitude I feel, knowing how much he cares, how hard he's trying, is enormous. I think Henry feels it too, but neither he nor I are able to express it at that point.

I give Henry a grocery bag with a Star Wars t-shirt in it and the secretary lets him use the office bathroom to change. When he comes out, he holds the bag with the offensive pajama top in it by two fingers and hands it over to me like it's toxic waste. He dries his eyes and blows his nose, then Mr. Danforth walks him back to class.

When I get to work I call John. There was a time when an irrational meltdown like this would have sent me into tears just as it did Henry, but now I'm more frustrated than emotional.

"Should I have said 'no' to watching the last few innings of the game last night?" I ask.

"Absolutely not," John replies. "Henry loved watching the game."

I'm thrilled when Henry asks to do something off his normal schedule, like stay up past bedtime or eat something not included in his usual repertoire. I view it as progress. But then we have moments like this one, and I wonder if the trade-off is worth it.

"It's like preschool all over again," I say. "One day all is well, but the next is a disaster." Maybe the volatility of approaching adolescence and its accompanying hormonal surges are causing Henry's ups and downs, or maybe it's just an increasing awareness that he's different from the other kids. He knows things that they don't—statistics and facts. But they know things he doesn't—how to identify sarcasm, tell a joke, and make friends. The facts and statistics can only take him so far; he wants to know how to be a kid now, a typical tween. But first he has to master the complicated social system that his peers are operating within. It's an insurmountable task for a kid like Henry. The rules are too fluid. He can't memorize them the way he's absorbed presidential history or the fundamentals of baseball. What constitutes an appropriate greeting or response to one person is unacceptable to another; what's okay behavior in one situation is rude in the next. These monumental, nonsensical complexities seem to destine him to fail. As if he'll forever linger on the fringes of inclusion. At the back of the classroom. On the perimeter of the playground. In a dark corner of an abandoned cafeteria. This is what Henry has come to believe about himself in relation to his peers at school, and I'm starting to believe it, too. It's how I viewed my own experience for much of my childhood and adolescence, resigned to loneliness and isolation. But I can't accept it for my son. I *won't* accept it.

The System is Reactive, not Proactive

The school schedules Henry's last IEP meeting of fifth grade for shortly before summer break. A guidance counselor from the middle school will attend to answer questions about the curriculum. John and I have serious concerns about Henry's transition to middle school. We haven't found it to be a particularly warm, nurturing place during Danielle's first two years there. She's a well-adjusted kid; even so, she's experienced some problems. Her locker-mate made snide comments to her and others on a regular basis at the beginning of this school year. Fortunately, Danielle came to the middle school with a solid group of friends in her own grade and several acquaintances in upper grades, thanks to three seasons of playing town softball. When the bully recognized that Danielle was not vulnerable to intimidation she stood down. But I know that all bullies don't back off so easily.

Everyone who's present at the IEP meeting assures us that Henry will do fine at the middle school. But they can't offer him an educational aide or even designate a staff member who would be responsible for guiding him through the most challenging parts of this new environment. No one person will be available to him if things don't go well. I reiterate that Henry's last developmental evaluation indicated that he needed minimal transitions during the day and consistent guidance. But I'm told that there is no way to alter the middle school schedule for Henry. The bell will ring every fifty minutes and Henry will be expected to gather his things, follow the massive crowd into the hallway, get to his locker and to the bathroom, if necessary, and then make it to his next class. All in under five minutes. This is a ridiculous expectation even for a kid without any additional challenges. Given Henry's self-imposed rituals just to get through lunch and recess at the elementary school, as well as manage the occasional transitions out of his regular classroom and into the music or art room, I can't envision seven changes a day going smoothly without additional help.

"There isn't an aide or paraprofessional that could at least help him get from one class to another for the first few weeks of each trimester?" I ask. "Just to help him get his bearings and create a routine for himself?"

"He doesn't qualify for that level of assistance," the IEP team leader says. "However, if he is unsuccessful in adapting to the new routine, we can readdress it then." *So my kid needs to fail, to crash and burn, before he'll get any help here.* If that happens, I'm not sure Henry will recover from it. When something goes seriously wrong, Henry classifies the associated activity into a category of his mind, *the bad place*, where it stays, permanently. He decides the activity is not for him, not to be attempted again. Riding a bike, roller skating, and petting dogs (he was knocked down by an overly exuberant one in our neighborhood a few years back) have all been relegated to this category. School is not optional and therefore has remained out of *the bad place*, but I wonder what Henry will do if a mandatory activity becomes unbearable. Where will it go in his mind? Where will *he* go?

After the meeting concludes, I turn to Mr. Danforth. "I'm worried," I say.

"I am, too," he replies.

John heads back to work. I return home, dejected. We recently received information in the mail from the two small charter schools in the area; one is a twenty-five-minute drive from us, and the other is only ten minutes away. I fill out the paperwork for both of them so Henry's name will be entered in their admission lotteries. There are two criteria that push a kid's name higher up on the list—having a sibling who currently attends the school or being an incoming kindergartener rather than an older student—and Henry has neither of these advantages. These charter schools serve over thirty communities combined, including four districts where the public schools are notoriously underfunded and underperforming. Most of the students start in kindergarten and remain throughout their primary education, so there are few openings in upper grades and the waiting lists are extensive. It's a longshot, but worth a try.

I spend the rest of that afternoon on the computer looking into private schools, but I find that many of them are financially impossible for us. They're also ill-equipped to deal with a student who requires accommodations—private schools are not required by law to service kids with disabilities the way public schools, including public charter schools, are. Private schools can pick and choose whom they accept, but charter schools are supposed to admit any child from the communities they serve as long as there's space. Many parents believe that not all charter schools honor this obligation though. Some feel that children are denied available spots if the school is aware that they'll require special education services, because those kids cost more money to educate. And there's some evidence to support these parents' allegations.

A Government Accountability Office report from 2012 found that, at a national level, charter schools were serving fewer students with disabilities than traditional district-run schools. A 2020 study that examined enrollment levels of students with disabilities in Colorado charter schools found that the charter schools enrolled children with disabilities at a lower rate than the state's traditional public schools. These findings prompted Disability Law Colorado to file legal complaints with the U.S. Department of Education's Office for Civil Rights, which identified twenty-nine charter schools in the state whose applications contained questions about a child's disability status. In response, Colorado passed a rule in 2022 prohibiting charter schools from asking on their applications whether students would require special education services.

It didn't occur to me that Henry might be discriminated against as I sought a better educational fit for him. I simply wanted access to some options that I knew other schools offered—a smaller facility, improved teacher-to-student ratios, more progressive programming.

* * *

For the last six months, Henry has been attending a weekly autism support group that a local psychologist facilitates. It meets from 5-6 p.m., and most of the parents spend the hour in a separate waiting area of the office even if they live nearby, because the rush-hour traffic makes it impossible to run errands or go back home. During a chat with another parent in that waiting room, I learn that her town's school district provides a specific program for middle schoolers with high-functioning autism (or what will much later be referred to as "Level 1 autism"). The school offers classrooms with one teacher and no more than ten students. The kids stay in that room for all subjects except art and gym and the occasional science lab, minimizing the stressful transitions but still encouraging social interaction. Her son is a year older than Henry and he's thriving in the program. John and I had looked at homes in that area back when we were house-hunting, and I silently curse our decision to buy a property less than a mile over the town line in the other direction.

Massachusetts has had a school choice law on the books since the early 1990s that presumes all school districts in the state will admit non-resident students on a space-available basis. But the reality is quite different. A town's school committee makes the final determination as to whether or not their district will participate in the program. They can choose to opt out or opt in each year during a public meeting. When this conversation with my fellow parent takes place, not one school district in my county is participating in school choice—they've all opted out each year.

In 2017, two districts in our area approved school choice. Both districts are relatively rural; school choice became a method by which to bring in more funds and mitigate diminishing enrollment in these towns. For the 2021-2022 school year, 170 school districts across Massachusetts participated in school choice—53 percent of the state's total. Our home district repeatedly opted out until the 2022-2023 school year, when it too began suffering from decreased enrollment and therefore decreased funding. And the adjacent district that had such a great program for middle schoolers on the autism spectrum back when Henry was a fifth grader? They finally voted to participate in school choice in February 2023 and started accepting up to five non-resident students per grade for the 2023-2024 school year. Henry will graduate from college before families can apply to those few available spots. I can't help but question the original intentions and ultimate outcomes of this 1991 law and whether it was ever really about choice at all.

As I become more acquainted with other parents who are navigating the special education system, I hear of families who rent the tiniest one-room apartments they can find in towns whose schools offer solid special-needs programs. These families never live in the apartments, but the rentals give them a "permanent" address in the town and therefore provide their children with a legal right to attend its schools. Given the inconsistencies across public school districts and the limited choices outside of them, this can be the best educational option, not to mention the least expensive one, if a kid's current school isn't up to par and the parents aren't in a position to move the entire family to a new location. Renting a single room in the area is less expensive, by far, than paying private school tuition or buying a house in a better funded district.

In just one hour-long IEP meeting, our public middle school has become my last choice, if I have any choices at all. Even with a teacher as understanding as Mr. Danforth, Henry still suffers from occasional bouts of extreme anxiety about school. Unsupervised social settings continue to be landmines for him, and the middle school environment will create countless more.

Later that June evening, while Henry and Finn play catch in the backyard, I summarize that month's events with John.

At the very end of the school year, after seven years of special education within this system and most recently in a class with a caring, competent teacher, I still had to drive to the school with a new shirt because Henry couldn't move forward with his day wearing the one he had on. This isn't the school's fault, I know; this is autism. Public school isn't causing all of Henry's problems, but it isn't helping them either. Nothing I heard in that day's IEP meeting reassured me that the situation will improve at the middle school.

Danielle has been listening to our conversation from the other room. She interrupts and confides that she heard about the pajama top incident from friends who have younger siblings in Henry's school. The kids think Henry is weird because, "What fifth grader cries over wearing a pajama top?" Danielle knows it's impossible to explain it to them—she's been living with this as long as we have. "If you don't live with an autistic person, you don't get it," she says.

I sit silently for a moment, encompassed by an overwhelming sense of defeat. Then I say it—the truth—untainted by anyone else's opinion of what the next course of action *should* be. "I can't do it. I can't send him to the middle school next year. I just can't."

John lets out a sigh, nodding. "I know."

The results of the charter school lotteries are months away, and Henry's chances of getting a spot are slim. I won't wait. After one last-ditch effort to find a small, private school that we can afford and that would accommodate Henry, with no success, I begin to research homeschooling. I dive into this task with the urgency of a captain at the helm of a sinking ship. I have to find a solution, a way out, and I have to find it fast.

I scour the internet for homeschool groups in the New England area. I ask to be included on their mailing lists and to join their online forums. I read every article I can find on the subject. I review our state's laws on education. With another parent's help, I find our school district's homeschooling policy, buried deep within the viscera of its website. This is important, because in my research I learn that each state has its own guidelines on homeschooling and each district within that state can enforce their own rules around it. Some schools make it easy for parents; others make it difficult, requiring pages and pages of initial paperwork, in-home visits to ensure the student has an "appropriate educational environment," and quarterly progress reports. Our district seems to lean closer to the "easy" side. On a five-page form, we must list the education and experience of any person who will be teaching Henry, provide an education plan for the upcoming school year, and identify any texts and other curricula we'll be using for each subject. If the district initially denies our application to homeschool, we have thirty days to appeal that decision and provide additional information.

One afternoon later that week, I join Henry in the living room where the last inning of a Red Sox home game is playing out. When it ends with a favorable result displayed on the scoreboard, I ask him, "What do you think about homeschooling?"

"I don't think I'd like that."

Great. We're out of options, Buddy.

I counter, "But, Henry, I feel like you're nervous about going to the middle school next year, and that's part of why you've been so sad and upset lately."

"Yeah, maybe. I don't really want to go there."

"Okay, but the soonest you could get into one of the charter schools is a year away—seventh grade—and it's just pure luck whether or not they'll pull your number out of their database. We can still hope for that, but we need to make a decision for now, for what we'll do this September."

"So, I would stay home with you?"

"Yes. But we could try and find some outside classes too, maybe with other homeschoolers. The classes would be smaller. And you wouldn't get so tired at the end of the day because we could take breaks when you need them, and working together one-on-one we could get more done in less time."

"The school day would be shorter?"

"Definitely." I almost add that we might arrange our schedule so he can watch these one o'clock baseball games in their entirety, rather than just the last inning or two, but that would give homeschooling a seriously unfair advantage. I want to maintain the belief that this is at least partly his decision and not completely coerced by me. I want his buy-in, his input—something our district's special education system and the larger IEP process never asked for or desired, even as his transition to middle school approached.

"Okay. I guess we can try it."

I search for curricula. I have no experience in teaching and I have no idea what features I should be looking for. There are a fair number of religious curricula available, which I don't want. I'm surprised to find that the sort of traditional textbooks public schools use are nearly impossible for a parent to purchase independently. They're sold in bulk to school systems, not to individual purchasers.

I send out questions to homeschool forums and find that most parents are creating their own programs from multiple sources. But after reading through Massachusetts' core standards, I feel overwhelmed by the idea of developing materials on my own that will meet the criteria for each subject. I identify several online learning tools, but when I have Henry do the sample lessons, he doesn't like the format.

Eventually, I find a California company that offers an all-inclusive sixth grade curriculum, including evaluations by professional teachers. We rent the textbooks for the school year, which the company ships to us directly, and their staff customizes the curriculum based on Henry's particular strengths and weaknesses. They include a daily schedule for us to follow. Each month, I'll send completed work back to them and a teacher employed there will, in turn, correct the assignments and provide a progress report. At the end of the school year, we'll receive an official transcript that I can provide to our district. Their fee for these services is affordable. This is the first option I've come across that feels manageable. I print out the forms and set them aside while I prepare our homeschool application.

I tell Mr. Danforth our plan. He explains that even if we homeschool, Henry should still qualify for the speech therapy the school offered us—the only service they determined Henry was eligible for in the upcoming year. I contact the guidance counselor who attended our recent IEP meeting; she confirms Mr. Danforth's assumption and promises to call me in September to set up times when I can bring Henry into the middle school for a half-hour of pragmatic speech therapy twice a week.

As word spreads of our decision among school staff, I receive phone calls and emails urging me to reconsider. The IEP team leader insists Henry needs to be "socialized" and that removing him from the school setting could destroy any progress he's made. *What progress?* I want to ask. He has no more friends now than he had five years ago and his ability to manage the school day has not improved, maybe even gotten worse. Henry's psychologist is equally discouraging, concerned that homeschooling will allow Henry to descend into his own world and disengage further.

At Henry's ten-year checkup, his pediatrician cautions that I'll need to make sure Henry is getting regular physical activity and seeing plenty of other children. *Do all these professionals think I'm going to lock my son in a room with a textbook all day and close him off from the world?* Of course Henry needs opportunities to socialize with other kids and engage in group activities, both academic and physical. But he needs *positive* social engagement, not the negative social experiences he so often encounters within public education.

In the flurry of final-week-of-school activities for Danielle and Finn, and amidst the urgency to get Henry's homeschool paperwork filed before the end of the school year, Henry announces, "I need a baseball." Not just any baseball, either; I'm not going to find it by taking a quick trip to the local sporting goods store.

Henry and Mr. Danforth often discuss the ongoing major league season during breaks in the school day. At some point, Mr. Danforth told Henry a story about how he'd attended dozens of Red Sox games when he was a kid, carrying a baseball or a notebook with him, hoping for the autograph of his favorite player—Dwight Evans. Sadly, he was never able to score that autograph. So, for an end-of-school gift, Henry is determined to get it for him. Typically when I ask Henry what we should get for his teacher for the holidays or at the conclusion of a school year, he replies, "I don't know." So I end up purchasing a gift certificate or a coffee mug and have Henry add his name to the accompanying card. This is the first time Henry has approached me with such a defined idea. And he is adamant.

We call sports memorabilia and hobby shops. We search online stores. I even write to the Red Sox and the talent agency that represents Evans, all with no luck. Then I get an email notification. Just like with The Wiggles dolls that brought Henry so much joy years before, an eBay seller has come through. Someone has put a Dwight Evans autographed ball up for auction. Research proves that it's genuine. I obtain a certificate of authenticity for the ball and confirm the date it was signed. This gift breaks the school district's rules on acceptable spending for a teacher gift, but it's just a baseball, I rationalize, the signature only worth something to a person who deems it valuable. It also breaks our family budget for teacher gifts, but it's hard to put a price on what Mr. Danforth did for Henry that year.

We purchase a glass display case for the ball and wrap it up. It's too fragile to send in on the bus, so I ask Mr. Danforth if he'll be available after school on the last day for just a few minutes. I meet Henry outside his classroom after the other kids have left to start their summer vacations. Henry takes the gift from me and brings it to his teacher with genuine delight. When Mr. Danforth unwraps it and realizes what he's holding, he gets choked up. "This is the best gift anyone has ever given me, Henry."

Henry says his goodbyes and heads out into the hallway. As I turn to follow, Mr. Danforth softly speaks to me, "You have a pretty special kid there." *Yes, I sure do.*

LESSON 19

Say No to the Status Quo

Our application to homeschool is approved in late July. I request a meeting with my manager, with the intention of giving my two weeks' notice. John and I will sorely miss my paycheck in our family budget, but there's no way I can work during the week and homeschool too, come September. When I explain the situation, my manager asks, "What if I swap out some of your duties and have you focus on payroll? That's a weekend job, Friday through Sunday. I could get you a company laptop and you could do the work from home." Like Mr. Danforth's quiet interventions, this accommodation makes a world of difference for our family.

I continue to search for outside extracurricular activities, academic classes, and social opportunities for homeschoolers in my area. If they're out there, they are not well advertised, and I come up short. Meanwhile, the kids participate in their usual summer vacation activities—baseball games, day trips, camp—and all goes well. Henry seems genuinely more at ease, and I attribute his relaxed demeanor to the fact that he knows he won't have to attend the public middle school in the fall.

However, in late August, when Henry's new teammates in his fall recreational baseball league begin asking who he got for teachers and which middle school "house" he was placed in, he walks away and doesn't respond. He's embarrassed to tell anyone that he'll be homeschooled. I advise Henry to simply tell the kids that he's not attending the town middle school. There are plenty of kids on the team who go to local parochial or private schools, so he isn't the only one going down a different path. But when he tries that, the kids don't let up. They want to know which school, what town, where he'll be.

I don't blame Henry for feeling self-conscious about this decision. We don't know anyone else who homeschools. When I mention our plan to a few friends and family, they stare at me like I've gone mad, so I feel apprehensive too. I want to help Henry feel less ostracized by removing him from the traditional school environment, but sometimes doubt creeps in and I second-guess myself—will I be making the situation worse?

Our packaged curriculum hasn't yet arrived by the time Danielle and Finn start school. I received the district's approval to homeschool in August. Then I completed the lengthy surveys so the mail-order middle school could appropriately customize Henry's program. They said it would take three to four weeks to put the curriculum together and send it out to us.

That first day of school, once John is off to work and Danielle and Finn are safely on their way to their respective classes, I walk back across our yard from the bus stop. I enter the house to find Henry standing waiting for me. We look at each other quizzically. Henry says, "What do we do now?"

I pour myself a second cup of coffee and we sit at the kitchen table. With me in my sweats and he still in his pajamas, pencils in hand, we start going through a sixth grade English workbook that I picked up in the education section of the local Barnes and Noble the day before.

We learn. About suffixes and prefixes.

And we laugh. About the silly, simple words that the publishers chose to illustrate the concepts, words that are grades below Henry's current vocabulary level.

Henry talks to me, asks me questions, and challenges himself to see how many answers he can get right in fifteen minutes, ten minutes, five.

We take breaks when we need to.

We have lunch together.

And instead of Henry being exhausted and irritable at the end of the school day, he has a skip in his step. A new boy has moved in down the street—a foster child my neighbor is caring for. Henry wonders aloud if maybe we can invite him over. I'm flabbergasted. Henry never asks for anyone to come over to play, even the one or two kids from baseball with whom he seems comfortable. Just trying to get himself through a day of traditional school drained every ounce of energy he had.

I know, at the end of our very first day of homeschooling, that we made the right decision. Henry and I will get through this, maybe even do better than just get through.

Later that week, my neighbor mentions that she met a mother at her kids' soccer game who also homeschools. She got the woman's number for me, and I call. Her name is Melissa. She's a part-time anthropology professor and has taught all four of her kids at home. Her youngest is now six years older than Henry and they've mostly moved on from the homeschooling community, but she knows of a local group that gets together for recreation and field trips. She still has the email address of the organizer.

We arrive at a local park the following week to meet the group. Henry hangs a few steps behind me. He's nervous. So am I. After so many dire warnings from educators, doctors, family and friends, I'm not sure what to expect. But soon it becomes clear that they're just parents like me, moms and dads who have decided to homeschool for many reasons. The first person I meet is a military spouse whose family moves so often that she deems it too disruptive to put the kids in traditional school. Another is a college professor who rotates homeschooling duties with her spouse, who is also a professor, so the family can all have school breaks at the same time and make better use of university sabbaticals.

I introduce myself to the group leader. She calls several boys over. One of them approaches Henry. "Hi, I'm Evan. What's your name?"

Evan pulls Henry into whatever game the kids were engrossed in before we interrupted, and within an hour, Henry is running and hollering and laughing alongside them.

While Henry plays, I join a group of adults who are congregated in a corner of the playground area watching over younger children. I ask a lot of questions, curious about what motivated them to homeschool their kids. Many of the parents want to incorporate travel and extended community-based opportunities into their children's educations in a way the traditional school curriculum doesn't allow for. Some of their kids also have special dietary needs or allergies that proved too difficult for their respective school districts to handle. A few kids struggle with dyslexia or attention deficit disorder and find it easier to learn at their own pace rather than at a speed forced upon them. Others have a special interest or entrepreneurial spirit that a traditional school day can't accommodate. It is a whole new world—an underground network of creative kids and innovative parent educators.

By the end of that year, Henry has made more friends, true

friends, than he had in seven years of public school. Instead of a twenty-minute recess where Henry hides under a tree trying to tune out the chaos, he has more than two hours to play with a small group of ten or twelve other children his age, along with both older and younger kids. They are forging real relationships and learning how to compromise, with plenty of adults present to guide them in appropriate social behavior. This multi-age, multi-grade format makes more sense to me than the modern single-grade system in traditional schools. These homeschooled kids seem more independent, more capable of advanced decision-making and critical thinking than their similarly aged peers in public school.

According to a 2015 article in the *Journal of Educational and Social Research*, multiple studies show that "multi-grade education is as effective as single-grade schooling in terms of academic achievement and better in terms of social learning." Although a multi-grade structure is also more economical, it has long been out of style in U.S. public schools. One reason for this is the outside-the-box teaching and creative lesson planning it requires, because standardized curricula and mainstream textbooks aren't very useful in a multi-age setting. Other reasons cited are the differing maturity levels of students in a multi-age classroom that can make discipline difficult, and the increased work multi-grade education creates for administrators in terms of scheduling, staffing, and communication.

Members of that first homeschooling group we join tell us about other groups, including formal programs that offer additional recreational and field trip opportunities, academic classes, and workshop events. One of those resources is a homeschool creative writing course that I think might be good for Henry.

Like many children on the autism spectrum, writing is a challenge for Henry, and he avoids it whenever possible. He has difficulty organizing his thoughts into a clear paragraph, much less an entire paper, and he struggles with the physical muscle strength and motor skills necessary for the task. He holds his pencil so awkwardly that it looks painful when he sits down to practice penmanship—an art that I'm still insisting on, however antiquated my thinking is for the digital age we now live in. Years of occupational therapy within the public school system did not correct this problem, though Henry says it doesn't actually hurt but only makes the process slower. When he sits down to his first writing assignment from the packaged curriculum we bought, he's close to tears. I'd requested that the company supply us with a Language Arts text that includes many sports-related subjects, and they complied. So, Henry chooses a topic that interests him and we break up the assignment, piece-by-piece, into manageable sections. He ends up with a two-page report on a favorite baseball player. Henry has never written two pages in one sitting before. It was extraordinarily tedious for him, but he did it.

The next writing assignment isn't quite so daunting, and just a few months later Henry can write a two- to three-page report without any intervention from me. But creative writing is an entirely different challenge. Henry thinks in literal terms; little to no imagination is involved. He reads only biographies, history, and science-related books. He has no use for fiction.

Several other homeschoolers have taken a course with a woman they call "Miss Lucy," and the parents rave about her. Miss Lucy rents a conference room at the local Audubon Society and teaches multiple Language Arts classes, including "Creative Writing for Middle Schoolers who Hate to Write."

I sign Henry up. On the registration form, Miss Lucy asks the students to write one paragraph and bring it with them to the first class. They can write about any subject or idea that interests them, but it has to be fiction, something from their own imaginations. She mentions that each student will read his or her paragraph out loud.

Henry is a wreck. He dislikes being the center of attention, and he's particularly disturbed by the notion of reading something to the class that he's made up himself. He can share baseball stats or Star Wars trivia when asked, but fiction of his own making? No way. He agonizes over the assignment for days. When he finally gets a paragraph written, he won't let me read it.

On the first day of class, we drive to the Audubon Society building in silence. Henry is too anxious to chat. Miss Lucy greets him in the foyer and introduces herself. He barely looks at her.

"Something wrong, Henry?" she asks.

"I don't want to read out loud," he mumbles.

"Okay," Miss Lucy says. "I'll read it for you. How's that?"

When Henry emerges from the conference room ninety minutes later, he's trying to stifle a smile, as if he doesn't want to reveal that this class may have been something other than torturous.

"How'd it go?" I ask.

"It was … fun."

Creative writing was fun?

Miss Lucy began that first session by asking for one student's paragraph. She then went around the table and challenged the eight other students to keep the story going by adding a sentence or two of their own.

Two months into this course, the kids are narrating lengthy cooperative stories, devising ever more complicated plot lines, and creating characters based on one another. They elevate a classmate to fearless hero one week, kill them off the next, and then bring one or another of them back as the villain in the subsequent go-around. Many meet tragic fates: someone is smothered by the fluffy tail of a giant squirrel or accidentally scorched by the fiery breath of an overexuberant dragon-dinosaur hybrid, then comes back to life in the following story as a fiendish ferret or a diabolical donkey (DNA mix-ups and scientific abominations are popular with this crowd). I wait for Henry in the visitors' area of the small building each week and rejoice in the raucous laughter emanating from the classroom.

At some point Miss Lucy asks the kids if they think they ought to write down some of the stories they've come up with in class, so they won't be forgotten. Her cooperative creative writing strategy is nothing short of brilliant in my mind. Next she introduces poetry. Henry writes an epic poem about why he hates poetry. He toils over every single word to get the tone and rhythm exactly right. Miss Lucy finds this subject matter perfectly acceptable, as well as amusing; I doubt other middle school Language Arts teachers would be so tolerant.

Miss Lucy is exceptional in many ways, but her creativity and motivation are not unique in the homeschooling world. We find a professor from MIT who teaches biology and anatomy at a Boston-area educational enrichment center one day a week. The class considers bacteria and bugs and other icky things. The teacher provides no grades, only constructive feedback. He's an entertaining and engaging instructor, and the kids are fascinated. He offers them an optional assignment of researching their favorite virus and doing a presentation on it.

Every student in the class accepts the challenge and then they all engage in a friendly competition to find the most obscure pathogen possible. They build disturbing models of half-eaten flesh and display videos of multiplying invasive organisms. Though many of the parents cringe, myself included, the kids find it all incredibly cool. I've never seen children so captivated by biological science. These teachers, who measure learning and achievement by their ability to engage their students rather than by the students' ability to absorb traditionally delivered curricula, are a revelation to me.

The center where the biology class is held occupies half a floor of an old mill building that's almost an hour's drive from our house. I can't drop Henry off and go home for a bit. A few other parents are in the same situation and we sit together in a makeshift lounge area with a worn-out sofa, a couple of stained reception chairs, and a well-used oak coffee table pocked with scratches and beverage rings. By then I've learned that homeschool classes are often held in low-rent neighborhoods and that whatever furniture they have is secondhand. Money is carefully spent, and the modest tuition we pay for this class goes toward the purchase and maintenance of microscopes and materials for the students, not toward superficial frills. I'm fine with that.

The other parents and I chat for a few minutes and then we open our laptops. Two other mothers and a father stay, in addition to me. One mother is a full-time homeschooling parent, and she spends the class time reviewing her daughter's assignments in other subjects. The second mom and the dad both work primarily from home and are on the clock for these two hours, answering emails and getting projects done. I've recently embarked on finishing a degree in communications through continuing education classes—a degree begun many years ago before marriage and kids—so I use the time for my own homework.

The woman who runs the enrichment program has a degree in education and a love for teaching. The center offers homeschool classes as well as after-school and summer programs in science, technology, and industrial arts for public school students in the economically struggling area where it's located. She lives in a tiny house, built on someone else's farm. Her husband is a carpenter and, in lieu of rent, the two of them do handiwork and help care for the land the house sits upon. They live by their own rules, follow their own callings, and I admire them for it.

During spring break of that sixth grade homeschooling year, I sign Henry up for a one-week workshop where kids build a mock town government from scratch. They elect officials, create fiscal budgets, and prioritize public needs. By the end of the week Henry has made a good friend with whom he remains in contact with after the class is over. That's as important to me as the fact that at age eleven, he has a better understanding of civics than most American high school graduates. The majority of homeschooling parents are discerning, and if a program or teacher isn't both informative and creative, no students will attend. The bar for quality is high. Thanks to engaging instructors, personal attention, and the diversity of his school days, Henry is no longer overwhelmed and exhausted in the evenings. Danielle is now in eighth grade and she comes home from school with two hours of homework almost every night, but Henry is finished by three o'clock each day. And yet he is receiving as good an education as his sister is, maybe even a better one.

I learn a lot that year, too. I accompany Henry on a conservation field trip where we both handle and study birds of prey at a wildlife refuge. We tour a farm where we participate in making maple syrup, from tree-tapping to bottling to marketing the product. We visit museums and living history centers. We attend "Science Saturdays" at MIT's Lincoln Laboratory. I'm delighted to see Henry participate in all of these incredible learning experiences. But that gratification doesn't compare to the joy of watching Henry's confidence grow as he is free to be himself, not in occasional small windows, but all the time, every day.

All through public school, we focused on Henry's weaknesses. The services provided to him were designed to make him better fit the norm. Now we celebrate his strengths, let him pursue his intense interests in depth, and embrace his individuality. Henry is no longer surrounded by people who are trying to "fix" him. No one treats him as if he were broken. That shift in thinking changes everything—the way he engages with others, his enthusiasm for academic and even some physical challenges, and his willingness to try new things. After years of watching Henry struggle and feeling helpless to improve his daily life, much less his education, this transformation is as miraculous for me as it is for him.

I never experienced such a shift as a child. I eventually learned to assimilate well enough in most situations. I laughed along with the crowd even when I didn't get the joke. I avoided physical activities where my clumsiness would be on display. I listened to the music my peers liked, watched the popular movies and TV shows, and tried to keep my intense interests to myself.

Sometimes, though, the pretending became too exhausting

and my disguise started to crack, at which point I'd hide out for a couple of days, feigning illness. If I didn't catch those cracks quick enough, they became caverns, and I'd melt down, say something I shouldn't, and lose whatever "friends" I had in the process. Then I was alone again, starting over. This cycle has repeated itself dozens of times in both my personal and professional life. I've only recently acknowledged the pattern and am still figuring out how to stop it. When you spend decades disguised as someone you're not, it's difficult to remember who you actually are on the inside. I couldn't fight for myself when I was young; I had no language for my experience. The term "neurodivergent" hadn't been coined yet. The word "autism" was reserved for severely disabled people with serious intellectual challenges. I was just "different" or "weird," depending on who you asked. It wasn't until I became a mother that I found my inner advocate—for both my children and myself. In fighting for the educational experience that Henry, and every kid, deserves, I honor the little girl I once was.

LESSON 20

Risks Can Pay Dividends

Henry is terrified of flying. I don't know where or when this fear began, but he's felt this way as long as I can remember. He's never been on a plane, and no one we know has had a terrible experience with air travel. Regardless, in his mind, the technology that sends an aircraft thirty-six-thousand feet into the air is inadequate. He doesn't trust it. But we aren't going to Disney World in May if Henry won't get on a plane.

I do contemplate driving, initially. "Three days in a car with three kids? Are you kidding me?" John says. I agree that's too much to put us all through, especially when we can be there in three hours on a nonstop flight. So when John takes a business trip in March, I pick him up at the airport and bring Henry along. We explore the terminal and watch the planes come and go. I do the same in April with the hopes of persuading Henry that air travel is routine for lots of people. But he still isn't convinced. John and I try a new strategy. We put the kids in charge of choosing which parks we'll visit in Florida and how much time we'll spend in each. We gather a collection of Orlando guidebooks for them and they go to work. They pore through the materials every night after dinner. Henry really, really wants to go to Legoland, and he resolves that getting on a plane is a necessary means, albeit an unpleasant one, to that end.

A couple of summers ago, John introduced the kids to the original Star Wars trilogy and Henry became an instant fan. My mother gave him a stuffed Yoda that Christmas. He became very attached to it. Yoda went almost everywhere with Henry back then, except to the public elementary school (because the kids would make fun of a boy his age bringing a stuffed toy to class). Now Yoda has become Henry's surrogate in situations that make him uncomfortable. Henry uses a different voice for Yoda, and it is that eighteen-inch-tall stuffed green alien who offers me a "Goodnight, Mommy" every evening, held out at a full arm's length from Henry's own body. Yoda wishes people a "Happy Birthday," not Henry. Yoda hugs the grandparents. It is Yoda who is so very sad when John's father—the kids' Pépère—passes away. And it is Yoda who boards the plane first that May, frightened but resolute. Extended family think Henry's attachment to Yoda is cute, but I know it's about much more than that.

The flight hits minor turbulence an hour or so in. I nervously look toward John who's sitting in between Henry and Finn, across the aisle from Danielle and me. Henry pulls the window shade down and holds Yoda tight. I watch in astonishment as Henry says, "It's okay, Yoda. We'll be alright." Henry continues to hold tightly to Yoda while he focuses on the new book he brought with him, then on the Nintendo DS handheld game that he and Finn share, then back to the book again. He's using these diversions as a coping mechanism. There's no meltdown. Neither John nor I have to intervene. Henry understood that his anxiety was building and he implemented a strategy in response. It strikes me that he couldn't learn how to do this within public school, not only because comforts like a stuffed Yoda were deemed socially unacceptable but also because his senses were so constantly bombarded that he was unable to successfully separate out the offending stimuli and calmly mitigate them. Removed from some of the daily chaos and negative social interactions, he could start to understand and work on the situations that upset him the most. Yoda is a tool for responding rationally to irrational fears.

Our rental car is a minivan like the one we drive at home, but our vacation lodgings are far more luxurious than what we live in every day. I'd found a spacious, modern, fully equipped condo just outside downtown Orlando, where all the kids have their own rooms. Henry settles into the space fine, but I'm not sure how he'll do at the parks. Legoland is a manageable size, easily done in a day, but the Disney parks are massive. I'm afraid he'll become exhausted well before Danielle and Finn are ready to call it a day, and then John and I will find ourselves negotiating who'll go back to the car with him and who'll keep exploring with the other two.

Turns out, it isn't an issue. As when we were in D.C., Henry keeps going. He wants to try every ride. The distrust that fuels his fear of airplane machinery somehow doesn't translate to speeding roller coasters and death-defying drops. Maybe the physics of land-bound amusement park rides make more sense to him than a plane soaring through the air; I don't know. Regardless, Henry spends most of our first day at the Magic Kingdom asking Danielle to accompany him on thrill rides. If he meets the height requirements he rides, whether or not any of us are willing to join him. Later in the week, he even sits with a stranger in order to take another spin on the new Expedition Everest coaster, when the rest of us cannot handle one more jolt, loop, or drop.

I'm terrified that Henry will be thrown seventy feet into the air from one of these intense thrill rides. He may be tall enough, but he's a lanky rail, all skin and bones, in the twenty-sixth percentile for weight at his last checkup. I complain to John that the rides should have weight guidelines, not just height standards.

"Maybe he gets his irrational fears from you," John mutters.

The condo we rented is cheaper and far roomier than a Disney hotel room. It also allows us to make most of our meals in the full kitchen and pack sandwiches for the parks. We tell the kids that we'll eat out twice during our vacation and we'll all have to agree on the restaurants. The only rule: no dining at chains we have at home—we must try something new. Danielle proposes an Irish pub at Disney for the first meal, where there's live step dancing and audience participation. During dinner, Henry sits quietly as Finn is singled out for a quick lesson and then performs on stage with the dancers and a few other kid volunteers. We eat the second meal at a Cuban restaurant outside the main tourist area, with a menu that includes no mac and cheese or chicken tenders. We try small plates of alligator meat, oxtail stew, plantains, and other exotic-to-us dishes. Maybe Henry is just hungry or maybe this trip is convincing him that sometimes trying new things pays off, but he samples them all. Some he likes; some he doesn't. But he tries, and that's a victory.

When it's time to go home we're all ready, consumed with a happy exhaustion. Henry's eager to get back to his own room, his own bed, and his regular routine, but he had a great time. He still doesn't like to fly. However, even with the turbulence on that maiden voyage, air travel didn't get moved into *the bad place*. Rather it became a fear he could overcome. It's one of many activities that transition from out-of-the-question to relatively manageable that year, and *the bad place* eventually becomes just a memory, a symbol of the before-homeschooling Henry. Whether it's his new educational environment, his growing maturity, or a combination of the two, I'm not sure, but Henry is newly empowered. Withdrawing into his own world is no longer so alluring.

LESSON 21

One Size Does Not Fit All

The summer after sixth grade, Henry goes back to the academic camp he loves, but when September comes around again, he doesn't have to wish school was more like camp. It's a reality now. I decide that we can figure out seventh grade on our own, so I don't buy another packaged curriculum. Thanks to a tip from the speech therapist at the middle school, I discover the district has extra books to lend, and we're able to borrow the entire seventh grade set. We supplement those with the next level of Miss Lucy's creative writing class, continued Latin and science classes at enrichment centers, and an additional online pre-algebra course.

We take field trips that align with Henry's current interests, and I let him dwell on the academic topics that inspire him. If he wants to spend a week working on a computer programming task or translating a certain text from Latin, he does. I don't force fifty-minute blocks of each subject on him. When we talk about the Civil Rights Movement in American History, I let him use the integration of Major League Baseball as a portal to explore it. For literary analysis, we examine Star Wars movies and Marvel comics. Steinbeck and Shakespeare will come, but first we need to define symbolism and theme in a way that holds meaning for Henry.

Danielle has started her first year of high school. But when I take Finn to the open house at the school where he'll attend third grade, the same school Henry had attended, he's less than thrilled. He's a creative kid—bright and entrepreneurial—and the opportunities to exercise those talents fade in the higher grades. He starts asking to be homeschooled like his brother, but I suspect this request has more to do with envying the extra time I spend with Henry than it does with any real desire to learn at home. Finn is intuitive, social, and adaptable. He'd be surrounded by people twenty-four-seven if we let him, and he's been doing great in school. He thrives in the classroom. Homeschooling doesn't seem like a good fit for him and, frankly, I'm not sure I have the energy to keep him engaged at home. Henry is a natural independent learner; Finn learns best within a group dynamic.

So, when Finn asks if we can go to an open house at the small private school our neighbor's kids attend, I agree. I don't think he'll like it—not enough people, not enough going on. But we're both smitten within minutes of walking through the front door. The school is small, personal, and thanks to an abundance of floor-to-ceiling windows, bright and cheerful. It only serves kids in grades kindergarten through fifth, but they teach up to an eighth grade curriculum. Students are allowed to advance as much as their intellect and curiosity will let them. We aren't even out of the parking lot when Finn says, "Mommy, I don't know how much this school costs, but you can have all the money in my piggy bank if I can go here."

It will require more sacrifices and more freelance work on top of my Friday through Sunday job, but after changing our lives to homeschool Henry, how can I tell Finn no? He deserves the same opportunity to thrive. Danielle is well suited to public school. She can brush off the small annoyances, take full advantage of the honors and AP offerings, and engage with the handful of great teachers who will challenge her to do her best. She's already joined clubs and earned a spot on the junior varsity softball team. She's a kid who will attend every game and theater production, decorate the gym for pep rallies, and host team dinners. Neither of my boys are as good a fit. Unlike Henry, Finn would have done well enough if he continued in public school. But after witnessing Henry's transformation over the last year, "well enough" isn't acceptable to me anymore.

The private school holds an ice cream social the week before classes officially start. Finn plays with the other kids and makes his own sundae, while the parents get an introduction to a typical day at the school. "We believe in frequent breaks here," the director says, "so the kids have two recesses—one mid-morning after snack time and another after lunch." I agree with this philosophy whole-heartedly. The three lead teachers explain that the classes are blended, with kindergarteners and first graders in one room; second and third graders in another; then fourth and fifth graders grouped together. The kids in the older class mentor "buddies" from the younger class. I love that responsibility and leadership skills are consciously taught versus allowing leaders to emerge organically via the "survival of the fittest" mentality that prevails in so many education systems. I'm also thrilled with the multi-grade classrooms—a structure that Henry's homeschool programs have convinced me is superior to the traditional single-grade system.

There will be just eleven kids in Finn's class, and his teacher is experienced and enthusiastic. The environment could not be more different from the chaos and congestion at our public school complex. I still fear that there may be too few people for Finn here, not enough action, but he's excited for it. And I appreciate the flexibility this small school offers. They have after-school care, but unlike at the public school where you have to commit to a certain schedule in August for the entire school year, I can call same-day if Henry and I are running late from a class, and Finn can stay and play at school until I get there, for a nominal daily fee.

That's not to say it's all easy. Danielle and Finn are very aware that they don't get some of the things they want due to Henry's needs. Henry gets more of my time and more treats during the day because we're so often on the road. He doesn't have homework the way the other two do; his evenings are free for watching TV or reading for pleasure. And his siblings are envious. In addition to these disparities, Henry's psychologist-led autism support group meets weekly but is not covered by our health insurance. This is true of almost every service for improving Henry's social and adaptive skills, so a substantial amount of our income goes to his medical and academic needs. My kids don't have cell phones and iPads and brand-name clothes like many of their friends do, and that trip to Disney World is the one and only major family vacation we'll ever take.

It takes a toll on me, as well. I'm one person trying to meet the needs of three children who all have their unique personalities, while also being supportive of my husband's growing career, being present for my aging parents, and managing part-time paid work.

Our relationship with John's side of the family has become more difficult over time and causes additional stress. My sister-in-law and her husband have disowned us. John and I aren't sure what real or perceived transgression instigated this, and I continued to send them holiday cards, email updates about the kids, etc. for a while, thinking they'd come to their senses. But they stopped acknowledging John and me altogether, and they cut off all communication with the kids as well—no phone calls, no birthday cards, no visits. Whatever grievances or disagreements they had with us, they were now making the kids pay for, too. This was especially difficult to explain to Danielle, who was eleven at the time and old enough to notice the complete disappearance of her aunt and uncle from her life.

After my father-in-law passes away, John's motivation to maintain a relationship with his family diminishes. He's had enough of the emotional strain, as have I, but I still extend invitations to John's older sister and to my mother-in-law so they can celebrate birthdays and holidays with the kids. We're now excluded from family gatherings on John's side—if John's youngest sister and brother-in-law will be in attendance, our family is not invited. So the only times my kids see their paternal grandmother and other aunt are when I host something, which I do, multiple times a year, for their benefit. Maintaining what's left of those connections has become my responsibility, on top of everything else.

I work long days on Friday, Saturday, and Sunday in order to be home during the week to homeschool Henry. I miss sports games, special events, and weekend get-togethers—John takes the kids to all of those things. It's an exhausting routine for John and me, and we're in over our heads most of the time, both emotionally and financially. At one point, finances get so bad that our family budget becomes a precarious house of cards, borrowing from one credit card to pay another. But I never consider sending Henry or Finn back to public school.

All three kids seem to be exactly where they belong, and that offers me a peace of mind I haven't enjoyed in years. The social and emotional ease outweighs my monetary anxiety.

It's different for John. He's continuously stressed about our low bank account balances and feels enormous pressure to provide us with more financial security. Ensuring my kids find their own place in the world, their perfect "fit," may be priceless to me, primary to my priorities, because I never found it for myself.

I get along alright with the parents of my kids' school friends, but I've never found a consistent group of fellow parents in town with whom to find mutual support and fellowship. The lives of parents whose children attend public schools are often rooted in the routines and schedules of the educational system, and in its extracurriculars. People meet one another at class open houses, concerts, and field days. They socialize in the bleachers at football, basketball, softball, and volleyball games and at theater, cheerleading, and band practices. Their kids carpool to these events and hang out at each other's homes afterward. If you're not an active part of these systems as a parent, it's difficult to find a social footing. I'm not present at the public schools enough to build those relationships. On the occasions when I do attend a game or event there, I feel like a stranger.

I meet some nice people within the broader homeschool community, but I find no consistent social group there, either. Many of the homeschooling families I come in contact with are baffled by my choices. They don't understand how I could function with two children in traditional education systems and one in the homeschooling world, or why I'd want to. For many of them, homeschooling is a lifestyle choice. They wouldn't take on the work of that while at the same time being bound to a public or private school's schedule. They have a point. I was so lost for so long when I was young, it does now cross my mind that I'm overcompensating, holding myself to too high a standard of individualized parenting. This ideal may not be sustainable.

Yet even if I didn't overextend myself, my social life might not be any different. I've always been socially anxious and prefer to be alone over spending time as part of a group. A specific profession might have become a passion for me and mitigated some of my loneliness had I found my calling sooner, but it took me over twenty years to discover an occupation that I was both good at and enjoyed. I worked in service most of my life until I earned my college degree at forty-five years old, followed by a master's degree at forty-eight. Only in mid-life did I consider the possibility of building a fulfilling career that combined both my individual strengths and intense interests. Unfortunately, despite motivational speakers asserting otherwise, it can be too late to pursue some of your dreams. Many careers have an expected trajectory of education, accomplishments, and promotions—good luck if you take a different route, especially if you're middle aged or older. I don't want my own kids to be similarly disadvantaged; I've learned that encouragement and exposure to a wide range of educational opportunities are critical to a better outcome for them.

I thought something was wrong with me when I was in middle and high school. Maybe I just wasn't "book smart." Or maybe I wasn't smart, period. No one offered an alternative outside of traditional public systems. When I started attending a local college's continuing education classes at night as an adult, the teachers praised my work and I earned high marks.

For the first time in my life, I felt competent in academics. In the continuing education program, I attended one or two night classes a week and did the remainder of the work on my own. I excelled when I could decide how I'd best learn the subject matter and then implement the system and schedule that worked for me. But by then I was a self-supporting adult. Making a living was my primary responsibility. I couldn't turn back the clock and become a college-bound eighteen-year-old, as much as I sometimes wished I could.

We are all unique beings, and our journeys to a place of professional satisfaction and personal joy vary widely. One size does not fit all, and it never has, but many of the systems within our society still operate as if it does.

It's a Journey, Not a Destination

The phone rings as I walk through the door. I rush in, set down my grocery bags and schoolbooks, and answer it.

Henry and I have been gone since morning. Thursdays are our longest day of the week. We sat for forty minutes in expressway traffic so I could stop in at the office and drop off paperwork from my weekend job. Then we traveled another twenty-five minutes to Latin class. We ate bagged lunches at Henry's weekly homeschool recreation afternoon, and then got on the road again for the forty-five-minute drive to Finn's school. It was even slower today, because Henry recently got his learner's permit and I let him drive.

"Mrs. Mackin? It's Lisa from A-Plus Driving School. Do you have a minute to talk?"

A call like this is never good news when it comes to Henry. No one calls to say that he's doing fantastic, exceeding all expectations, acing this or that task. But when I see the driving school's name on the caller i.d., I assume they need to reschedule one of Henry's lessons. I've let my guard down—Henry has been doing so well for so long with his classes, his friends, and even engaging in some volunteer work.

Lisa says that Henry's driving instructor has "concerns." She conferences in the instructor, Bruce, to elaborate. Henry grips the wheel too tight, Bruce explains, takes his corners in starts and stops rather than in one smooth motion, and seems unusually anxious when driving. They question if John and I are doing our required hours of supervised driving with him. "He's homeschooled," I say. "He's getting more road time with us than our daughter ever did." But I assure them we'll do more.

I put the phone down and slump onto the couch. I thought we were past this, but I was fooling myself. Autism is never done. The challenges change, and the communication gets better, but it's always going to put an extra obstacle in the way of whatever Henry tries to achieve. It's estimated that 15 to 20 percent of humans exhibit some form of neurodivergence. If that's true, then the other 80 to 85 percent are neurotypical. This doesn't mean we shouldn't advocate for better awareness, sensitivity, and flexibility, or expect reasonable accommodations, but systems will always be designed around the needs of the majority. The judgments people make, the conclusions that they come to, are based on the perceptions of that 80 to 85 percent.

Danielle is in her freshman year of college now, and I'm hoping to transfer to a better job within my organization to help pay the tuition bills. But a new, more lucrative position means commuting into Boston every day, not working from home, and with Danielle living on a campus four and a half hours away, Henry will have to help with driving duties. He'll need to drive himself to his classes and activities and drive Finn home from school a couple of days a week. I need him to drive competently and be comfortable doing it. So from then on, I have him drive. Everywhere. And on the weekends, John drags Henry out on every errand and makes him take the wheel.

Despite continued trepidation on the part of the driving school, Henry is scheduled for the driving test in February—the Registry of Motor Vehicles' first available timeslot. The day arrives and the forecast is for snow and sleet. *This poor kid can't catch a break*, I think. Bruce arrives on time and beeps from the driveway. The car is white like the weather, but there's no missing it—the driving school's cherry red and electric blue logo is painted on both sides of the body, across the hood, and on the trunk. It's obnoxious, and I wish our hatchback looked just like it. No one's going to accidentally rear-end that thing. Unfortunately, the little secondhand Subaru we bought last year for Danielle to drive to school and sports practices, and for Henry to drive around when he's ready, is a dark gray with no conspicuous markings. On a rainy day you can barely see it if the headlights aren't on.

I know Henry will be careful when he drives on his own, logical and precise, but I also know that many of the other drivers on the road around him won't be so conscientious. The texters, the folks who've had too many drinks, the commuters who are in a constant rush. They terrify me. What people say about Massachusetts drivers is largely true—generally speaking, we're an impatient, inconsiderate bunch when we're in our vehicles, and it takes particular skills to drive in the Boston area. I ordered a slew of neon yellow "student driver" magnets to affix to the Subaru as well as to our minivan when Henry borrows it, hoping these warnings will encourage other drivers to back off. John and all three kids think I'm being ridiculous. Danielle proclaims, "I'm taking every one of those signs off when I have the car."

The instructor walks around to the passenger side and

Henry settles into the driver's seat. Then he backs out of our snow-covered driveway. I told him to text me as soon as it was over, and I glance at my phone every couple of minutes throughout the next two hours until a notification lights up the screen. "I passed," it reads.

He passed. On the first try. In a snowstorm. Maybe we've all underestimated him. Again.

Life is Full of Surprises

In the autumn of Henry's junior year of homeschooled high school, we go on our first road trip to visit Danielle at college. It's "family weekend," and the college will be offering free concerts, campus tours, and lunchtime barbeques. The school is in Vermont and the off-campus outdoor activity options are numerous. On our last day, we go apple picking at a local orchard before saying our goodbyes and dropping Danielle back at her dorm.

John navigates our minivan onto the last stretch of highway that will take us home. Henry says nonchalantly, "I think maybe I'll live at college."

Wait, what?

When Henry was younger, he insisted that he only wanted to look at colleges that he could commute to. College is not optional for our kids; John and I made that decision early on. We'd had our own career growth hindered too many times due to a lack of higher education. Danielle couldn't wait to move away and live on campus, and Finn recently did a school project on Denmark, which prompted him to declare that this small country is where he will receive his college education and probably live permanently. He hasn't figured out the logistics of that plan yet. Only twelve years old, he has time, I remind him.

Henry is less excited about the idea of college. He's been adamant that if he is to get his education as we insist, he'll live at home while doing it. He will maintain his essential routines—sleep in his own room, eat breakfast and dinner in our kitchen, and go to classes during the day. That's fine with us. We live within a commutable distance of both Boston and Providence; there are fantastic choices in both those cities and in many of the suburbs in between.

"You think living at college would be fun?" I ask Henry when I get over the initial shock of his statement.

"It just seems easier," he says. "You know, just being able to get up fifteen minutes before class in the morning and walk to whatever building it's in."

The joys of the unlimited college meal plan that he'd recently been exposed to probably have something to do with it, too. The kid likes to eat. Not cook or do dishes, mind you, but eat. At least in that way he's a stereotypical teenager.

I look over at John, my eyebrows raised. He smiles.

With this revelation, Henry's choices expand significantly. We need to explore as many options as we can. College tours and information sessions were a scheduling nightmare when Danielle was looking because the public school allowed students only five school days in their entire senior year for this purpose. If you're traveling to another part of the country to tour schools, these five days are easily used up in just one trip. But with Henry homeschooling, we have a lot of flexibility, at least for the time being, and I'm motivated to use that advantage to its fullest. Now that Henry is driving and doing all of his schoolwork through homeschool enrichment centers, community college courses, and online classes, I've applied for several full-time jobs both inside my current organization and outside of it. If one of those comes through, that will be the end of my free weekdays.

Just like Danielle had, Henry asks to look at campuses when school is in session to get a sense of the student culture, so weekends and semester breaks are out. He wants to be sure that any school he's considering has a relaxed, low-key atmosphere, rather than a chaotic or competitive one. For this reason he rules out the Ivy Leagues, though his transcripts, together with his SAT and ACT scores, qualify him to apply. He's learned that mountains of schoolwork and traditional hierarchies don't necessarily correlate to success, at least not to his success, and he assigns no value to prestige.

Henry placed in the top one percent on the standardized tests he sat for, without any formal preparation. And he's already completed three levels of calculus at the community college as a dual-enrollment student—a program that allows kids with unique circumstances to take courses at their local state school. He's currently taking statistics there and the professor asked him to lead a Saturday study group, because Henry is the only student in the course who got a 100 on the mid-term. He likes helping the other students, who range from twenty-somethings to retirees. One of Henry's strengths is a complete absence of preconceptions about people. He accepts everyone as they are, until they prove themselves to be unkind or untrustworthy. It's what I most admire about him.

I sometimes like to look at Henry's academic excellence and fantastic work ethic as a validation of my choice to home-school, as a marker of our success. But the truth is I had little to do with developing either of these traits in him. All I did was remove a few obstacles, the public school environment being one of them. He taught himself advanced mathematics and computer programming. I didn't help him study for the SATs; I didn't even pay for one of those expensive preparatory classes that are now common for college-bound students. He looked over the workbook the College Board sent with the registration materials and then scored a 790 in math, out of a possible 800. Considering I barely made it through Algebra I in high school, I knew I had no hand in that success.

Henry's intellect and impartiality is a combination most of us wish our leaders possessed. Unfortunately, our society gives more weight to charisma—a quality Henry has very little of. He's not interested in persuading people; he just wants others to innately do the right thing by each other, society, and the environment, and to pursue progress ethically and rationally. We need more people like Henry to serve in public office or lead corporations, but it seems that those jobs attract and are awarded to the boastful and charming. Americans seem more interested in sales pitches than evidence-based solutions, both in industry and government, and John and I are concerned about Henry's future job prospects because of it.

In early spring, Henry and I visit a mid-sized business school outside of Boston. It has a great reputation for preparing students for the modern workforce and offers an exceptional career services program. Freshmen start writing cover letters, crafting resumes, and practicing interview skills from the very first semester. While many colleges don't even want to see students in the career services department until their junior year, this school gives us an entire presentation on why these skills should be built much sooner. It appeals to Henry. During the presentation, he writes numerous comments in the notebook that he's brought with him. He never says it out loud, but I think he understands that he'll need this extra assistance to land a professional job.

The business school fits in other ways, too. It's an enclosed suburban campus, with room to breathe. It isn't crowded like the city schools we've looked at, and there are many private nooks throughout the university where a student can study or take a break. The faculty seem friendly and approachable, and the students appear relaxed. There are a lot of people eating alone in the cafeteria or walking to class by themselves, and it feels like a place where Henry can define how much social interaction he wants, rather than it being forced upon him.

"So, what do you think?" I ask as we drive out of the visitors' lot. I've kept my opinions to myself on every college tour so far. I don't want to sway Henry one way or another. I'm underestimating him again; he knows what he wants in a school and why. My thoughts aren't going to influence his assessment.

"I like their internship program and the likelihood that I'll have a job lined up when I graduate. And I like the campus. I can see myself here," he says. "I think this is my first choice so far."

He can see himself here. At college. Living on his own. Managing all his own needs and academic schedules and internships. I can see him here, too.

* * *

Two months later, a suitable job comes through for me. Henry begins picking up his brother at school a few days a week, rotating the responsibility with my father. When John and I occasionally run late on our commute home, Henry makes dinner for himself and Finn, albeit boxed macaroni and cheese or frozen chicken patties. He drives himself to his classes. He does his own laundry and cleans the bathroom that he and his brother share. He grunts when I ask him how his day was, the grunt many parents of teenagers would recognize. We tour multiple colleges, and he compiles a spreadsheet of pros and cons that ultimately becomes a tiered list of his choices. When acceptance letters arrive, he's ready to make an informed decision.

Sitting around the kitchen table one night, Henry contemplates the big changes coming and we talk about dormitory options. Henry's open to having one roommate, especially if there are plenty of other private places on campus to escape to, but we both think an individual room would be best. Having his own space to decompress after a busy or stressful day is ideal.

"If you want a single room, you might have to tell the administration that you're on the autism spectrum," I say.

Henry doesn't generally disclose this to people. He resists this label and any other. Autism, or neurodivergence, isn't part of his personal identity the way it is for some.

"Hmmm. That might be worth it," he says. "No one else has to know."

That's true. With all the time we've spent focusing on this disorder, or *difference* as I've come to think of it now, and with all the file folders full of IEPs, developmental evaluations, physical assessments, and educational recommendations that still clutter my home office, no one else has to know. Like homeschooling was six years earlier, college will be another fresh start. But this new chapter of Henry's life won't unfold within the shadows of developmental clinics and therapists' offices. He won't be defined by a specific set of behaviors or a medical diagnosis before he even begins to build a social network. Because people don't look at him and see autism anymore. They just see Henry.

And that's all he, or I, ever wanted.

EPILOGUE

In July 2023, the Pew Research Center released a report revealing that the number of students in the American special education system has doubled over the past four decades, from about 3.6 million in the 1976-77 school year to approximately 7.3 million in 2021-22, and that schools are struggling to hire enough professionals to serve this growing population.

The COVID-19 pandemic was devastating for special education students who need in-person tactile assistance. But for some students who receive special education services due to conditions that fall under the neurodivergent umbrella, learning from home provided a welcome relief from the challenging social environments of public school, resulting in improved academic performance and lower stress. Media coverage and public discussion of this phenomenon is sparse, but state departments of education should take a closer look to identify opportunities that would make public schools work better for all children, including those who have neurodivergent conditions.

Today's special education system engages a vast range of disabilities, and school districts often can't keep up. In March 2023, for the first time in over twenty years, my home state of Massachusetts updated its IEP resources. This came after nine years of review, and Massachusetts is still one of only a few states that have made any substantial updates to their special education programs since the 1990s. Improving the system is a multifaceted challenge that's exacerbated by teacher shortages and inequitable funding across districts, systemic bias, lack of training initiatives for current teachers and paraprofessionals, and a decline in college students entering the field. The list goes on.

Many kids who have challenges that require an IEP do best with face-to-face support in structured settings like school. But few education experts acknowledge that traditional classroom environments can impede the progress of some special education students, particularly those who have neurodivergent conditions, by constructing barriers to alternatives that would help these kids succeed.

When Henry left the public system, I created a customized hybrid education primarily based on his abilities and interests, rather than on a diagnosis, and utilized all of the resources available in our area as well as online learning options. I had to do it alone. Through my independent research and outreach, I built a network of public and private school teachers, mission-driven educational entrepreneurs, community college staff, local museum educators, secular homeschool groups, and several university professors who all participated in educating my son. Henry's classroom was an extraordinary success, but it wouldn't have been possible if I hadn't had the time to invest in finding these professionals, if I didn't have a spouse with a full-time job and healthcare benefits.

Homeschooling is not a long-term solution for meeting the needs of students like Henry. I was able to manage his alternative education around part-time work and my other kids' schedules. And I was privileged to live in an area with myriad resources to supplement and diversify his academic experience. Many parents aren't so fortunate. But the types of partnerships that I initiated to facilitate my son's learning could be instituted on a much larger level, filling the gap that exists between what schools can offer and the services children—especially children with disabilities—need to thrive, without asking parents to become full-time instructors and curriculum designers themselves.

This is not an argument to privatize public schools, but rather to offer families flexible options that position community resources and schools as partners—an arrangement the Brookings Institution refers to as "Powered-up Schools" in a 2020 report outlining ways that public education could emerge from the pandemic stronger than before. In the U.K., students in some districts participate in what's called "flexi-schooling." This system allows a child to be a fully funded public school student while spending part of the week homeschooled and/or attending off-site programs. I know that having access to this flexibility would have been beneficial for my own family, and parents of children who do have access to this system report positive outcomes.

Hybrid public education models were unheard of when Henry was younger, but a small number of districts are considering them now, post-pandemic. Some families don't want to return to the status quo, and a few school administrators are listening. But in most of the U.S., how we educate our children is still a binary choice: traditional school or homeschooling. It's not "both/and"; it's "either/or."

To meet the goal of ensuring that every student receives an appropriate and comprehensive education, we need to break away from traditional structures that haven't changed much in the last several decades and start building more creative, nimble solutions that don't take nine years of discussion and analysis to actualize. We learned to pivot quickly when a global pandemic gave us no choice; let's embrace those lessons and create educational systems that allow for individual flexibility and innovative engagement beyond school walls. This is how we build a more equitable, diverse, and inclusive society.

The same goes for workplaces. Success in corporate spaces is often rooted in outdated ideas about social behavior. Before the COVID-19 public health crisis, the university I worked for was very resistant to work-from-home options. A department hired me as an individual contributor, but I was assigned project manager responsibilities once I was onboarded. I'm organized and can keep a project on track, but the constant in-person meetings drained my energy. Zoom meetings end at a designated time, but in-person meetings often spill out into the hallway or rekindle at the coffee station, and people frequently stop by others' cubicles to discuss projects further. I sometimes found myself hiding in a ladies' room stall just to delay assaults on the quiet, focused times of my workday that I so desperately needed to stay on task. I stopped taking public transportation to work and started driving—a two-hour commute each way in rush hour traffic—just so I could sit in my car alone at midday and eat my lunch in peace. When I tried to speak to my manager about how I could minimize some of these meetings and interruptions in order to get back to the productive work I was hired to do, I was told "that's just the job." My coworkers lamented the inability to meet in person once the pandemic temporarily closed our office. I silently rejoiced. But it was clear that I would not be able to advance my career there if I wanted to work from home permanently, even if only for part of the week.

As a kid, I was socially isolated with few friends, and I

hated school. I was viciously bullied and perpetually uncomfortable in those spaces, which made learning difficult. But I hadn't considered how these challenges may have followed me into adulthood and affected my ability to get and keep a job. I experienced frequent burnout when I was young, single, and supporting only myself. But I attributed that to boredom. My secretarial skills were in demand and the job market was good, so I'd just find a new position somewhere else when I got restless. It wasn't until my kids were older and I went back to work full time that I began to understand how negatively the office environment impacted me. When COVID-19 sent me and my coworkers home three years after that, I realized how much more productive I am in a remote setting. Despite the pandemic-related anxieties and stressors so many of us experienced during that time, my mental and physical health significantly improved.

These recognitions and what I'd learned as Henry's mother caused me to suspect that I, too, was in some way neurodivergent. But getting a formal diagnosis isn't easy. Conditions such as autism, ADHD, dyscalculia (difficulty with math), dysgraphia (difficulty with writing), dyslexia (difficulty with reading), dyspraxia (difficulty with coordination), and sensory processing disorders can look very different in adults who've been masking the symptoms their entire lives in order to survive and make a living. And few doctors are trained in diagnosing autism or associated disorders in adults. Most of the tools for evaluating these conditions were designed for children, including the latest versions of the Autism Diagnostic Interview (ADI) and the Childhood Autism Rating Schedule (CARS). These surveys are typically completed by parents, but by the time adults seek diagnostic screening for themselves, their parents are often elderly, infirm, or deceased. If this is the case, the person being evaluated is asked to recall their own development from their early life. How many of us in our 40s, 50s, or 60s can recall when we first walked, talked, ate solid foods, or learned to read? Did we exhibit functional impairments in social communication and social reciprocity in elementary school? Did we experience sensory anomalies?

Adult women, in particular, are difficult to diagnose. Research shows that women engage in masking, or what scientists refer to as "camouflaging," at a significantly higher rate than men. This is attributed to societal gender norms—a cultural mandate that expects women to "fit in" and encourages men to "stand out." The consistent, elaborate effort among women to mask their symptoms often results in chronic physical exhaustion, mental stress, and extreme anxiety. It also contributes to a lack of diagnosis in women that limits their access to therapeutic programs and support. Holding eye contact with a colleague is uncomfortable for me, but I've trained myself to do it. I often find formal networking at conferences and working lunches enormously stressful, but I've learned to summon a measure of visible ease in these situations in order not to stand out or appear too awkward. I use tools like clothing and makeup to help me put on my "professional" persona or my "socializing with friends" persona. And I adhere to daily structured routines as much as possible to help me avoid overwhelm. But everyone adjusts to some extent when they interact with different people and environments. It's difficult to know what an abnormal level of this adaptation looks like.

For me, the exhaustion Henry experienced after a full day of traditional school provides some scale. Danielle and Finn came home energized—excited to drop their backpacks, have a snack, and go off to their respective extracurriculars. They needed swim practice, gymnastics class, softball or soccer to burn off excess energy, to run and play and socialize. Henry needed to rest and to be alone. I'm useless at the end of a busy onsite workday. I have no desire to go out and "blow off some steam" like many of my coworkers do. I have no energy to do necessary tasks like laundry or dinner preparation or yard work, much less to socialize and engage in small talk. But I can't afford to burn out at another job or be deemed "not a team player" as I have in the past—I've got two kids in college, and I carry the healthcare benefits for my entire family through my employer. Most of my job requires independent research, writing, and editing, all of which can be done digitally, online and via email, and I'm very competent at this work. I resent having to disclose my personal challenges so that I may do my job in a setting that allows me to be successful, productive, and relatively comfortable. These environmental expectations seem reasonable to me even without a medical diagnosis, especially in a post-pandemic era when many of us have demonstrated that we can work effectively from offsite locations. But many managers are stuck in a factory mindset, just like so many school systems.

Some organizations that claim diversity, equity, and inclusion (DEI) are absolute priorities for them nevertheless routinely create barriers and bureaucracy for neurodivergent employees, consciously or not. Even when the focus is on community building versus increased supervision, there's often no acknowledgment or understanding that many of these well-intentioned policies do not provide positive bonding opportunities for some employees. To advance their careers while simultaneously maintaining their mental health and/

or managing symptoms, many neurodivergent people have to disclose personal health information to their employers and possibly to coworkers. They also need an official diagnosis to ask for what constitutes a "disability accommodation." I fear Henry will, too, when he's on the job market. But diagnoses and disclosures can backfire.

A 2015 report based on two large longitudinal studies found that the unemployment rate among young adults on the autism spectrum is at least 42 percent. The unemployment rate in the general population hovered around 4 percent at this time. The unemployment rate among people with other documented disabilities is about 10.5 percent. Several agencies have investigated this further and, regardless of the specific numbers, they all point to the same conclusion: people with autism who are otherwise willing and able to work, many of whom also hold advanced degrees, are unemployed or under-employed at a far greater rate than the general population, and at a higher rate than even other segments of the disabled community. This is not usually due to a lack of intelligence, skills, or work ethic, but rather to a series of systemic, discriminatory practices in the workplace, beginning with hiring processes, which form barriers to neurodivergent people's success.

A 2022 article in *Harvard Business Review* noted, "Autistic professionals can be up to 140 percent more productive than the typical employee when properly matched to jobs." That may be true, but the statistics show a significant number of these professionals aren't getting into appropriate jobs in order to prove it. This is primarily due to false stereotypes that find their way into our workplaces, where there is little to no training or policies to contradict them. A 2020 report from the Institute of Leadership summarizes recent research findings on these challenges, including a study that revealed half of employers surveyed in the U.K. would not hire a person who they knew had a neurodivergent condition.

Henry's classroom will soon become Henry's office, and we need to expand the breadth and vision of American workplace culture just as we need to continue to improve that of our educational systems. It's time for corporations to include neurodiversity in their DEI plans and to revisit hiring processes that present barriers for people who have disabilities and/or neurological differences that are not overtly visible or disclosed. Competent, comprehensive, flexible education programs are needed within our schools, along with meaningful policies and training within our workplaces, before we can realize a more inclusive society that values and reflects the multitude of talent and experiences that exist in every corner of this country and beyond.

* * *

I arrange the six-foot Italian submarine sandwich on a folding table beneath the party tent we rented. It was Henry's only food request for his high school graduation celebration, but I add an assortment of regular sandwiches, salads, and chips for those who may not find this monstrosity appetizing. The cake—a large block featuring his chosen college's mascot—remains in the fridge, so the frosting doesn't melt in the sun. As I attach balloon bouquets in the college's signature colors to our deck and fenceposts, I'm reminded of that party sixteen years ago and the unexpected joy I felt when Henry gleefully wrapped his tiny arms around the Elmo impersonator. And I remember the many discouraging birthday parties that followed, when parents of Henry's classmates said their kids would attend but then never showed up. Large cakes that went uneaten. Party favors that were never distributed. Hearts broken and put back together again and again.

We left those particular disappointments behind with our decision to leave traditional classrooms. Soon our yard will be filled with Henry's friends—young people he's met through all the different homeschooling activities he's joined throughout the region. Unlike Henry's siblings, he won't take part in any graduation procession. There will be no cap and gown. No one will miss those ceremonial formalities but me. I'm still working at modifying my expectations and letting go of the status quo for all of us, especially for myself. But Henry is already there.

NOTES

Prologue

For general information on the history of school counseling, see materials provided by the American School Counselor Association at https://www.schoolcounselor.org.

Meyer, Katharine and Lindsay C. Page, et al. "The School Counselor Staffing Landscape: Policies and Practice." Brookings, 9 Feb. 2023, https://www.brookings.edu/blog/brown-center-chalkboard/2023/02/09/the-school-counselor-staffing-landscape-policies-and-practice.

Carley, Kathryn. "Not Enough School Counselors to Meet Needs of MA Students." *Public News Service*, 13 Oct. 2022, https://www.publicnewsservice.org/2022-10-13/mental-health/not-enough-school-counselors-to-meet-needs-of-ma-students/a81018-1.

"School Counselor Roles & Ratios." American School Counselor Association, https://www.schoolcounselor.org/About-School-Counseling/School-Counselor-Roles-Ratios.

Brown, Carleton H., and David S. Knight. "Student-to-School Counselor Ratios: Understanding the History and Ethics behind Professional Staffing Recommendations and Realities in the United States." *Ethics & Behavior*, 1-19, 2024, https://doi.org/10.1080/10508422.2024.2342520.

To learn more about the evolution of disability services and the parental activism that instigated legislation, see Valerie Leiter's article, "Parental Activism, Professional Dominance, and Early Childhood Disability," in *Disability Studies Quarterly*, Vol. 24(2), 2004, https://dsq-sds.org/index.php/dsq/article/view/483/660.

For more information on the Individuals with Disabilities Education Act (IDEA) and its various iterations, see materials from the Office of Special Education and Rehabilitative Services, U.S. Department of Education, at https://sites.ed.gov/idea/IDEA-History.

Lesson 1

Alicke, Mark. "Willful Ignorance and Self-Deception." *Psychology Today*, 10 Sept. 2017, https://www.psychologytoday.com/us/blog/why-we-blame/201709/willful-ignorance-and-self-deception.

Grose, Jessica. *Screaming on the Inside: The Unsustainability of American Motherhood*. HarperCollins, 2022.

Lesson 2

"Rights of Massachusetts Youth with Disabilities Regarding Transportation to School." Mental Health Legal Advisors Committee, 2012, https://mhlac.org/wp-content/uploads/2018/10/ed_sped_transportation.pdf.

Glasmeier, Amy K. "Living Wage Calculator." Massachusetts Institute of Technology, 2024, https://livingwage.mit.edu/states/25.

Hogan, Dennis. *Family Consequences of Children's Disabilities.* Russell Sage Foundation, 2012.

Kliff, Sarah. "A Stunning Chart Shows the True Cause of the Gender Wage Gap." *Vox*, 19 Feb. 2018, https://www.vox.com/2018/2/19/17018380/gender-wage-gap-childcare-penalty.

Klevin, Henrik, Landais, Camille, and Jakob Søgaard. "Children and Gender Inequality: Evidence from Denmark." *American Economic Journal: Applied Economics*, vol 11(4), 2019, doi:10.1257/app.20180010.

"E-16. Unemployment Rates by Age, Sex, Race, and Hispanic or Latino Ethnicity." Labor Force Statistics from the Current Population Survey, U.S. Bureau of Labor Statistics, https://www.bls.gov/web/empsit/cpsee_e16.htm.

McKinsey & Company produced several studies during the pandemic period revealing the impact on working women, including: Jablonska, Justine (ed.). "Seven Charts that Show Covid-19's Impact on Women's Employment." McKinsey & Company, 8 Mar. 2021, https://www.mckinsey.com/featured-insights/diversity-and-inclusion/seven-charts-that-show-covid-19s-impact-on-womens-employment.

"Pandemic Sets Back Women's Progress in Workforce." *All Things Considered*, NPR, 14 Feb. 2021, https://www.npr.org/2021/02/14/967917836/pandemic-sets-back-womens-progress-in-workforce.

"American Community Survey (ACS), Census.gov." U.S. Census Bureau, 2024, https://www.census.gov/ programs-surveys/acs.

"40% of Lawyers Are Women. 7% Are Black. America's Workforce in Charts. *The Wall Street Journal*, 9 Feb. 2024, https://www.wsj.com/economy/jobs/ workers-america-jobs-demographics-charts-94a5ff6c.

Elsesser, Kim. "Kindergarten Teachers Are Women, Research Shows – Here's How to Attract More Men." *Forbes*, 12 Feb. 2024, https://www.forbes.com/sites/ kimelsesser/2024/02/12/over-96-of-kindergarten-teachers-are-women-research-shows-heres-how-to-attract-more-men.

For more information on the challenges neurodivergent people experience in the medical system, see this study and the related ones listed at its conclusion: Wilson, Shelby A. and Catherine C. Peterson. "Medical care experiences of children with autism and their parents: A scoping review." *Child Care Health and Development*, vol 44(6), 2018, doi:10.1111/cch.12611. Also see Mason, D., Ingham, B., Urbanowicz, A., Michael, C., Birtles, H., Woodbury-Smith, M., Brown, T., James, I., Scarlett, C., Nicolaidis, C., and J.R. Parr. "A Systematic Review of What Barriers and Facilitators Prevent and Enable Physical Healthcare Services Access for Autistic Adults." *Journal of Autism and Developmental Disorders*, vol 49(8), 2019, doi:10.1007/s10803-019-04049-2. PMID: 31124030; PMCID: PMC6647496.

Lesson 3

Catalá-López, F., Hutton, B., Page, M.J., et al. "Mortality in Persons with Autism Spectrum Disorder or Attention-Deficit/Hyperactivity Disorder: A Systematic Review and Meta-analysis." *JAMA Pediatrics*, vol 176(4), 2022, doi:10.1001/jamapediatrics.2021.6401.

Lesson 4

For more details on and history of the myringotomy procedure, see (1) Mangat, K.S., Morrison G.A., and T.M. Ganniwalla. "T-tubes: a retrospective review of 1274 insertions over a 4-year period." *International Journal of Pediatric Otorhinolaryngology*, vol 25(1-3), 1993, doi:10.1016/0165-5876(93)90044-4; and (2) Rimmer J., Giddings, C.E., and N. Weir. "The History of Myringotomy and Grommets." *Ear, Nose & Throat Journal*, vol 99(1_suppl), 2020, doi:10.1177/0145561320914438.

Dubin, Minna. "The Rage Mothers Don't Talk About." *The New York Times*, 16 Apr. 2020, https://www.nytimes.com/2020/04/15/parenting/mother-rage.html.

Heggeness, Misty L., Fields, Jason, García Trejo, Yazmin A., and Anthony Schulzetenberg. "Tracking Job Losses for Mothers of School-Age Children During a Health Crisis." Census.Gov, 8 Oct. 2021, https://www.census.gov/library/stories/2021/03/moms-work-and-the-pandemic.html.

Suarez-Angelino, Lena. "How to Deal with Mom Rage – Practical Tips from a Therapist." *ChoosingTherapy.com*, 1 June 2023, https://www.choosingtherapy.com/mom-rage.

Aarntzen, Lianne, Derks, Belle, van Steenbergen, Elianne, Ryan, Michelle, and van der Lippe, Tanja. "Work-family guilt as a straightjacket. An interview and diary study on consequences of mothers' work-family guilt." *Journal of Vocational Behavior*, vol 115, 2019, doi:10.1016/j.jvb.2019.103336.

Mills, Kim. "What's the difference between guilt and shame? With June Tangney, PhD." Speaking of Psychology (podcast), episode 255, Sep. 2023, *American Psychological Association*, https://www.apa.org/news/podcasts/speaking-of-psychology/guilt-shame.

Ward, Libby. "It's Not a You Thing." *TikTok*, 29 May 2022, https://www.tiktok.com/@diaryofanhonestmom/video/7103160826479119621.

Thornston, Amber. "The Default Parent Syndrome: More than Just a TikTok Trend." *Psychology Today*, 14 Nov. 2022, https://www.psychologytoday.com/us/blog/the-balanced-working-mama/202211/the-default-parent-syndrome-more-just-tiktok-trend.

Fry, Richard, Aragão, Carolina, Hurst, Kiley, and Kim Parker. "In a Growing Share of U.S. Marriages, Husbands and Wives Earn about the Same." Pew Research Center's Social & Demographic Trends Project, Pew Research Center, 13 Apr. 2023, https://www.pewresearch.org/social-trends/2023/04/13/in-a-growing-share-of-u-s-marriages-husbands-and-wives-earn-about-the-same.

Buzard, Kristy, Gee, Laura, and Olga Stoddard. "Who You Gonna Call? Gender Inequality in External Demands for

Parental Involvement." *Social Science Research Network*, 22 May 2023 (abstract of work in progress), https://papers. ssrn.com/sol3/papers.cfm?abstract_id=4456100.

Billotte Verhoff, China, Hosek, Angela M. and Jessica Cherry. "'A Fire in My Belly:' Conceptualizing U.S. Women's Experiences of 'Mom Rage.'" *Sex Roles*, vol 88(11-12), 2023.

Ou, Christine H. and Wendy A. Hall. "Anger in the context of postnatal depression: An integrative review." *Birth*, vol 45(4), 2018, doi:10.1111/birt.12356.

Lesson 5

Heller, Kalman. "The Challenge of Children with Special Needs." *Psych Central*, 17 May 2016, https://psychcentral. com/lib/the-challenge-of-children-with-special-needs#6.

Schwartzman, J.M., Millan, M.E., Uljarevic, M., and Gengoux, G. "Resilience Intervention for Parents of Children with Autism: Findings from a Randomized Controlled Trial of the AMOR Method." *Journal of Autism and Developmental Disorders*, vol 52, 2021, doi:10.1007/s10803-021-04977-y/

Sharma, S., Govindan, R., Kommu, J.V.S. "Effectiveness of Parent-to-Parent Support Group in Reduction of Anxiety and Stress Among Parents of Children with Autism and Attention Deficit Hyperactivity Disorder." *Indian Journal of Psychological Medicine*, vol 44(6), 2022, doi:10.1177/02537176211072984.

Chimeh, N., Pouretemad, H.R., and R. Khoramabadi. "Need assessment of mothers with autistic children." *Journal of*

Family Research, vol 3, 2007.

Faraji-Khiavi, F., Zahiri M., Amiri, E., Dindamal, B., and N. Pirani. "The experiences of families raising autistic children: A phenomenological study." *Journal of Education and Health Promotion*, vol 10:78, 2021, doi:10.4103/jehp. jehp_837_20.

Hastings, R.P. "Behavioural adjustment of siblings of children with autism engaged in applied behavior analysis early intervention programs: the moderating role of social support." *Journal of Autism and Developmental Disorders*, vol 33, 2003, doi:10.1037/e334202004-002.

Petalas M.A., Hastings, R.P., Nash, S., Reilly, D., and A. Dowey. "The perceptions and experiences of adolescent siblings with a brother with autism spectrum disorder." *Journal of Intellectual & Developmental Disability*, vol 37, 2012, doi:10 .3109/13668250.2012.734603.

Petalas, M.A., Hastings, R.P., Nash, S., Dowey, A., and D. Reilly. "I like that he always shows who he is": the perceptions and experiences of siblings with a brother with autism spectrum disorder. *International Journal of Disability, Development and Education*, vol 56(4), 2009, doi:10.1080/10349120903306715.

Lesson 6

Suskind, Ron. *Life, Animated: A Story of Sidekicks, Heroes, and Autism*. Kingswell, 2016.

Lesson 7

Dubin, Minna. *Mom Rage: The Everyday Crisis of Modern Motherhood.* Seal Press, 2023.

Krebs G. and Isobel Heyman. "Obsessive-compulsive disorder in children and adolescents." *Archives of Disease in Childhood*, vol 100(5), 2015, doi:10.1136/archdischild-2014-306934.

For more information on neurodivergent comorbidities, see (1) Vasa, R.A., Keefer, A., McDonald, R.G., Hunsche, M.C., and C.M. Kerns. "A Scoping Review of Anxiety in Young Children with Autism Spectrum Disorder." *Autism Research*, vol 13(12), 2020, doi:10.1002/aur.2395; (2) Garcia, A.M., Freeman, J.B., Himle, M.B., et al. "Phenomenology of Early Childhood Onset Obsessive Compulsive Disorder." *Journal of Psychopathology and Behavioral Assessment*, vol 31, 2008, doi:10.1007/s10862-008-9094-0; (3) Yuhas, Daisy. "Untangling the Ties between Autism and Obsessive-Compulsive Disorder." *Spectrum*, 7 June 2022, doi:10.53053/PEUU3791; and (4) Kirby, Amanda. "Is There a Link between Neurodiversity and Mental Health?" *Psychology Today*, 26 Aug. 2021, https://www.psychologytoday.com/au/blog/pathways-progress/202108/is-there-link-between-neurodiversity-and-mental-health.

Ivarsson, T. and K. Melin. "Autism spectrum traits in children and adolescents with obsessive-compulsive disorder (OCD)." *Journal of Anxiety Disorders*, vol 22(6), 2008, doi:10.1016/j.janxdis.2007.10.003.

Lesson 8

"Mental health in the United States: Parental report of diagnosed autism in children aged 4-17 years – United States, 2003-2004." *Morbidity and Mortality Weekly Report*, vol 55(17), 2006, Centers for Disease Control and Prevention, https://www.cdc.gov/mmwr/preview/mmwrhtml/mm5517a3.htm.

Lesson 9

Kaiser Permanente. "Autism risk in younger children increases if they have older sibling with disorder." *ScienceDaily*, vol 5, 2016, https://www.sciencedaily.com/releases/2016/08/160805230101.htm

Lockwood, Estrin G., Milner, V., Spain, D., Happé, F., and E. Colvert. "Barriers to Autism Spectrum Disorder Diagnosis for Young Women and Girls: a Systematic Review." *Review Journal of Autism and Developmental Disorders*, vol 8(4), 2021, doi:10.1007/s40489-020-00225-8.

Hansen, S.N., Schendel, D.E., Francis, R.W., Windham, G.C., Bresnahan, M., Levine, S.Z., Reichenberg, A., Gissler, M., Kodesh, A., Bai, D., Yip, B.H.K., Leonard, H., Sandin, S., Buxbaum, J.D., Hultman, C., Sourander, A., Glasson, E.J., Wong, K., Öberg, R., and E. T. Parner. "Recurrence Risk of Autism in Siblings and Cousins: A Multinational, Population-Based Study." *Journal of American Academy of Child & Adolescent Psychiatry*, vol 58(9), 2019, doi:10.1016/j.jaac.2018.11.017.

Lesson 10

U.S. Department of Education. "A history of the individuals with disabilities education act (2023)." *Individuals with Disabilities Education Act*, https://sites.ed.gov/idea/IDEA-History.

Sonnenschein S., Stites, M.L., Grossman, J.A., and S.H. Galczyk. "This will likely affect his entire life": Parents' views of special education services during COVID-19." *International Journal of Education Research*, vol 112:101941, 2022, doi:10.1016/j.ijer.2022.101941.

Turner, C. and R. Klein. "After months of special education turmoil, families say schools owe them." Morning Edition, NPR, 16 June 2021, https://www.npr.org/2021/06/16/994587239/after-months-of-special-education-turmoil-families-say-schools-owe-them.

Taketa, K. "Families endure costly legal fights trying to get the right special education services." *Los Angeles Times*, 6 Oct. 2019, https://www.latimes.com/california/story/2019-10-06/legal-fights-families-special-education-services.

"Broken Promises: The Underfunding of IDEA." National Council on Disability, 7 Feb. 2018, page 11, https://ncd.gov/assets/uploads/docs/ ncd-brokenpromises-508.pdf.

"U.S. Commission on Civil Rights Recommendations for the Reauthorization of the Individuals with Disabilities Education Act." U.S. Commission on Civil Rights, May 2002, https://www.usccr.gov/files/pubs/idea/recs.htm.

"Van Hollen, Huffman Introduce Bill to Fully Fund Special Education." Senator Chris Hollen's Office, 10 July 2023, https://www.vanhollen.senate.gov/news/press-releases/van-hollen-huffman-introduce-bill-to-fully-fund-special-education.

Blackwell, W.H., and V.V. Blackwell. "A Longitudinal Study of Special Education Due Process Hearings in Massachusetts: Issues, Representation, and Student Characteristics." Sage Open, 2015, vol 5(1), doi.org/10.1177/2158244015577669.

"Federal officials question Mass. oversight of special education." *The Boston Globe*, 5 Oct. 2023, https://www.bostonglobe.com/2023/10/05/metro/special-eduction-massachusetts.

Lesson 13

Villarreal, Yvonne. "'Parenthood' Told a Flawed Autism Story. This Time, Jason Katims Vowed to 'Do Better.'" *Los Angeles Times*, 21 Jan. 2022, www.latimes.com/entertainment-arts/tv/story/2022-01-21/as-we-see-it-amazon-jason-katims-friday-night-lights-parenthood.

Harris, J. "The mother of neurodiversity: How Judy Singer changed the world." *The Guardian*, 5 July 2023, https://www.theguardian.com/world/2023/jul/05/the-mother-of-neurodiversity-how-judy-singer-changed-the-world.

Rawe, Julie. "The 13 disability categories under IDEA." *Understood.org*, 9 Apr. 2024, https://www.understood.org/en/articles/conditions-covered-under-idea.

Lesson 15

Greenfield, S. "The internet has changed bullying – for the worse." *Psychology Today*, 1 Dec. 2015, https://www. psychologytoday.com/us/blog/mind-change/201512/ the-internet-has-changed-bullying-the-worse.

Sasson, N.J., Faso, D.J., Nugent, J., Lovell, S., Kennedy, D.P., and R.B. Grossman. "Neurotypical Peers are Less Willing to Interact with Those with Autism based on Thin Slice Judgments." *Nature: Scientific Reports*, 2017, vol 7:40700, doi:10.1038/srep40700.

"How Schools Can Support Neurodiverse Students." Child Mind Institute, 23 Aug. 2023, https://childmind.org/ article/how-schools-can-support-neurodiverse-students/.

Anderson, Connie. "IAN Research Report: Bullying and Children with ASD." IAN Research Report: Bullying and Children with ASD, Kennedy Krieger Institute, 26 Mar. 2012, https://www.kennedykrieger. org/stories/interactive-autism-network-ian/ ian_research_report_bullying.

Hoover, D.W. and J. Kaufman. "Adverse childhood experiences in children with autism spectrum disorder." *Current Opinion in Psychiatry*, vol 31(2), 2018, doi:10.1097/ YCO.0000000000000390.

For more information on the frequency and impact of bullying on neurodivergent children, see: (1) Hwang, S., Kim, Y.S., Koh, Y.J., and B.L. Leventhal. "Autism Spectrum Disorder and School Bullying: Who is the Victim? Who is the Perpetrator?" *Journal of Autism and Developmental Disorders*, vol 48(1), 2018, doi:10.1007/s10803-017-3285-z; and (2) Käld, E., Beckman, L., Eapen, V., and P. Lin. "Exploring Potential Modifiers of the Association Between Neurodevelopmental Disorders and Risk of Bullying Exposure." *JAMA Pediatrics*, vol 176(9), 2022, doi:10.1001/jamapediatrics.2022.1755.

Soke, G.N., Rosenberg, S.A., Hamman, R.F., Fingerlin, T., Robinson, C., Carpenter, L., Giarelli, E., Lee, L.C., Wiggins, L.D., Durkin, M.S., and C. DiGuiseppi. "Brief Report: Prevalence of Self-injurious Behaviors among Children with Autism Spectrum Disorder – A Population-Based Study." *Journal of Autism and Developmental Disorders*, vol 46(11), 2016, doi:10.1007/s10803-016-2879-1.

For more information on special education staffing shortages, see (1) Jung, Carrie. "A shortage of special education staff leaves many students without services they need." WBUR, 17 Dec. 2021, https://www.wbur.org/news/2021/12/13/labor-shortage-special-education; (2) Lieberman, Mark. "Contractors Are Filling Staffing Gaps in Schools. Know the Benefits and the Drawbacks." *Education Week*, 29 June 2022, https://www.edweek.org/leadership/contractors-are-filling-staffing-gaps-in-schools-know-the-benefits-and-the-drawbacks/2022/06; (3) Randazzo, S. and M. Barnum. "A Record Number of Kids Are in Special Education – and It's Getting Harder to Help Them All." *The Wall Street Journal*, 20 June 2024, https://www.wsj.com/us-news/education/special-education-student-growth-teachers-understaffed-20efa9da; and (4) Blad, Evie. "Retention Is the Missing Ingredient in Special Education Staffing." *Education Week*, 13 May 2024, https://www.edweek.org/leadership/retention-is-the-missing-ingredient-in-special-education-staffing/2024/05.

Lesson 16

Sohn, Emily. "How Abuse Mars the Lives of Autistic People." *Spectrum/Autism Research News*, 5 Feb. 2020, https://www.spectrumnews.org/features/deep-dive/how-abuse-mars-the-lives-of-autistic-people.

The man who spoke at my daughter's school was John Halligan. For more information, see his website at https://www.ryanpatrickhalligan.org.

Kõlves, K., Fitzgerald, C., Nordentoft, M., Wood, S.J., and A. Erlangsen. "Assessment of Suicidal Behaviors Among Individuals with Autism Spectrum Disorder in Denmark." *JAMA Network*, vol 4(1):e2033565, 2021, doi:10.1001/jamanetworkopen.2020.33565.

"Reducing biases about autism may increase social inclusion, study finds." *Science Daily*, University of Texas at Dallas, 8 Feb. 2021, https://www.sciencedaily.com/releases/2021/02/210208085441.htm.

Grosjean, B., MD. "Autistic Psychiatrist: Oxymoron or Superpower?" Stanford Neurodiversity Summit, Stanford University, 3 Oct. 2023, Stanford, CA.

Miller, Carrie E. and Steven A. Myers. "Disparities in School Discipline Practices for Students with Emotional and Learning Disabilities and Autism." *Journal of Education and Human Development*, vol 4(1), 2015, doi:10.15640/jehd.v4n1a23.

Botha, M., Dibb, B., and D.M. Frost. "'Autism is me': An investigation of how autistic individuals make sense of autism and stigma." *Disability & Society*, vol 37(3), 2022, doi:10.1080/09687599.2020.18227.

Miller, D., Rees, J., and A. Pearson. "Masking Is Life: Experiences of Masking in Autistic and Nonautistic Adults." *Autism Adulthood*, vol 3(4), 2021, doi:10.1089/aut.2020.0083.

Lesson 18

"Charter Schools: Additional Federal Attention Needed to Help Protect Access for Students with Disabilities." U.S. Government Accountability Office, 6 June 2012, https://www.gao.gov/products/gao-12-543.

"Shared Responsibility, Shared Accountability: An Analysis of Enrollment of Students with Disabilities in Colorado's Charter School Sector." National Center for Special Education in Charter School, Nov. 2020, https://coauthorizers.org/wp-content/uploads/2021/06/Shared-Responsibility-Shared-Accountability-An-Analysis-of-Enrollment-of-Students-with-Disabilities-in-Colorados-Charter-Sector-002.pdf.

Meltzer, Erica. "Colorado charter schools seek more authority over special education." *Chalkbeat*, 27 Mar. 2022, https://co.chalkbeat.org/2022/3/27/22997038/colorado-charter-schools-seek-more-authority-over-special-education.

Meltzer, Erica. "Colorado: Charter school applications can't ask about disability." *Chalkbeat*, 13 Jan. 2022, https://co.chalkbeat.org/2022/1/13/22881155/colorado-charter-school-applications-cant-ask-about-disability.

Bergman, Peter and Isaac McFarlin, Jr., "Education for all? A Nationwide Audit Study of School Choice." National Bureau of Economic Research, Dec. 2018 and revised Jan. 2020, https://www.nber.org/system/files/working_papers/w25396/w25396.pdf.

Greene, Peter, "Charter Schools Fight for Their Right to Discriminate." *Forbes*, 10 Nov. 2021, https://www.forbes.com/sites/petergreene/2021/11/10/charter-schools-fight-for-their-right-to-discriminate/?sh=715583ce6c78.

Prothero, Arianna, "Charter Schools More Likely to Ignore Special Education Applicants, Study Finds." *Education Week*, 20 Dec. 2018, https://www.edweek.org/leadership/charter-schools-more-likely-to-ignore-special-education-applicants-study-finds/2018/12.

Riley, Jeffrey. "Advisory on Inter-District School Choice pursuant to G.L. C. 76, §12B - Education Laws and Regulations." Massachusetts Department of Elementary and Secondary Education, 23 Apr. 2019, https://www.doe.mass.edu/lawsregs/advisory/2019-0423glc76s12b.

"Massachusetts School Choice Roadmap." National School Choice Week, 29 Oct. 2019, https://schoolchoiceweek.com/guide-school-choice-massachusetts.

Lesson 19

Saqlain, Nadeem. "A Comprehensive Look at Multi-Age Education." *Journal of Educational and Social Research*, vol 5(2), 2015, doi:10.5901/jesr.2015.v5n2p285.

Braff, D. "The Pros and Cons of Multiage Classrooms."
U.S. News & World Report, 24 Jan. 2023, https://
www.usnews.com/education/k12/articles/
the-pros-and-cons-of-multiage-classrooms.

Lesson 22

"Neurodiversity." National Cancer Institute, Division of
Cancer & Epidemiology Genetics, 25 Apr. 2022,
https://dceg.cancer.gov/about/diversity-inclusion/
inclusivity-minute/2022/neurodiversity.

Epilogue

Schaeffer, Katherine. "What Federal Education Data Shows
about Students with Disabilities in the U.S." Pew Research
Center, 24 July 2023, https://www.pewresearch.org/short-
reads/2023/07/24/what-federal-education-data-shows-
about-students-with-disabilities-in-the-us/.

Ingram, Noble. "The Unexpected Benefits of Remote
Learning for Neurodivergent Students." *EdSurge*, 4
Aug. 2021, https://www.edsurge.com/news/2021-08-
04-the-unexpected-benefits-of-remote-learning-for-
neurodivergent-students.

"A Guide to the Individualized Education Program." Office
of Special Education and Rehabilitative Services, U.S.
Department of Education, July 2000, https://www2.
ed.gov/parents/needs/speced/iepguide/index.html.

Lieberman, Mark. "Special Education Is Getting More
Expensive, Forcing Schools to Make Cuts Elsewhere."

Education Week, 20 Apr. 2023, https://www.edweek.org/leadership/special-education-is-getting-more-expensive-forcing-schools-to-make-cuts-elsewhere/2023/04.

National Center for Learning Disabilities, ncld.org.

Mader, Jackie. "How Teacher Training Hinders Special-Needs Students." *The Atlantic*, 1 Mar. 2017, https://www.theatlantic.com/education/archive/2017/03/how-teacher-training-hinders-special-needs-students/518286.

Flannery, Mary Ellen. "Missing: Future Teachers in Colleges of Education." *NEA Today*, 29 Mar. 2022, https://www.nea.org/nea-today/all-news-articles/missing-future-teachers-colleges-education.

Vegas, Emiliana and Rebecca Winthrop. "Beyond Reopening Schools: How Education Can Emerge Stronger than before COVID-19." Brookings, 8 Sept. 2020, https://www.brookings.edu/articles/beyond-reopening-schools-how-education-can-emerge-stronger-than-before-covid-19.

"Flexi School." Home Education UK, https://www.home-education.org.uk/articles/article-flexi-schooling.pdf.

Ray, Brian D. "Parents' Perspectives on Flexischooling Their Autistic Children." *National Home Education Research Institute Blog*, vol 34(1), 31 Dec 2018, https://www.nheri.org/parents-perspectives-on-flexischooling-their-autistic-children.

Zerbo, O., Massolo, M.L., and Y. Qian, et al. "A Study of Physician Knowledge and Experience with Autism in Adults in a Large Integrated Healthcare System." *Journal of Autism and Developmental Disorders*, vol 45, 2015, doi:10.1007/s10803-015-2579-2.

The U.K.'s National Autistic Society provides an online guide of the various diagnostic tools used to evaluate autism here: https://www.autism.org.uk/advice-and-guidance/topics/diagnosis/assessment-and-diagnosis/criteria-and-tools-used-in-an-autism-assessment. Additionally, this study, published in 2022, provides a list of widely used diagnostic tools for autism spectrum disorder: Fekar, Gharamaleki F., Bahrami, B., and J. Masumi. "Autism screening tests: A narrative review." *Journal of Public Health Research*, vol 11(1), 2021, doi:10.4081/jphr.2021.2308.

"The autism dilemma for women diagnosis." Organization for Autism Research, 26 Oct. 2018, https://researchautism.org/audience/research/the-autism-dilemma-for-women-diagnosis.

Schuck, Rachel K., Flores, Ryan E., and Lawrence K. Fung. "Brief Report: Sex/Gender Differences in Symptomology and Camouflaging in Adults with Autism Spectrum Disorder," *Journal of Autism and Developmental Disorders*, vol 49, 2019 , doi: 10.1007/s10803-019-03998-y.

Russo, Francine. "The Costs of Camouflaging Autism." *The Transmitter*, 21 Feb. 2018, https://doi.org/10.53053/ZNSG1811.

"Understanding undiagnosed autism in adult females." UCLA Health, 12 Oct. 2023, https://www.uclahealth.org/news/article/understanding-undiagnosed-autism-adult-females.

"Employment outcomes of young adults on the autism

spectrum." A.J. Drexel Autism Institute, Life Course Outcomes Research Program, Drexel University, 31 Aug. 2015, https://drexel.edu/autismoutcomes/publications-and-reports/publications/Employment-Outcomes-of-Young-Adults-on-the-Autism-Spectrum.

"Autism and Employment Statistics – Update 2023." *MyDisabilityJobs.com*, 29 Aug. 2022, https://mydisabilityjobs.com/statistics/autism-employment.

"Persons with a Disability: Labor Force Characteristics Summary." U.S. Bureau of Labor Statistics, 23 Feb. 2023, https://www.bls.gov/news.release/disabl.nr0.htm.

Frank, F., Jablotschkin, M., Arthen, T., Riedel, A., Fangmeier, T., Hölzel, L.P., and L. Tebartz van Elst, "Education and employment status of adults with autism spectrum disorders in Germany – a cross-sectional-survey." *BMC Psychiatry*, vol 18, 2018, doi:10.1186/s12888-018-1645-7.

Praslova, L.N. "Autism doesn't hold people back at work. Discrimination does." *Harvard Business Review*, 13 Dec. 2021, https://hbr.org/2021/12/autism-doesnt-hold-people-back-at-work-discrimination-does.

"Workplace Neurodiversity: The Power of Difference." The Institute of Leadership, https://leadership.global/resourceLibrary/workplace-neurodiversity-the-power-of-difference.html.

Owen, Jonathan. "Half of Managers Uncomfortable Employing a Neurodivergent Worker, Report Finds." *People Management*, 2020, https://www.peoplemanagement.co.uk/article/1742920/

half-of-managers-uncomfortable-employing-a-
neurodivergent-worker.

Davies, J., Heasman, B., Livesey, A., Walker, A., Pellicano, E.,
and A. Remington. "Access to employment: A comparison
of autistic, neurodivergent and neurotypical adults'
experiences of hiring processes in the United Kingdom."
Autism, vol 27(6), 2023, doi:10.1177/13623613221145377.

"50% Employers Admit They Won't Hire Neurodivergent
Talent." *Fair Play Talks*, 3 Nov. 2020, https://www.
fairplaytalks.com/2020/11/03/50-employers-admit-they-
wont-hire-neurodivergent-talent-reveals-ilm-study.

ACKNOWLEDGMENTS

On a September evening in 2012, I walked into James Morrison's *Writing for Print and Online Media* class at Curry College. This was a required course for the undergraduate degree that I'd been pursuing for over twenty years—attending evening and weekend classes as work and family schedules allowed. When Professor Morrison directed us to write a long-form personal essay that we would spend the semester critiquing and revising, I had no choice but to write about the difficulties Henry experienced within public education; my then recent decision to take him out of school was all consuming. This memoir originated in that classroom, spurred on by my fellow students and our fearless instructor. Thank you!

I'm so grateful to the faculty and alumnae at Vermont College of Fine Arts, who are an endless source of insight, guidance, and inspiration through this writing life. Special thanks to stellar advisors Sue William Silverman and Patrick Madden for helping me shape this narrative in its later stages, and to Connie May Fowler for rightly noting early on that the work needed some lightness and humor.

Appreciation goes to Kevin Atticks and the Apprentice House team for making this dream a reality, and to the past and present Apprentice House authors who welcomed me into the fold and were willing to share information about the small-press publishing process.

Professor and journalist Nell Lake provided comprehensive

final edits (in a very short timeframe!) that made this book so much better. I'm fortunate to count her as a professional colleague.

Much gratitude is given to the following publications in which some excerpts of this book were originally published in slightly different forms: *The Atlantic*, "How My Autistic Son Got Lost in the Public School System," January 2013; *The Shriver Report*, "Homeschooling: The Benefits for My Son, and the Added Responsibilities for Me," October 2013; *Watershed Review*, "Fish Bowl," Spring 2021; and *Sand Hills Literary Magazine*, "Sunny Day," Vol. XLV, No. 1, Spring 2021.

I gained a sense of self from my family of origin that was indispensable in figuring out who I would become as an adult and later as a parent. My mother taught me the value of service to others. My brother modeled endurance through the day-to-day struggles of life. And I always felt that I had a place to softly land when my plans went awry, thanks to my father's unwavering commitment to family. Dad responded, no matter the circumstances, every single time he was called. We don't always agree, but now in his late 80s he's still got my back whenever life hits hard. The effect that his care and reliability have had on me, over a lifetime, is impossible to measure.

My husband John is my first reader of everything. His patience, unending support, and honest critiques were essential to the completion of this written work. More importantly, his love and understanding continue to be vital, every day, to my human work-in-progress.

Finally, to my three amazing children, without whom this story and so many others would not exist: Motherhood has been and continues to be my greatest challenge in life. Standing by you as you achieve goals and celebrate milestones fills me with immeasurable joy. Watching you struggle with failure, disappointment, and heartbreak shatters me. But as you learn resilience, so do I. You are my best teachers.

ABOUT THE AUTHOR

Amy Mackin writes at the intersection of education, cultural history, public health, and social equity. Her work has appeared in outlets such as *The Atlantic, Chalkbeat, The Washington Post, Witness,* and *The Shriver Report.* She earned her MA in American Studies from the University of Massachusetts and her MFA in Nonfiction Writing from Vermont College of Fine Arts. Over the last several years, she has held leadership writing roles in the public health, science, and higher education sectors. Amy loves the fickle weather and spectacular landscapes of New England, where she resides with her family and always at least one friendly feline.

Apprentice
House Press
Loyola University Maryland

Apprentice House is the country's only campus-based, student-staffed book publishing company. Directed by professors and industry professionals, it is a nonprofit activity of the Communication and Media Department at Loyola University Maryland.

Using state-of-the-art technology and an experiential learning model of education, Apprentice House publishes books in untraditional ways. This dual responsibility as publishers and educators creates an unprecedented collaborative environment among faculty and students, while teaching tomorrow's editors, designers, and marketers.

Eclectic and provocative, Apprentice House titles intend to entertain as well as spark dialogue on a variety of topics. Financial contributions to sustain the press's work are welcomed. Contributions are tax deductible to the fullest extent allowed by the IRS.

To learn more about Apprentice House books or to obtain submission guidelines, please visit www.apprenticehouse.com.

Apprentice House Press
Communication and Media Department
Loyola University Maryland
4501 N. Charles Street
Baltimore, MD 21210
Ph: 410-617-5265
info@apprenticehouse.com • www.apprenticehouse.com